SO-ATE-689

DISCARDED

The Marshall Cavendish Illustrated History of

POPULAR MUSIC

Volume 20

MARSHALL CAVENDISH
NEW YORK, LONDON, TORONTO, SYDNEY

Reference Edition Published 1990

Published by Marshall Cavendish Corporation
147 West Merrick Road
Freeport, Long Island
N.Y. 11520

Printed and Bound in Italy by L.E.G.O. S.p.a. Vicenza.

All rights reserved. No part of this book may be reproduced or
utilized in any form or by means electronic or mechanical,
including photocopying, recording, or by an information storage
and retrieval system, without permission from the copyright
holders.

Reference edition produced by DPM Services.

© Orbis Publishing Ltd.MCMLXXXIX
© Marshall Cavendish Ltd.MCMLXXXIX

Set ISBN 1-85436-015-3

Library of Congress Cataloging in Publication Data

The Marshall Cavendish history of popular music.
     p.   cm.
   Includes index.
   ISBN 1-85435-099-4 (vol. 20)
   1. Popular music – History and criticism. 2. Rock music – History
and Criticism. I. Marshall Cavendish Corporation. II. Title:
History of popular music.
ML 3470. M36 1988
784. 5' 009 – dc19   88-21076
                              CIP
                              MN

Editorial Staff

Editor	Ashley Brown
Executive Editors	Adrian Gilbert
	Michael Heatley
Consultant Editors	Richard Williams
	Peter Brookesmith
Editorial Director	Brian Innes

Reference Edition Staff

Reference Editor	Mark Dartford
Revision Editor	Fran Jones
Consultant Editor	Michael Heatley
Art Editor	Graham Beehag

CONTENTS

CONTRIBUTORS

CLIVE ANDERSON

Co-author of *The Soul Book* and contributor to *Encyclopedia of Rock,* he has also written for *Black Music, Black Echoes, New Kommotion* and other magazines.

STEPHEN BARNARD

Has contributed to *Atlantic Rock, Melody Maker* and the *Rock Files* series. He also lectures at the City University, London.

DICK BRADLEY

Completed his PhD thesis on *British Popular Music in the Fifties* at the Centre of Contemporary Cultural Studies in Birmingham, England, and has also written articles for *Media, Culture & Society.*

JOHN BROVEN

Author of *Walking to New Orleans* and *South of Louisiana,* he has also contributed to *Nothing but the Blues* and *Encyclopedia of Rock.* He writes for *Blues Unlimited* and has also compiled several New Orleans rhythm and blues anthologies

ROB FINNIS

Author of *The Phil Spector Story* and *The Gene Vincent Story,* he has contributed to the major rock journals and runs a specialist record shop.

SIMON FRITH

A lecturer at the University of Warwick, England, he has built up a reputation over the last 15 years as one of the leading international commentators on rock music. He has co-edited the *Rock File* series, and written *The Sociology of Rock.*

PETER GURALNIK

Author of *Feel Like Going Home, Lost Highway* and *Nighthawk Blues,* his articles on blues, country and rock have appeared in *Rolling Stone,* the *Village Voice, Country Music, Living Blues,* the *New York Times* and the *Boston Phoenix.*

BILL HARRY

Founder member of UK's *Mersey Beat,* he later became news editor of *Record Mirror* and music columnist for *Weekend.* He is currently an independent PR for such artists as Suzi Quatro and Kim Wilde.

MARTIN HAWKINS

An acknowledged expert on the Sun era of rock'n'roll (author of *The Sun Story*), he writes for *Melody Maker, Time Barrier Express* and *Country Music*

BRIAN HOGG

Publisher of *Bam Balam,* which concentrates on US and UK bands of the Sixties, he has also written for such magazines as *New York Rocker* and *Record Collector.*

PETER JONES

Was editor of UK's *Record Mirror* from 1961 to 1969. He then became UK News editor of *Billboard* in 1977 and later UK and European Editor.

ROBIN KATZ

After 10 years in the Motown Press Office, she now writes freelance for *New Sound, New Styles, International Musician* and *Smash Hits.*

JOE McEWEN

An acknowledged authority on soul music, he has written for *Rolling Stone, Phonograph Record, Black Music,* the *Boston Phoenix* and Boston's *Real Paper.*

BILL MILLAR

As a freelance journalist he writes for *Melody Maker* and other rock papers. He is the author of *The Drifters* and *The Coasters.*

DAVID MORSE

Author of *Motown,* he lectures at the School of English and American Studies at Sussex University, England.

TONY RUSSELL

Editor of *Old Time Music* from 1971, he contributes regularly to *Blues Unlimited* and *Jazz Journal* and is the author of *Blacks, Whites and Blues.*

ROBERT SHELTON

Has written about blues, country and folk for the *New York Times ,* London *Times, Listener, Time Out* and *Melody Maker.*

NICK TOSCHES

Author of *Hellfire,* a biography of Jerry Lee Lewis, he also writes for *New York Times* and *Village Voice.*

MICHAEL WATTS

Writes on popular arts for *The Los Angeles Times* and London *Times* and is rock columnist for *Records and Recording Magazine.*

ADAM WHITE

Has written about Motown for *Music Week* and *Black Echoes,* and scripted a six-hour documentary about the company and its music for US radio. Also worked as managing editor of *Billboard* magazine in New York.

Entertainment USA

Variety was the keynote of the American music scene as the Seventies ended

IT TOOK THE United States almost five years to respond to the changes in rock brought about by the UK punk explosion of 1977. Only then did most American record buyers take to the new generation of British music makers who, ironically, had taken their original inspiration from the mid-Seventies New York scene of Television, Richard Hell *et al*.

US resistance to the spirit of 1977 had hardly been surprising at the time. The world's largest music market was marching to the tune of a different drummer, one playing at 130 beats per minute. Disco ruled America in the late Seventies, encouraging even rock's superstars – the Rolling Stones, Rod Stewart, Kiss – to flirt with the dictates of the dance floor.

One act which embodied some of the British punk sensibilities, Blondie, *did* break through in the US during 1979. The irony was that they did so with a dance-oriented item, 'Heart Of Glass', produced by ace popster Mike Chapman. Chapman also produced the same year's most bogus imitation-punk hit, 'My Sharona' by the Knack. The public's eventual reaction against such a contrived sound was to blight the careers of many beat-oriented bands, both British and American.

Dead or alive?

Conspiring, however subconsciously, to keep the new music from fully penetrating the American market were the programmes of adult-oriented rock (AOR) radio. Increasingly conservative, they preferred to play the music of Led Zeppelin, Eric Clapton, the Who, Jimi Hendrix, the Doors and other luminaries of the late Sixties and early Seventies, dead or alive, to contemporary sounds.

Fortunately, the new and the fresh remained a staple of hundreds of college radio stations and small rock clubs across the US throughout this period. Ian Copeland, founder and head of the Frontier Booking International (FBI) agency, was one of the few entrepreneurs who recognised and nourished the 'new underground' with a series of low-cost, no-frills tours by adventurous British rockers like Squeeze and the Police.

FBI's pioneering work combined in 1981 with a pair of other significant developments: the introduction of a 'new music' rock format on Los Angeles radio station KROQ-FM, and a national debut of Music Television (MTV), a cable channel which played nothing but rock video clips around the clock.

In origin, the two could not have been further apart. KROQ was owned by maverick broadcasters who were having licence renewal problems; MTV was owned jointly by Warner Communications and American Express. But both attracted listeners and viewers respectively at the expense of AOR radio, and began to change the sounds and sight of rock'n'roll.

Creative competition

By mid-1982, the KROQ format was beating its local AOR competition in the ratings and being syndicated to other stations across the US, while MTV was playing more new music than dozens of radio stations combined – and becoming the talk of the television and music industries in the process.

The competition between video and radio was generally seen as good for the music business, both commercially *and* creatively. If no single medium had a monopoly on exposing new talent, as radio did in the Seventies, that talent had, it seemed, a better chance of gaining the public's attention and acceptance.

ADAM WHITE

David Byrne, the enigmatic and egocentric leader of the Talking Heads who proved to be one of the most innovative and influential American bands of the late Seventies.

FEAR OF MUSIC

Who's afraid of Talking Heads?

THE NAME TALKING HEADS is mediaspeak – a phrase found in a TV guide by a friend of the band's, describing the framed heads of a television talk show. The name defines the band's preoccupations accurately: the 'global village' of mass electronic communication, with its lack of privacy and attendant paranoias; materialism; home appliances and all the other trappings of middle-class American life.

The band originated with three friends from the Rhode Island School of Design, Chris Frantz, Martina Weymouth and David Byrne. They all came from rich, upper middle-class backgrounds: Tina was from a naval family, Chris Frantz a general's son. Byrne came from Baltimore, although he was born in Scotland. Well-travelled, well-read and highly educated, the trio seemed suited to the hothouse artistic environment of RISD.

Frustrated with the élitism of the art world, however, Byrne dropped out before finishing his course. He had already played in a band, the Artistics, with Frantz (some of their numbers would later be played by Talking Heads). Moving to New York, he worked as a short-order cook while performing at a number of fringe events – at one, he played violin with a plastic bird on the end of the bow, and shaved off his beard on stage with cold beer.

Frantz and Weymouth joined him after finishing their degrees in 1974. The three of them moved into a loft on the Lower East Side, and Byrne and Frantz decided to start a band. Although they couldn't find a suitable bass player, it was a while before it occurred to them to teach Tina, although she could already play guitar. 'Rock'n'roll is thought of as a male music,' Byrne said later. 'I wasn't sure how it would be received.'

Tina played down the problems she had in establishing herself as a respected member of the group – after the band got their recording contract, Byrne made her audition all over again for her job as bass player. In a 1981 interview with the *Face*, she said: 'One thing I did that I'm glad about in retrospect is that I never talked about the problems of being a woman. I didn't want to discourage anyone who had the same idea. I didn't want to make it look like an uphill trek, which it was.'

Talking Heads were soon playing regularly at CBGB's, the regular haunt of many US new wave bands like the Ramones, Television and the Patti Smith Group. The bare, angular sound of the three-piece band, with Chris on drums, Tina on bass and David on 12-string acoustic guitar, complemented Byrne's anxious vocals and manic, jittery stage

Remain in light – the Talking Heads pose against an urban skyline, from left Jerry Harrison, Tina Weymouth, Chris Frantz and David Byrne.

presence. This intense nervous energy, which immediately marked out Talking Heads as a band to watch, stemmed from Byrne's own shy, uncomfortable nature. 'I'm getting a bit better now at normal relations,' he remarked in 1981, 'like saying please and thank you, things like that.'

The band turned down several offers of a recording contract until they felt they were ready, eventually signing to Sire in 1977. Their first single, 'Love Goes To A Building On Fire', appeared early that year, and shortly afterwards, Jerry Harrison was recruited as a second guitarist and keyboard player. Harrison had been a member of Jonathan Richman's original Modern Lovers, a band that – along with the Velvet Underground – had been a crucial influence on Talking Heads. The wide-eyed naivety with which Richman viewed everyday situations so that they appeared strange and alien also characterised a number of Talking Heads songs like 'Don't Worry About The Government'.

Their debut album, *Talking Heads: 77*, was released that July to rave reviews. The band's quirky, eccentric sound was captured on tracks like 'Uh-Oh, Love Comes To Town', which took an ambivalent look at romance, the haunting, Lou Reed-like 'Happy Day' and the song that was virtually to become their anthem, 'Psycho Killer'. Also released as a single, 'Psycho Killer' took Byrne's jittery presence to its extreme: 'I can't seem to face up to the facts/I'm tense and nervous and I can't relax/I can't sleep 'cos my bed's on fire/Don't touch me I'm a real live wire . . .'

The kids of today

Although they were pushed as a 'punk' band by their record company, Sire, the band's image was studiedly ordinary – clean slacks and checked shirts – in keeping with their lyrical preoccupations, the neuroses lying beneath the surface of Middle-American life. They spurned the hysterical praise showered on them by the music press, and kept a low profile publically. But, paradoxically, Byrne's idea of the function of the rock singer was not that far removed from the concept of the shaman that the Doors' Jim Morrison had believed in: 'In most rock'n'roll there's the emphasis on the front person living out this mythical archetype. They are given this role that they become possessed by and they live out that role in front of the audience.'

Byrne certainly sang like a man possessed. This tension between the material and the spiritual, the 'Seen And Not Seen', to quote one of their song titles, lay at the heart of their music. The second Talking Heads LP, produced in collaboration with former Roxy Music synthesiser-player Brian Eno, elaborated their familiar obsessions, as its title, *More Songs About Buildings And Food* (1978), mockingly suggested.

Eno and Byrne got on well – so well, Tina commented ironically, that they were soon copying one another's clothes and trying to impress each other 'like 14-year-olds'. Eno's influence on this LP, however, was relatively subtle. He fed the sound of the band through his synthesiser, and then mixed the treated sound in with the original.

The result emphasised rather than altered the band's style. Tina and Chris – who had married the previous year – were developing into a powerful, funky rhythm section, and the overall sound of the record was a bigger, more confident version of its predecessor. The album also contained a surprise hit single, a cover of soul singer Al Green's 'Take Me To The River'. Sung with all the intensity Byrne could muster, the single entered the US Top Thirty that year, reaching Number 26.

Tales of urban tension

The collaboration with Brian Eno was extended on the next LP, *Fear Of Music* (1979). The record also showed the band's growing interest in funk and African music – although the band members disagreed over who first introduced this element. 'I Zimbra', a frantic, driving track with nonsense lyrics from a poem by Hugo Ball, featured a pair of African drummers, and King Crimson guitarist Robert Fripp added some experimental noises at Eno's invitation. 'Cities' set Byrne's familiar persona – the outsider surveying ordinary people going about their lives, to this new, energetic beat, while 'Life During Wartime' – released as a single – was a description of urban tension written, according to Tina, 'from the point of view of a terrorist': 'This ain't no party, this ain't no disco,' sang Byrne grimly.

Byrne then went on to make a very strange, experimental album with Eno, *My Life In The Bush Of Ghosts*. Travelling the country, they recorded the voices of radio evangelists – a peculiarly American phenomenon, and set them to their own backing tracks, along with the chants of Middle-Eastern musicians and other 'found' material. The results – which included an exorcism that took place on the air – reflected Byrne's preoccupation with modern mass communications, spirituality and possession, together with his and Eno's interest in ethnic music.

Although the album's release was delayed until 1981, due to legal problems with the estate of one of the evangelists (whose voice was eventually deleted), this project influenced the next Talking Heads album, *Remain In Light* (1980). Using the latest digital recording equipment, the band built up rhythm patterns from tape loops made from studio jam sessions. Gradually, layer after layer of intricate cross-rhythms were added to these basic, one-chord jams. Other musicians were brought in to fill out the sound: Adrian Belew, David Bowie's tour guitarist; former LaBelle vocalist Nona Hendryx; a horn section, arranged by Jon Hassell. To complete the all-star cast, there was even a guest appearance by singer Robert Palmer on percussion.

Inset right: David Byrne (left) and Brian Eno, who first collaborated together on the Talking Heads' second LP. Inset below: The augmented band on stage in Paris, 1980. Below: Tina Weymouth.

The rich, orchestral funk that resulted was far removed from the frail, brittle textures of *Talking Heads: 77*. Byrne then added lyrics, many of them adapted from the radio evangelists he and Eno had recorded for *My Life In The Bush Of Ghosts*: 'And you may ask yourself/Am I right? . . . Am I wrong?/And you may say to yourself/ MY GOD! . . . WHAT HAVE I DONE?' ('Once In A Lifetime'). That particular track brought the band their first UK Top Twenty hit in early 1981.

When it came to presenting this material on stage, it was necessary to assemble an even larger collection of musicians: a second bassist, Busta Cherry Jones; Parliament keyboard-player Bernie Worrell; veteran soul percussionist Steven Scales; vocalist Dolette MacDonald; and Adrian Belew. With such a large group, the focus inevitably shifted away from David Byrne as the lonely, tormented lead vocalist to a more joyful, communal form of music-making. 'On a good night,' Byrne

Heads studio LP (although a live album, *The Name Of This Band Is Talking Heads*, appeared in 1982).

In 1981, the Byrne/Eno record *My Life In The Bush Of Ghosts* finally surfaced, while Tina Weymouth and Chris Frantz went off to the Bahamas where they recorded their *Tom Tom Club* LP. Like *Remain In Light*, it took a communal approach to music making and used a vast array of musicians: Adrian Belew, Tina's sisters, Loric, Lani and Laura, and reggae session star Tyrone Downie, among others. Unlike the Talking Heads LP, which was full of nervous energy, *Tom Tom Club* was a delightfully relaxed, summery record. It was also a massive commercial success, remaining in the US charts for 30 weeks. A single taken from it, 'Wordy Rappinghood', reached Number 7 in the UK.

Fun and fireworks
Jerry Harrison, meanwhile, had made an intriguing solo album, *The Red And The Black* (1981), while David Byrne teamed up with modern dance choreographer Twyla Tharp on a ballet called *The Catherine Wheel*. The subject matter, the tensions within the all-American nuclear family, was right up Byrne's street, and prompted some of his best work. The songs from the ballet were released as an LP, also called *The Catherine Wheel* (1982). Byrne also produced the B-52's mini LP *Mesopotamia* (1982), and the Fun Boy Three's second LP, *Waiting* (1983). The British vocal trio used an all-women band of instrumentalists, which Byrne – having changed his tune somewhat – described as 'real sharp thinking'.

1983 saw another Tom Tom Club LP, *Close To The Bone*, and a single, a cover of the Drifters' 'Under The Boardwalk'. All this independent activity fuelled rumours of the Talking Heads' imminent demise, so the release of the LP *Speaking In Tongues* took many people by surprise. In many ways a return to their earlier, simpler style, it included the manic single 'Burning Down The House'. A live LP and a film, both called *Stop Making Sense*, followed in 1984. Their next studio LP, *Little Creatures* (1985), showed the band at their most relaxed; the song 'Road To Nowhere', with its delightful mock-gospel chorus, was released as a single and made the UK Top Ten.

'I wanted to emphasise the pop songs again,' Byrne said disarmingly. 'I enjoy singing, I sing along at home to other people's records and I thought, "You haven't written any of your own you can sing for ages."'

CHRIS SCHÜLER

Talking Heads Recommended Listening

Talking Heads: 77 (Sire 9103 328) (Includes: Tentative Decisions, Psycho Killer, Uh-Oh, Love Comes To Town, Happy Day, The Book I Read, Don't Worry About The Government): *Fear Of Music* (Sire K56707) (Includes: Heaven, Life During Wartime, Memories Can't Wait, Cities, Electric Guitar, Drugs).

remarked, 'you are all sort of locked together into one complicated groove that has nothing to do with one single personality . . .'

The old folks at home
Ironically, it was over *Remain In Light* that the tensions within the group exploded. Byrne and Eno felt that the LP was their creation. 'Brian's very insular,' Tina commented. 'You begin to feel you've been pinpointed as an innovator . . . He's gotten into an élitist ivory tower. He doesn't realise those ideas are in the air.' Worried about his influence on David Byrne, she added sharply: 'I can see them when they're 80 years old and all alone. There'll be David Bowie, David Byrne and Brian Eno and they'll just talk to each other.'

The rest of the band felt that Byrne and Eno had taken too much credit for the compositions on the album sleeve, and the second pressing was altered accordingly. The next two years saw no new Talking

Kitsch style and dance rhythms from the B-52's

WHEN THEY FIRST APPEARED on the rock scene towards the end of the Seventies, the B-52's seemed a little like an alien landing. Their music was a bizarre and intriguing blend of styles, a subtle but stirring mixture of the Ronettes, Captain Beefheart's Magic Band and Cuban drum music, while their style was centred around bad science-fiction and fearful 'beach party' movies of the Fifties and Sixties. If there was one asset the B-52's possessed, in apparently limitless quantities, it was humour. 'Their songs,' suggested *Time Out* magazine in 1980, 'explore intensely personal "real life" dramas as if in celebration of the old adage: he who laughs has not yet heard the terrible news.'

Bongos over Athens

The B-52's – Fred Schneider (vocals), Kate Pierson (keyboards and vocals), Cindy Wilson (vocals), Ricky Wilson (guitar) and Keith Strickland (drums) – were formed in Athens, Georgia, in late 1976. Repelled by the slick, uneventful rock fare of such acts as Jackson Browne and the Eagles, the various band members had whiled away the early Seventies ransacking the bargain bins of record stores for early pop classics. They also drained the local thrift shops of kitsch fashion accessories, for which they had developed an insatiable appetite. Regular visits were paid to an Athens disco, where the student friends' assembly of fake leopard-skin clothes, trimmed with fun-fur, and lampshades or baskets – sometimes even *shoes* – for headwear always guaranteed a frosty reception. 'People often threw bricks at us,' Schneider recalled years later.

In 1976, they decided to put their eccentric dress sense and shared unorthodox musical taste to positive advantage by forming a band and, taking their name from a Sixties slang term for the lofty, beehive hairstyle favoured by the girls; they made their debut appearance at a St Valentine's Day dance the following year.

In much the same way as British punk had taken off, the B-52's' utter contempt for contemporary style and complete inability to play their instruments rapidly made them a big draw on the local club circuit. Their early sound (which was hardly to change), consisted of a brisk, top-heavy drum beat and deep synthesised bass over which were spread the unlikely chords of a four-stringed electric guitar. A collection of bongos, wireless receivers and toy percussion filled in the cracks, all of which gave a free rein to the unsettling vocal delivery of Fred Schneider. Gangling,

Above: The B-52's, from left Keith Strickland, Cindy Wilson, Kate Pierson, Fred Schneider and Ricky Wilson. Above left: Their first LP.

bug-eyed and a look-alike of English comic actor Kenneth Williams, he applied himself with great relish to producing words about giant birds, colossal sea creatures, poodles with dyed green fur and whatever else took his fancy. This provided ample opportunity for various loopy vocal additions by the two girls, who quickly became renowned for their tacky on-stage attire

WHAMMY!

and was so adamantly opposed to meat-eating that he formed a 'vegetarian patrol' in his native Athens, scouring the streets for unsuspecting 'burger hogs' and, upon sighting one, letting off an old police siren strapped to the roof of his car. The girls were just as entertaining: Kate Pierson talked non-stop about her love for cheap horror movies like *Destroy All Monsters* and *The Attack Of The Fifty Foot Woman*, while Cindy Wilson recalled her days as a soda waitress at Athens' own Whirly Q Munch Out. Better credentials for 'hip credibility' were hard to imagine.

The B-52's was a remarkably fresh and entertaining debut LP, full of batty dance tunes like 'Dance This Mess Around' and '606 0842', all fuelled by Ricky Wilson's chopping guitar, Pierson's squeaky organ and Schneider's eccentric vocal delivery. With the help of a group appearance on TV's 'Saturday Night Live', the album sold reasonably well in the US and, later in 1979, the B-52's arrived in Europe to promote the record. Although the intricate details of their songs were completely lost on Continental audiences – whose sole consolation was an ultimately monotonous dance beat – crowds in London lapped them up and the band were, for a brief spell, the hippest thing in town. But it was in Australia that the B-52's made most impact. A re-recorded version of 'Rock Lobster' made that country's Top Ten in 1979, while a 1980 tour sold out.

Life is a party
A second album, *Wild Planet*, was released in September 1980 and proved to be a major disappointment; only the occasional track like 'Quiche Lorraine' recalled the verve of its predecessor and, at the end of 1981, the B-52's balloon began to deflate. They had moved from Georgia to a big dormitory house in the northern suburbs of New York, had put out *Party Mix*, a six-track mini-LP of early favourites, heavily remixed for the disco turntable, but had failed to come up with any new material. In the spring of 1982, another six-track stop-gap, *Mesopotamia*, was released; flatly produced by the Talking Heads' David Byrne, this contained but one palatable number, 'Throw That Beat In The Garbage Can' – which, for the rest of the songs, seemed pretty sound advice.

1983's Whammy proved disappointing, while the death of Ricky Wilson from cancer on 12 October 1985 seemed likely to end the story. But they regrouped in 1987 with the typically wacky album *Bouncing Off The Satellites*.   MARK ELLEN

which included bee-hive wigs, pendulous earrings, gaudy slacks and wrap-around Lycra skirts.

Early 1978 saw the release of a debut single, 'Rock Lobster'/'52 Girls', on the band's own Boofant label; in the summer they headed for the breaking grounds of Max's Kansas City and CBGB's in New York to put a toe in the water of current popular taste. Audiences and critics alike welcomed the group with open arms, and they were swiftly signed to Warner Brothers in the US, and Island for the rest of the world, on the basis of their 'ocean

cartoon' 'Rock Lobster' and a handful of other song-sketches.

Dance this mess around
In June 1979, the group's first album, *The B-52's*, produced by Island's Chris Blackwell, was released and further established the band as a 'hip' commodity. They were the critics' dream – a group that sounded new but was constructed almost entirely from familiar components. In addition, their dry, obtuse manner made for excellent copy: Fred claimed on many occasions that 'fluorescent lighting causes cancer'

The B-52's
Recommended Listening

The B-52's (Island ILPS 9580) (Includes: Planet Claire, 52 Girls, Rock Lobster, Lava, Hero Worship, Dance This Mess Around); *Whammy!* (Island ILPS 9759) (Includes: Legal Tender, Whammy Kiss, Work That Skirt, Big Bird, Trism, Butterbean).

SHAKE SOME *Action*

The bands that put the Bomp in US beat

IN THE MID SIXTIES, within the music of groups like the Kinks, the Byrds and the Who, musical aggression and melodic invention had co-existed. But with the rise of 'underground' rock music later in the decade, pop became increasingly clean and unthreatening. Harsh, powerful sounds were now the preserve of the hard rockers and pop could offer little more than lightweight tunes and studio artifice. In Britain, raw teenage pop made a brief – and contrived – re-appearance with the glitter of T. Rex and Sweet in the early Seventies, but in America, the form slumbered.

Feelin' groovy
But there were *some* US acts who attempted to revive the verve and spirit of Sixties pop music. The most committed and uncompromising of all power pop, or pop-rock acts, were the Flamin' Groovies. Formed as the Chosen Few in San Francisco in 1965, they started out, like a host of like-minded garage bands of the time, playing raw and raucous rock'n'roll and British beat cover versions. Yet when acid rock began to bubble in San Francisco towards the end of 1966, and the group's contemporaries started to take off on psychedelic excursions, the Flamin' Groovies remained true to their roots. They even dressed the part of mid-Sixties popsters and, as a result, the hippies of Haight-Ashbury and beyond remained aloof from their charms for some considerable time.

'The main reason we didn't make it in San Francisco,' said founder member Cyril Jordan years later, 'was because we'd walk on stage in front of a bunch of hippies and we'd have velvet coats on. Now, right there, we were saying "we're better than you." But all we were *really* saying was that ever since the Beatles and the Stones and the Who and the Kinks were over, there was nothing as heavy in its place. There was nothing put out after 1968 that was half as heavy as the Searchers or something in the Sixties.'

Playing short, fast and furious beat music during the 'summer of love' was distinctly uncool but with record companies frothing to sign *any* SF band, the Flamin' Groovies got a deal with Epic. After one incompetently-produced album, *Supersnazz* (1969), they moved to Kama Sutra and recorded *Teenage Head* (1971), a classic blend of deranged rock'n'roll and power beat.

Top: Dwight Twilley. Above: Cyril Jordan (left) and Chris Wilson of the Flamin' Groovies. Twilley and the Groovies were among the most committed pop revivalists of the early Seventies. Opposite: The late Seventies saw bands like the Real Kids (top), the Pop (centre) and the Knack (bottom) blend punk energy with pop hooks.

The early Seventies found others following the Flamin' Groovies backwards into the Sixties. In 1972, in Memphis, Alex Chilton, ex-singer with pop-soul outfit the Box Tops, formed Big Star. Signed to Stax subsidiary label Ardent, the group recorded two albums, *No 1 Record* (1972) and *Radio City* (1973), which were glorious, modern-sounding incorporations of the styles of the Byrds, the Beatles, the Kinks and the Beach Boys; as Chilton said in 1978: 'I quit school at 16 to be in the Box Tops and so I left my own peer group completely. So what I was writing about on the Big Star albums was just going back and trying to catch myself up. I was 21 at the time but I was writing like I was 16 or 17.'

Twilley don't mind
Meanwhile, in Tulsa, Dwight Twilley and Phil Seymour, who had formed a musical partnership in 1968, were exploring similar musical territory. 'There we were in Tulsa with no influences besides AM radio hits and the Beatles,' Twilley recalled in 1977. 'We weren't old enough to be aware of what Elvis was. We liked him but we never put him on the level of the Beatles and we just followed our ears.' Twilley's first two albums for Shelter Records, *Sincerely* (1975) and *Twilley Don't Mind* (1977), were superbly vibrant evocations of Sixties pop, with quirky rhythms, shimmering power chords and breathy vocals dominating the sound. 'Dwight Twilley and Phil Seymour are pop stars, teen idols,' wrote journalist Greg Shaw in his own fanzine *Bomp!* in 1977.

This was a nice thought, but the trouble was that Twilley and Seymour were not really pop stars or teen idols at all because they sold precious few records. They *did* make the US singles charts in 1975 with 'I'm On Fire', which reached Number 16, but this proved to be just a flash in the pan; like the Flamin' Groovies, Big Star and other Sixties-oriented acts of the time – Blue Ash, Left End, Magic, Stroke, the Semonars – Dwight Twilley's music proved to be remarkably uncommercial.

Virtually the only band to profit from a Sixties sensibility during the early Seventies were Cleveland's the Raspberries, led by vocalist Eric Carmen. The Raspberries distilled all the most potent ingredients of Sixties pop – from the Beatles to girl groups, from the Beach Boys to bubblegum – into their sound and, for a time, the formula proved to be a winning one. In 1972, the Raspberries had US Top Twenty hits with 'Go All The Way' and 'Wanna Be With You'. Their first three albums, *Raspberries, Fresh* (both 1972) and *Side 3* (1973), all sold healthily, and in 1974 they released 'Overnight Sensation (Hit Record)', which remains a classic of pop-rock. '"Overnight Sensation" *is* the radio that leads to Carmen's street of dreams,' commented *Rolling Stone* magazine. 'In it, his vision of himself the true inheritor of the innocence of early-Sixties rock is justified completely.'

Unfortunately, because their records were played on AM radio and their faces were featured in the pages of *Tiger Beat* and other teen magazines, the Raspberries alienated their potential rock audience. By the mid Seventies, the divide between rock and pop had become too great to be bridged by nothing more than just good music.

Velvet covers

It was not until 1977, when punk rock had re-introduced the idea of the short, sharp song, that pop-rock showed signs of coming into its own. Suddenly, the Flamin' Groovies, who had had an exceedingly lean time of it since the failure of *Teenage Head*, were fashionable for the first time: dressed in Beatle boots and haircuts, velvet jackets and tight trousers, the Groovies covered the Beatles' 'There's A Place', the Byrds' 'Feel A Whole Lot Better' and recreated the Sixties in songs of their own like 'Shake Some Action', picking up an enthusiastic following. Meanwhile, other American bands arrived, blending the new energy of punk with a sense of the past – the Cretones, the Pop, the Know, Semblance and the Jerkheads, the Heaters, the Real Kids, the Marbles, 20/20 (produced by Phil Seymour) and a host of others.

For a spell, it seemed as if a new musical form was about to erupt. 'Punk rock is finished,' eccentric rock entrepreneur Kim Fowley announced on US TV's 'Tomorrow' show. 'The future of the new wave is power pop!' 'Radio wants to play new-wave records but they don't want to offend their audience with crude obnoxious music,' said *Bomp!* 'They're waiting for power pop. And so are the kids of America.'

This proved to be more wishful thinking than anything else, however. The only power-pop group to make any commercial showing were the Knack, whose heavy, bubblegum-influenced 'My Sharona' was a US Number 1 hit in 1979. The quartet, dressed in matching white shirts and slim black ties, played guitar-chiming songs of teenage lust – 'Good Girls Don't' (1979), 'Baby Talks Dirty' (1980) – but their reign of success proved remarkably short. The press railed against the band's calculated approach, and the public soon tired of them.

The American pop revival of 1977-78 faded rapidly, and although pop-rock could still be heard in the Eighties – in the mind-numbing glitter-stomp of Joan Jett and the Blackhearts or the wry, Byrdsian approach of the dB's or REM – it seemed that with the dawning of the video age, the ascent of MTV (the music-oriented cable TV station) and the conservatism of FM radio, American kids would continue to ignore the charms of pop's history.

TOM HIBBERT

From looking sharp with the
Stilettoes in 1974 (inset far left),
Debbie Harry gradually
developed an image as a punk sex
kitten (left). Inset above:
Blondie on stage, from left Chris
Stein, Harry, Nigel Harrison and
Frank Infante.

BLONDIE

From plastic punksters to Autoamericans

AT THE END OF the Seventies, pop went blonde in a big way with Abba, the Police and Blondie registering a three-way claim to be the biggest singles sellers of 1978-79. Of the three, Blondie were the surprise packet. They were deliberately uncategorisable: poppy one minute and arty-serious the next; a group with an unusually open mind whose style was a rag-bag of swiftly-assimilated influences. Punk, power pop, disco, reggae, rap – you name it, they did it, in an often exhilarating and wildly successful stab at world domination of the radio airwaves and poster shops.

In former Playboy Bunny Debbie Harry they had the undisputed female sex symbol of the time. In 1978's *Parallel Lines* they had one of those rare albums that sells and keeps on selling; more than a million copies were bought in the UK alone and the LP spent over 100 weeks in the charts. Their demise was almost as sudden as their rise, but their career was certainly fun while it lasted.

Dark roots
Blondie grew out of an occasional, jokey New York group called the Stilettoes. Variously described by Debbie as 'tacky', 'gaudy' and 'general chaos', the band generally included three girl singers, and therefore naturally tended towards early-Sixties pop material sung by girl groups such as the Shangri-las, the Ronettes and the Supremes. In the serious, slightly stodgy music biz of the early Seventies, this was considered a highly unusual basis from which to work.

The Stilettoes had not been Debbie's first group (she had even made an album in 1968 with a band called Wind in the Willows), but it was the first to feature her boyfriend, Chris Stein, who had more definite ideas about making a career out of what had started out as part-time fun. With the current Stilettoes rhythm section of Fred Smith and Billy O'Connor, they formed a group that, after playing under a variety of names, became Blondie in 1974, when, briefly, it had two blonde backing vocalists.

The name – best-known for Chic Young's long-running cartoon strip – was apt for a group that used imagery from cartoons, B movies and tabloid headlines as inspiration for most of its early songs: 'X Offender', 'A Shark In Jet's Clothing', 'Kung Fu Girls' and 'The Attack Of The Giant Ants' were among the sensationalist titles that featured on the first album, *Blondie* (1976).

By the time of its release, Blondie featured a new rhythm section. Gary Valentine came in on bass, Fred Smith having left to join Television, and Clem

Right: Blondie's blonde bombshell Debbie Harry, for several years the most influential female face and voice in rock.

Burke joined on drums. Burke was just 18 but already steeped in Sixties pop, English groups in general and Keith Moon in particular, and was clearly a valuable addition. As Debbie succinctly remarked: 'He fell in enthusiastically with our plans to form a pop group that aimed to modernise AM radio sounds. Clem never wanted anything else but to be a pop star.' This was the sort of single-mindedness a struggling group needs.

Pop and fun were the keywords to the early Blondie. Their songs were brief and to the point (three-and-a-half minutes was long by their standards) with lots of punch and few pretensions. The LP was produced by Richard Gottehrer for the small Private Stock label, later known among the band as Private Joke, and its impact was strictly local. It was not even released in Britain until 1978 when their new label Chrysalis issued it along with the second album, *Plastic Letters* (1978).

Outside New York, the first people to take more than a passing interest in Blondie were the Australians, who made 'In The Flesh' a Number 2 hit – the only success under the group's belt when Chrysalis decided to invest half-a-million dollars in its future. Chrysalis' gamble paid off with the release of the first 45 from *Plastic Letters* – 'Denis', a reverse-sex version of a 15-year-old American hit by Randy and the Rainbows, which Debbie chose against strong opposition from within the band.

The single was an immediate hit in the UK, rising to Number 2 with the aid of a startling first appearance on BBC-TV's 'Old Grey Whistle Test' which began a lasting affair between Debbie, cameras and the British public. 'Denis' was a beginning and an end – the final blast of the group's fascination with Sixties nostalgia and (until 1980's 'The Tide Is High'), their only non-original hit.

Blondie had already toured the UK with Television in 1977, but TV and press approval plus an aggressive marketing campaign by Chrysalis (in which, initially, Blondie seemed merely to be an alternative name for Debbie) quickly established their popularity. 1978's *Plastic Letters*, an altogether darker and more adventurous album than 'Denis' would seem to suggest, remained over a year in the UK charts, reaching Number 10. Its best track, '(I'm Always Touched By Your) Presence Dear', written by departed bass-player Gary Valentine, became a UK Number 10 hit in May.

By this time, the band – now six-strong with the addition of keyboardist Jimmy Destri and English bassist Nigel Harrison (which meant that Frank Infante shared the guitar-playing with Chris Stein) – was recording with a new producer, the famed 'hit machine' Mike Chapman. The decision to work with Chapman represented a

Above: Debbie imitates Marilyn Monroe's famous pose from The Seven Year Itch.

change in the band's direction, from post-punk to mainstream 'hit or bust' pop. Blondie's new, streamlined and accessible sound gave them a far better chance of receiving airplay on American radio – notoriously slow to pick up on new groups, especially if they were reputed to be 'punk' or 'new wave'.

Yesterday's papers
The LP that Blondie recorded with Chapman, *Parallel Lines* (1978) was one of those rare records that reflects the time it was made as perfectly as an old newspaper. It had great variety – not only in an egalitarian use of all six members among the songwriters, but in a wide range of styles both vocally and instrumentally, which gave a great many tracks the feel of a snappy hit single. Which is what no less than four of them successively became – 'Picture This', 'Hanging On The Telephone', 'Heart Of Glass' and 'Sunday Girl' – with the last two providing the group's first British Number 1 hits. In addition, the disco-flavoured 'Heart Of Glass' finally broke the band in the US. Disco was officially acceptable on American radio and 'Heart Of Glass' soon shot to Number 1.

By 1979, Blondie were getting more coverage in the *Sun* than they were in *Sounds*: they were a pop group with a capital P. Their 1979 album, again with Mike Chapman at the controls, was *Eat To The Beat*, one of the first albums to be simultaneously released as a video. A little strained in places by comparison with *Parallel Lines*, it was still a tremendous hit, a Number 1 album that yielded another three major hit singles in 'Dreaming', 'Union City Blue' and 'Atomic'.

'Union City Blue' was confusingly not used in *Union City* (1980), an appealing, low-budget black comedy that provided a first film role for Debbie and a first film score for Stein. *Union City* was the first sign of increasing outside interests for Blondie members. The group had also gone through a protracted change of manager from Peter Leeds to Shep Gordon, the power behind Alice Cooper's Seventies success.

High tide and lost souls
Some inter-group wrangling occurred over who should produce the next album, with Stein and Harry being in favour of Euro-disco producer Giorgio Moroder. In the event, Moroder did the transatlantic Number 1 'Call Me' as an independent single while Chapman was back at the mixing desk for *Autoamerican* (1980), which was generally better received in the US than the UK, although it made Number 3 in the British charts.

The album provided the group's last UK Number 1 hit with the muted reggae of 'The Tide Is High', while the jokey rapping of 'Rapture' took it to Number 5. This time, however, the variety of styles (the LP even included examples of movie-soundtrack music) seemed more wilful than adventurous. One of the few reminders of old-style Blondie pop, 'T-Birds', was curiously ignored as a single. The LP appeared particularly disappointing after the band's 1980 tour, which showed them at the peak of their form. In future, it seemed that Ms Harry was more likely to be seen on *The Muppet Show*, in jeans commercials or at the movies (she starred in the 1983 horror film *Videodrome*) than on stage.

The 1981 release of Debbie's solo collaboration with Chic's Nile Rodgers and Bernard Edwards, *Koo Koo*, seemed likely to signal the end of the band. Much of the record sounded disappointingly cold and mechanical and, although it reached Number 6 in the UK, it provided only one minor hit single, 'Backfired'.

In the event, there was to be one more Blondie record, the widely-derided 1982 release *The Hunter*, which had the sound and look of a contractual obligation, and saw Stein and Harry's fascination with rapping taken to ridiculous lengths. As the band began to go their separate ways, 'Island Of Lost Souls' looked certain to be the group's last UK Top Twenty success. Debbie Harry's 1986 comeback with her second solo LP *Rockbird* and the UK Number 8 'French Kissin' In The USA' followed a period of uncertainty as she nursed Stein back to health from a mysterious wasting illness.   ROB MACKIE

Blondie
Recommended Listening

Parallel Lines (EMI Fame FA 3089) (Includes: Hanging On The Telephone, Picture This, Heart Of Glass, Just Go Away, Pretty Baby, Fade Away And Radiate); *The Best Of Blondie* (Chrysalis CDL TV1) (Includes: Atomic, Rapture, Denis, Dreaming, Rip Her To Shreds, The Tide Is High).

Dancing chic to chic with August Darnell

ON STAGE at the Eighties club in New York are an unusual-looking group of musicians. The singer is clad in an outsize suit with a fedora tilted just so. His partner wears a towel wrapped around his head, jungle fatigues and combat boots. The three girl backing singers have contrived to lose most of their clothes and are wearing little more than the briefest of leopard-skin bikinis. The club is packed and its predominantly gay clientele are bopping about to the heady mix of calypso, swing reggae, soul and salsa laid down by Kid Creole and the Coconuts.

In the jungle
Kid Creole and the Coconuts was the brainchild of August Darnell, whose date and place of birth were to remain shrouded in mystery, although he admitted to being brought up in the Bronx. Having worked briefly as a teacher and then as a songwriter for Chappell Music, he formed his first group, Dr Buzzard's Original Savannah Band, with his half-brother, Stony Browder, in the mid Seventies. The band shot to fame with a US Top Forty hit, 'Whispering'/'Cherchez La Femme'/'Se Si Bon' in 1976, then proceeded to blow their fortunes on fast cars and wild living.

Down on his luck, Darnell decided to put together a band with an exotic image based on the glamour and seediness of Hollywood musicals and B movies. While living in the Bronx, Darnell had been nicknamed the Creole Kid; over dinner one night his girlfriend, future wife and head Coconut Adriana Kaegi suggested he change the name around, and Kid Creole was born.

A chance meeting with Michael Zilkha, boss of Ze Records, resulted in Darnell being employed as a house producer. He worked on records by James White, Black, Chance and Cristina, also contributing to albums by Gichy Dan among others. In-between assignments, Darnell and his partner Andy Hernandez (who became known as Coati Mundi) managed to put together the first Kid Creole and the Coconuts LP, *Off The Coast Of Me* (1980). Despite being praised by critics, the album received minimal airplay and sold poorly.

The positive public response the group had won on their few live appearances encouraged the band to work on a second album, *Fresh Fruit In Foreign Places* (1981). The LP chronicled the Kid's search for his erstwhile lover, Mimi (a story loosely based on Darnell's own experiences when his first wife left him). *Fresh Fruit In Foreign Places* was ecstatically received by the British press, and Darnell hailed as a 'modern-day soul genius'. Unfortunately the record got little radio airplay (though 'Me No Pop I' – a single credited to Kid Creole and the Coconuts present Coati Mundi – was a minor UK hit). The group were unable to capitalise on the enthusiasm of the British music press as the Ze

Opposite: Kid Creole and the Coconuts pose for the camera (above) and disport themselves manically on stage (below). Above: August Darnell based his style on the sleek urbanity of Forties bandleader Cab Calloway.

label lacked the funds to finance a UK tour. Despite the record's wit and verve, it flopped; the appeal of Darnell's polished, satirical updating of Hollywood high camp appeared to be limited to a cult following.

A world elsewhere
Darnell, accompanied by Adriana, finally visited the UK in the summer of 1982. He became the toast of the cocktail set, producing an album for Funkapolitan by day and frequenting London's Club for Heroes by night. On his return to New York, he set about turning his planned solo album into a Kid Creole and the Coconuts record. This step brought about a rift with Andy Hernandez whose contribution to the resultant LP, *Tropical Gangsters* (1982), was to be minimal.

The same week that *Tropical Gangsters* was released, it was announced that the group would tour the UK. Two weeks later the first single from the LP, 'I'm A Wonderful Thing, Baby' began to move up the UK charts, eventually reaching Number 4. The group's first show in May at Leeds University was a sellout as, indeed, was every concert they played that spring. British audiences had seen nothing like it

before – a modern-day big band, fronted by the Kid in his outrageous Zoot suit, flanked by the bald, manic vibes player Coati Mundi and the svelte, seductive Coconuts. A red-hot rhythm section and an extravagant horn section completed the line-up.

As the tour progressed, Granada TV recorded a one-hour spectacular by the band. It was transmitted on the last day of the tour: thus, in a single evening, Darnell's dream had reached over a million homes; Kid Creole and the Coconuts had arrived. By the end of the year, Darnell and his *compadrés* had completed another tour of Britain and Europe.

Tropical Gangsters ended the year as one of the UK's top-selling albums. Tickets for the band's London shows fetched up to £50 on the black market. Two further singles from the album, 'Stool Pidgeon' and 'Annie I'm Not Your Daddy' became sizeable hits, making Numbers 7 and 2 respectively. The band ended the year with a Number 27 UK hit, 'Dear Addy'.

Back in New York, Darnell began work on the Coconuts' solo LP. The three girls had become a marketable commodity in their own right and had been snapped up by the EMI America label; in addition Coati Mundi had signed a solo deal with Virgin Records. The resultant album by the Coconuts, *Don't Take My Coconuts* (1983), was a disappointing affair and was poorly received; Coati Mundi's album, entitled *Coati Mundi – The Former 12 Year Old Genius* (1983), also failed to sell and

Below: The slinky Coconuts, featuring Darnell's wife Adriana (centre). Right: 'Sugar-coated' Andy Hernandez, who plays the Kid's sidekick, Coati Mundi, on stage. Far right: Ladykiller Darnell, the biggest suit in the business.

was quickly deleted. Immediately after the release of the Coconuts' LP, Darnell started work on the fourth Kid Creole and the Coconuts record, *Doppelganger* (1983).

Zoot allure

Its release came at a critical point in the band's career. The Zoot suit – the epitome of chic fashion the previous year – was now passé and, more significantly, Darnell had recently been involved in a heavy schedule of touring, partying and recording. Evidence of a diminution of Darnell's creative energies seemed to be indicated by the fact that four of the LP's songs had been co-written with his half-brother Stoney, to whom Darnell had hardly spoken since the break-up of the Savannah Band. It was later to transpire, however, that the two had reconciled their differences and had once more joined forces, planning to write together for future projects. Although the record included two of his finest compositions, 'Back In The Field Again' and 'Bongo Eddie's Lament', it also contained a reworking of 'The Seven Year Itch' that compared poorly with the original Savannah Band version, which had been superbly sung by Cory Daye.

The story-line of *Doppelganger* was a continuation of the concept behind the band's first two albums – the Kid's adventures on his endless search for Mimi. Its release was greeted with little enthusiasm by the British media. Radio play for a single from the LP, 'There's Something Wrong in Paradise' (co-written with guitarist

Mark Mazur) was patchy, while the album was almost unanimously panned by the critics.

However the tour that coincided with the record's release sold out almost as soon as it was announced. For this series of shows, Darnell sought to stun the audience by the sheer scale and scope of the stage set alone. With a backdrop depicting urban New York, fronted by a cave (which the band used as a dressing-room and as a quick exit from the stage), two waterfalls, a jetty, a telephone kiosk and enough foliage to fill Kew Gardens, he succeeded. The band were as tight, the girls' routines as slick and the clothes for the main protagonists as extravagant as ever – Darnell alone underwent four costume changes. And yet, somehow, it all seemed as if there really *was* something wrong in paradise: although the group turned in some stunning performances, a certain air of calculation and predictability hung over the band.

Darnell had said that he would 'kill off' his *alter ego*, Kid Creole, when he tired of him; in the mid Eighties that remained a distinct possibility as Darnell set to work on a new project, a studio big band named Elbow Bones and the Racketeers, whose lush horn arrangements recalled the big bands of the Thirties and Forties. Whether the band's sound would click with the public remained to be seen. HEADLEY DOWN

Kid Creole and the Coconuts Recommended Listening

Fresh Fruit In Foreign Places (Island ILPS 7014) (Includes: Table Manners, In The Jungle, Animal Crackers, Going Places, With A Girl Like Mimi, Latin Music); *Tropical Gangsters* (Island ILPS 7016) (Includes: Annie, I'm Not Your Daddy, I'm A Wonderful Thing, Baby, The Love We Have, No Fish Today, Loving You Made A Fool Out Of Me, Stool Pidgeon).

Grace Jones: a talent to amaze

GRACE JONES is living proof of the importance of image in rock music. Throughout the metamorphoses her career has undergone – from cover girl to high-camp cabaret *chanteuse* to rock-disco superstar – she has displayed a breathtaking confidence in the power of glamour not only to disarm criticism but also to make statements every bit as subversive and 'political' as those contained in the songs of 'serious' rock artists.

Most rock musicians' work attempts to forge often spurious links between themselves and their fans. Grace, like David Bowie, has continually stressed her individuality and separateness from her audience. Her deliberately outrageous appearance undermines every stereotype of race and gender: her stage acts, which have seen her kitted out as a prizefighter or as a caged 'cat person' chewing on a piece of raw meat, ridicule preconceived ideas of taste and decorum, defy notions of how 'a star' should behave and redefine received notions of what is beautiful, grotesque or obscene. In the bizarre world of Grace Jones' music anything is possible, everything is permitted.

Ms Jones dresses to confuse (left) and sets out for a night on the tiles as an uncaged 'cat person' (below).

Grace glows and glowers in black leather (above) and models her favourite headgear (below left).

Unlimited capacity

Grace came from a wealthy, religious Jamaican family; both her father and her uncle were bishops. She recalled in *New Musical Express* in 1983: 'I had a strict religious upbringing. And, of course, I rebelled against all that. I was determined to try everything I'd ever dreamed of, and that's what I've done.'

Her family moved to Syracuse, New York, when she was 12. After a brief spell in college, she left home at 17 and began working for the Wilhelmina Model Agency. She also flirted with acting, appearing in the movie *Gordon's War* (1973). She then decided to join her brother in Paris. Her androgynous, black-panther-like exoticism fascinated the high-fashion world of Europe and she was soon appearing on the covers of *Elle, Vogue* and *Der Stern*. She was not content merely to be looked at, however, and was determined to express her forceful personality by becoming a singer. She first recorded in France, then signed with Island Records, a UK-based company.

Jones was initially treated as a strange and beautiful new toy by the international jet set and by the fast-growing gay disco scene in New York, centred on the exclusive Studio 54 club. Her performances saw her accompanied on stage by an assortment of male dancers, all in various states of semi-nudity; in Paris, 6000 fans reportedly rushed the stage in a frenzy and tore her few clothes off. She was fulsomely hailed as a 'secret night goddess' and 'the Dietrich of the New Decade'.

Her disco hits, such as 'What I Did For Love' and 'I Need A Man' from her first LP, *Portfolio* (1977), and 'Do Or Die' from *Fame* (1978), were extravagant exercises in kitsch with lush, decadent productions by Tom Moulton. The fact that her vocal abilities were minimal did not detract from her bizarre appeal, as her subsequent collaborator, the artist Jean-Paul Goude, recalled in his book *Jungle Fever*: 'She had been singing for less than two years and she wasn't an accomplished vocalist. But she had something much more important. She offered a whole new sensibility which was far more interesting to me than just an ability to sing properly.'

New extremes

With the commercial failure of her third LP, *Muse* (1979), which was never even released in the UK, Grace realised that changes had to be made. She and Jean-Paul, who by this time had become lovers (she had a son by him, christened Apollo), worked together on developing her image to new extremes. Goude designed clothes for her with huge padded shoulders; the femininity of her voluptuous mouth was strangely emphasised by a severe, flat-top, US Marine crew-cut. The look, combining strength and vulnerability, severity and sensuality, featured on the sleeve of her *Warm Leatherette* album in 1980.

The petulant authority of Grace's countenance on the cover was reflected by the LP's music, which was spare and commanding. Island Records' boss Chris Blackwell had decided to involve himself in shaping his signing's future, calling in the crack reggae rhythm section of drummer Sly Dunbar and bassist Robbie Shakespeare. Whereas her previous records had featured comatose camp standards like 'Send In The Clowns', 'La Vie En Rose' and 'Autumn Leaves', *Warm Leatherette* contained funk/reggae interpretations of songs by adventurous modern songwriters such as Bryan Ferry ('Love Is The Drug') and the Pretenders' Chrissie Hynde ('Private Life').

Grace no longer sounded like a closet Shirley Bassey, but adopted a sneering, monotone delivery that was both ironic and cutely sinister – nowhere more so than on the title track, originally a B-side by UK synthesiser wizard Daniel Miller's *alter ego* the Normal, that pondered the joys of having sex during a car crash. 'Private Life' became a UK Top Twenty hit, and Grace followed this success when she caused a sensation by whacking TV host Russell Harty for not paying her enough attention on his chat show.

Her next album, *Nightclubbing* (1981), consolidated her position as the queen of avant-garde disco-rock and was a *tour de force* of economy and power, once more pro-

duced by Blackwell and Alex Sadkin. The rhythmic clarity of 'Walking In The Rain' (containing the quintessential expression of Grace's persona in the line 'Feeling like a woman, looking like a man') and the drive of 'Pull Up To The Bumper' (co-written by Jones and Kookoo Baya) were particularly effective.

Sense of adventure

A softer side to Grace's personality was evident on *Living My Life* (1982), which was more relaxed in its use of reggae and rock rhythms and more adventurous in its arrangements than its predecessor. Its outstanding track was Melvin Van Peebles' 'The Apple Stretching', although the record's other songs – all with lyrics by Jones – were not far behind.

With *Living My Life* Grace Jones had

proved conclusively that she could stand on her own feet as a singer and writer, giving the lie to critical speculation that she was little more than a puppet. 'No one has ever told me wear this, do that, and I've always maintained complete control of my career. I'm not saying I've done it all myself because I've always collaborated with other artists, but my personality has always come through (in) my work.'

ALASTAIR DOUGALL

> **Grace Jones**
> **Recommended Listening**
>
> *Nightclubbing* (Island ILPS 9624) (Includes: Nightclubbing, Demolition Man, Walking In The Rain, Art Groupie, Fed Up, I've Done It Again); *Living My Life* (Island ILPS 9722) (Includes: My Jamaican Guy, Nipple To The Bottle, The Apple Stretching, Everybody Hold Still, Inspiration, Unlimited Capacity For Love).

The accordion provides a suitable prop for a 'Parisian' routine from Grace's One Man Show, designed by Jean-Paul Goude.

Electronically Yours

How the synthesiser eclipsed the guitar as the dominant sound in early-Eighties rock

By 1984, ELECTRONIC instruments had become an integral part of rock and pop music; it seemed hard to imagine that barely three years earlier, the Human League had been acclaimed as innovators when they reached the top of both the UK album and singles charts with two totally electronic records, *Dare* and 'Don't You Want Me'. During the early Eighties, the music industry absorbed and assimilated the new technology to the extent where the electronic hitmakers of 1983 – Blancmange, Eurythmics, Howard Jones – took synthesisers more or less for granted, blending them with more traditional instruments to produce a less stridently synthetic sound.

For all practical purposes, the synthesiser entered rock music in 1971 with the launch of Dr Robert Moog's Minimoog. Unlike his earlier models, it was small, compact and portable, and although it was monophonic – only capable of playing one note at a time – it caught on rapidly. The Minimoog was soon followed by the ARP Odyssey and the first British synth, the Putney (later EMS) VCS-3.

Europe and Japan
The new instruments were soon taken up by rock keyboard players like Rod Argent, Rick Wakeman, Keith Emerson and artists like Yes and Frank Zappa. But the first true synthesiser player was probably Brian Eno of Roxy Music. While his often classically-trained contemporaries transferred their piano or organ techniques to the new instruments, Eno began his musical dabblings on the VCS-3, using it to create startling new sound effects.

By the mid Seventies, electronic music had become both widespread and diverse. There was increasing interest in synths from jazz players like Chick Corea, George Duke and Herbie Hancock, and there was the growth of keyboard-oriented groups like Barclay James Harvest and Supertramp. There was also, from Germany, a group called Tangerine Dream, who converted to keyboards and grew to become one of the early giants of the genre.

Other significant events of this period included the release in 1973 of Mike Oldfield's *Tubular Bells* – an instrumental album which, although it did not use synthesisers, was based on the electronic treatment of other instruments – and, in 1975, of Tomita's *Snowflakes Are Dancing* and Kraftwerk's *Autobahn* albums. Isao Tomita from Japan, who used synthesisers to interpret the work of classical composers like Stravinsky or Debussy, was undoubtedly one of the early masters of electronic music. In Germany, Kraftwerk and producer Connie Plank exploited the cool modernism of electronic technology, creating a new kind of music that reflected the contemporary urban, industrial environment.

The second half of the Seventies was a period

of development both in the technology and the music which it could be used to create. Between 1976 and 1978, however, this growth was almost entirely overshadowed in Britain by the phenomenon of punk. Punk's message was that anyone who could afford £30 for a second-hand electric guitar could be in a band. But there was no such thing then as a £30 synthesiser – or a usable £300 synthesiser for that matter – so keyboards had little role to play in the movement and electronic music remained in the hands of established names like Vangelis, Patrick Moraz and Jean-Michel Jarre.

Sons of the silent age
In 1977, however, David Bowie collaborated with Brian Eno to produce two widely influential electronic albums, *Low* and *'Heroes'*. These records influenced and inspired a whole new wave of post-punk bands which were not afraid to use keyboards. Magazine, founded in 1977 by former Buzzcocks vocalist Howard Devoto, featured the intricate and dramatic keyboard-playing of Dave Formula. Along with bands like Ultravox! and the Human League (in their original line-ups), Magazine paved the way for many later developments. Jazz-rockers Landscape, meanwhile, traded their traditional instruments for synthesisers and became highly influential in the field.

The late Seventies also saw a number of technological innovations that paved the way for the musical developments of the Eighties. It was during this period that the first polyphonic-performance synthesisers – Moog's Polymoog, Sequential Circuits' Prophet 5 and Oberheim's OB-8 – came onto the market. Electronic rhythm machines, meanwhile,

Isao Tomita, the Japanese synthesiser pioneer, specialised in thoroughly modern interpretations of classical works. As synths became more accessible during the course of the Seventies, their influence extended into the field of commercial pop.

became more sophisticated and flexible. Much of the new equipment was programmable, allowing the user to create sounds or rhythms and store them on integrated-circuit memories. Sequencers, which could store whole passages of music, became more commonplace, particularly the remarkable Roland MC-8 Microcomposer (favoured by producer Martin Rushent, who was largely responsible for the Human League's phenomenal success). Drum synthesisers enjoyed a brief vogue at the beginning of the Eighties, when they saturated the pop and disco charts for a while.

But it was not until the introduction of the Electronic Dream Plant's Wasp in the late Seventies that there was a usable synthesiser comparable in price to a cheap electric guitar. It was the Wasp – and the spate of Japanese products that followed it – that brought the principle of punk to the keyboard scene, and made the instruments widely accessible. The availability of sequencers took the principle a stage further, for very little musical expertise was needed to play the instruments. An inexperienced musician could programme their tunes into the machine, note by note, and the sequencer would play them back in 'real time'.

Magic melodies

By the beginning of the Eighties, Japanese products dominated the popular market for synths and electronic instruments. The new interest in keyboards as a first instrument prompted electronics firms which had not previously been involved with music technology to launch their own products. The most notably successful company in this field was Casio, whose miniature and full-size keyboards were equally suited to use at home or on stage.

Japan also produced a notable electronic group in the form of Yellow Magic Orchestra, who blended the 'industrial' influence of Kraftwerk with a high degree of skill and an awareness of their particular ethnic background to create a unique and very stylish strain of music considered by many to be consistently ahead of the field. YMO were to be a big influence on British groups like Japan, and were to work with them and other pioneers in the field of electronics, notably Bill Nelson.

The UK, meanwhile, produced Gary Numan with his juvenile techno-fantasies, and a whole host of young 'electro-pop' outfits. Many of them first appeared on record on the *Some Bizarre* album early in 1981, including Soft Cell, Blancmange and Depeche Mode; these three went on to have major chart successes in their own right. The style of the new music was strictly danceable – an inevitable consequence of the level of the musicians' skills combined with the availability of drum computers and sequencers which could be most easily programmed to play strict dance tempos.

Among the new, keyboard-based bands of the early Eighties were the re-formed Ultravox, with Midge Ure on vocals, who enjoyed a massive hit in 1981 with their pseudo-classical 'Vienna', Visage, Orchestral Manoeuvres in the Dark and the Human League, now transformed from Kraftwerk-influenced experimentors to a classy, glamorous pop group in the

Abba mould. These bands were soon joined by Depeche Mode, Yazoo, the Thompson Twins, Yello and Eurythmics.

In America, the influence of electronics was more apparent in disco music, a notable milestone being Giorgio Moroder's production of Donna Summer's 1977 hit 'I Feel Love'. The next major development was the wave of electro-funk artists like Planet Patrol and the Jonzun Crew, the rappers and scratchers like Grandmaster Flash and Whodini, producers like Arthur Baker and the eccentric soul star Prince. The American developments fed back into British rock when New Order went to New York in 1983 to work with Arthur Baker on their single 'Confusion'.

By then, it had become extremely difficult to talk about 'electronic music' as a style apart from mainstream rock and pop, so completely had it been absorbed into the system. The self-

Opposite: Erstwhile jazzman Herbie Hancock combines vocal phrasing with his keyboard dexterity via a vocoder. Above: Brian Eno's pioneering work on a VCS-3 with Roxy Music showed that anyone could play synth. Right from top: European keyboards wizard Vangelis; the influential Japanese Yellow Magic Orchestra; and Depeche Mode, English popsters who chose synths over guitars.

conscious adoption of a cold, 'futuristic' sound and image, of which Gary Numan had been a classic example, had for the most part been abandoned in favour of a warmer, more 'natural' sound, and synthesisers were often used unselfconsciously alongside acoustic instruments. Despite a significant revival of guitar-based rock in the shape of Big Country and U2 in 1983, the synthesiser had become a standard feature of rock music.   IRVING KLAW

ROCK '81

1981 was a watershed year for pop in the UK. While the country was stricken with unemployment and torn by riots, the music scene polarised dramatically. On the one hand, there were the new romantics and their fellow travellers ABC, Soft Cell and Adam and the Ants, who wholeheartedly embraced the traditional escapism of the entertainment industry. It was the year of Antmania, of Soft Cell's 'Tainted Love' – the year's best-selling UK single – of nightclubbing, cocktails and outlandish clothes.

On the other hand, bands like the Specials, the Beat and UB40 preferred to confront the serious problems facing the country. Rejecting the froth and the fashion of the new romantics, the Specials scored an uncannily topical Number 1 hit with 'Ghost Town' that summer.

In the US, however, it was business as usual, and the charts were dominated by disco or arena-rock acts like REO Speedwagon and Air Supply. But there was a hint of things to come as UK bands like the Clash began to enjoy chart success in the States, presaging the new British Invasion of the following years. The New York scene, meanwhile, was producing flamboyant new non-mainstream acts like Grace Jones and Kid Creole and the Coconuts – although both, ironically, were to find far greater success in Britain and Europe than in the US.

January
2 David Lynch, one of the original members of the '50s vocal group the Platters, dies.
10 In the wake of John Lennon's murder, his classic song 'Imagine' reaches Number 1 in the UK chart.
12 The Sex Pistols' LP *Never Mind The Bollocks* is among 800 records given to the White House by the Recording Association of America.
16 Stevie Wonder plays in Washington DC as part of his campaign to have assassinated Civil Rights campaigner Martin Luther King's birthday (15 January) made a national holiday.
29 Barry Kramer, publisher of the rock magazine Creem, dies in Birmingham, Alabama, aged 37.

February
7 'Woman', by John Lennon, reaches Number 1 in the UK chart.
9 Bill Haley, one of rock'n'roll's founding

Left: In February the clock finally stopped for rocker Bill Haley. Above: April brought Eurovision success for Bucks Fizz, Britain's answer to Abba.

figures, dies of a heart attack at the age of 55 at his home in Harlingen, Texas.
13 Island Records release their '1+1' series of cassettes, featuring one side of music and one side of blank tape. This is soon condemned by the music industry watchdog the BPI as a 'blatant invitation' to home taping.
15 Blues guitarist Mike Bloomfield is found dead of a suspected heroin overdose in his car in San Francisco.
21 Joe Dolce's novelty song 'Shaddup You Face' reaches Number 1 in the UK.

March
14 'If it wasn't for people like us with ambition,' says Judas Priest's Kenny Downing, 'we'd all be on the dole like the other millions scavenging off the country.' Eric Clapton is hospitalized in St. Paul, Minnesota with bleeding ulcers. His US tour has to be cancelled.

April
4 British entry Bucks Fizz win the Eurovision Song Contest with 'Making

Your Mind Up', which goes to Number 1 in the UK the same month.

5 Canned Heat singer Bob Hite dies of a heart attack in Venice, California.

7 Kit Lambert, the Who's original manager, dies of head injuries after falling downstairs.

18 Progressive rockers Yes split up, although they were to reform in 1983.

20 John Phillips of the Mamas and the Papas is sentenced to eight years' imprisonment for dealing in drugs. All but 30 days of his sentence was suspended, however, on condition that he did community service and attended a drugs centre.

25 Guitarist Denny Laine leaves Paul McCartney's band Wings.

27 Ringo Starr marries actress Barbara Bach at London's Marylebone Register Office.

May

2 'I think England is very quickly falling out of love with me,' laments electro-pop star Gary Numan.

9 Adam and the Ants' 'Stand And Deliver' enters the UK charts at Number 1, the first record to do so since the Jam's 'Going Underground' a year earlier.

11 Bob Marley dies in a Miami hospital on his way home to Jamaica at the end of a long battle against cancer.

15 Fans riot at New York's Ritz Club as Public Image Ltd play behind a video screen, refusing to show themselves.

30 'I hope there will be time for a new romantic age,' says the Beat's singer Dave Wakeling, 'but it will be after young people have done something. Once we've made sure the world's going to last another 10 years, then we can all dress up and have a party.'

June

17 Singer Pauline Black plays her last show with the former 2-Tone band the Selecter.

21 Steely Dan's Donald Fagen and Walter Becker admit that their 14-year partnership has ended.

26 Bob Dylan plays the first of six nights at London's Earls' Court arena – his first UK dates since his conversion to Christianity.

27 Motorhead's *No Sleep Till Hammersmith* enters the UK album charts at Number 1.

30 Jerry Lee Lewis is rushed to hospital with a ruptured stomach and assorted ulcers.

July

2 Bruce Springsteen plays at the opening of the 21,000-seat Meadowlands Arena in New Jersey. It is the first of six shows which are all sold out in one day.

11 The Specials reach Number 1 in the UK charts with 'Ghost Town', a song that eerily captures the unrest of the times.

13 A black teenager is stabbed to death during a concert by reggae group Black

Uhuru at London's Rainbow Theatre.

16 Singer-songwriter Harry Chapin dies in a car crash on Long Island. A committed left winger who raised millions at benefit concerts, he had a worldwide hit with 'W.O.L.D.' in 1974.

August

1 'Green Door' gives Shakin' Stevens his second UK Number 1 single this year.

26 Lee Hays, co-author with Pete Seeger of 'If I Had A Hammer', dies of a heart attack at the age of 67.

29 Scottish folk singer Mary Sandeman scores a UK Number 1 hit with 'Japanese Boy' under the name Aneka.

September

5 'Tainted Love' by Soft Cell is Number 1 in the UK.

14 Walter 'Furry' Lewis, the bottleneck blues guitarist, dies of heart failure in

Top: Bob Marley's funeral was held at the National Arena, Kingston, on 21 May. Above: Mandolin-toting Joe Dolce.

Memphis at the age of 88.

18 'Prince Charming' by Adam and the Ants is Number 1 in the UK.

19 Simon and Garfunkel are reunited for the first time in 11 years at a concert in New York's Central Park. The occasion is both recorded and filmed.

October

10 'I'm disappointed,' Jerry Dammers says after Terry Hall, Lynval Golding and Neville Staples quit the Specials to form the Fun Boy Three, 'but I'm glad they stayed in the band long enough to record "Ghost Town".'

17 'It's My Party', by Dave Stewart and Barbara Gaskin, tops the UK chart, while 'Arthur's Theme (Best That You Can Do)' by Christopher Cross heads the *Billboard* listings.

18 A Rod Stewart concert at the Los Angeles Forum is broadcast live on TV around the world. It is watched by an estimated 35 million people. Sting cuts his hand during the filming of Dennis Potter's *Brimstone And Treacle*.

30 The Fun Boy Three release their first single, 'The Lunatics Have Taken Over The Asylum'.

November

21 'Under Pressure', a one-off single by David Bowie and Queen, is the new UK Number 1, while Olivia Newton-John's 'Physical' tops the US Hot Hundred.

December

6 Michael Dempsey, a publisher and former manager of punk band the Adverts, falls off a chair while changing a light bulb. He is found the next day and taken to hospital, where he dies of internal bleeding and a punctured liver.

12 'Don't You Want Me' by the Human League becomes the UK Christmas Number 1.

25 Christopher Tyrer, a heavy-metal fan from Staffordshire, dies in hospital. Eight days earlier he was paralysed and unable to speak after head-banging for three hours at a Saxon gig in Wolverhampton. A verdict of death by misadventure is recorded.

27 Broadway songwriter Hoagy Carmichael dies of a heart complaint at the age of 92 in California.

ANNETTE KENNERLEY, CHRIS SCHÜLER

WHO DARES WINS

The Human League: programmed for stardom

WITH ELECTRONIC POP music firmly entrenched in the charts and the public consciousness in the early Eighties, it was easy to forget that the form was a comparatively recent development. During the Seventies, the purposes to which electronic keyboards were put were self-consciously grandiose and their exponents were invariably trained musicians. At the end of the decade, however, a number of complete amateurs found success in the music business by tinkering with synthesisers and computers. This phenomenon was fostered by the prevailing attitudes of punk rock, which had preached that anyone could write and play music. The Human League and its offshoots were in the vanguard of this new development.

Logical songs
The Human League were formed in Sheffield in June 1977. The founders were Ian Craig Marsh (born 11 November 1956) and Martyn Ware (born 19 May 1956), a pair of computer operators with no musical training or experience but with a burning desire to start a modern electronic pop group. They were refreshingly blunt about their credentials for this undertaking: 'We're not musicians and we can't play guitars or anything like that. Instead we approach synthesisers using maths and logic.' The pair next approached an even more unlikely candidate – Philip Oakey (born 2 October 1955), who was working at the time as a hospital porter. The original quartet was completed by the arrival in March 1978 of Adrian Wright as 'visual director', a position merited by his deep interest in gadgets and obscure science-fiction films.

Their early live shows were chaotically engaging – triumphs of intent over technique. Marsh and Ware would stand lost in the gloom at the back of the stage, coaxing sounds out of a variety of machines, while Oakey maintained just enough of a profile to deliver some words. Meanwhile the focal point of the audience's attention was a screen on stage, upon which Wright pro-

The Human League started life as a highly experimental, multi-media group (opposite), but subsequently mutated into a more orthodox pop outfit (above).

jected a constant succession of slides from his 700-strong collection. The group's rationale for using the slides bordered on the pompous: 'We use the slides because they don't dictate a train of thought. They leave room for the imagination.' Nevertheless, this strange visual cocktail proved most effective and the group soon began to gather a sizeable cult following.

On the boil

The Human League formed an association with Bob Last, who had just formed the Edinburgh-based independent record label Fast Products. Accordingly, two tracks from among a number the group had recorded on a Sony two-track recorder were chosen for release as a single on Fast in June 1978 – 'Being Boiled' and 'Circus Of Death', collectively known as 'Electronically Yours'. Shortly after the release

of the single, they played their first London gig at the Music Machine. They supported the Rezillos, who contained within their ranks guitarist Jo Callis, later to become a member of the Human League.

The group got their first big break when they were invited to join Siouxsie and the Banshees on their UK tour. On 1 June 1979, the Human League released their second single for Fast entitled 'The Dignity Of Labour'. Like its predecessor, it made a respectable showing in the independent charts both in the UK and abroad. The group had signed to Virgin Records in April 1979, just after the completion of the second Fast single, and released their debut LP on Virgin in October 1979 after a European tour. Entitled *Reproduction*, the record sold poorly, a fact attributed in no small part to the group's peculiar choice of cover photograph – a selection of babies seen through broken glass. The rhythm tracks for the album were recorded at the group's own four-track studio, with producer Colin Thurston adding final overdubs at Red Bus studios. However the

subsequently Heaven 17, while Oakey and Wright were left with the rights to the Human League name. Oakey's reaction was predictable: 'I thought we were finished. The split wasn't very amicable and it was just rivalry that kept us going. We wanted to show the other two we could survive.' As events were to prove, the pair did rather more than that.

Boy meets girls

With an impending tour and only two band members, neither of whom could play anything, drastic measures were called for. Oakey immediately called on the services of Ian Burden, an old bass-playing friend from Sheffield, and recruited two girls, Joanne Catherall and Susanne Sulley, whom he met in Sheffield's Crazy Daisy

group still lacked the technical and musical ability to express its ideas fully – a fault that was amply demonstrated by a single taken from the LP, 'Empire State Human'.

In April 1980, the band released their second Virgin 45, a double single entitled 'Holiday 80' that contained five tracks: 'Nightclubbing', 'Dancevision', a new version of 'Being Boiled', a cover of Gary Glitter's 'Rock'n'Roll' and 'Marianne'. 'Holiday 80' reached Number 56 in the UK charts, representing a hopeful sign of things to come. In May, Virgin released the second Human League album, *Travelogue*; shortly afterwards, 'Empire State Human' gave the League a second, albeit lowly, chart entry at Number 62.

Although the Human League seemed to be poised for greater things, experienced observers of the group had long been aware of the friction, creative and otherwise, that had existed within their ranks. The band could be difficult – if entertaining – interviewees, often preferring to talk about films rather than music and refusing to be photographed because they had their own man in charge of visuals. One of the group's more controversial ideas was its 'disappearing' live act, whereby the audience would be entertained by pre-recorded tapes and slides while the band mingled with the audience or simply stayed at home in Sheffield. When news of this idea leaked out, it cost the group their support slot on a Talking Heads' UK tour.

On the eve of the Human League's UK tour in October 1980, it was announced that the group had split down the middle. Founder members Ware and Marsh left to form the British Electric Foundation and

Above: The band in the late Seventies, from left Phil Oakey, Adrian Wright, Ian Craig Marsh and Martyn Ware. Above right: Dare. Below: The Eighties League; (back row, from left) Jo Callis, Ian Burden and Oakey; (front row, from left) Joanne Catherall, Wright and Susanne Sulley.

disco, as backing singers, dancers and all-round centres of attention. The girls' initial response was hardly enthusiastic: 'There wasn't anything else that we'd set our hearts on doing. It was an opportunity to take a few weeks off school.'

This new line-up somehow managed to complete the tour. 1981 began with the release of a new single, 'Boys And Girls', which reached Number 44 in the charts, but more importantly established the new Human League sound. A follow-up single 'Sound Of The Crowd', released in April 1981 made Number 12, then July's 'Love Action' hit Number 3. By this time ex-Rezillo Jo Callis had joined the group; his composing debut was marked by the release of 'Open Your Heart', a Number 6 hit. Meanwhile, the Human League had been hard at work on their third LP with former Buzzcocks producer Martin Rushent.

Do or die
Released in October 1981, *Dare* was a pop classic. The material, written with one exception by combinations of Oakey, Burden and the experienced songwriter Callis, provided the hooks, while producer Rushent backed Oakey's tremulous bass voice with insistent Linndrum electronic percussion, repetitive keyboard riffs and synthesised basslines to create the necessary tension. The girls' voices were sparingly used, taking the lead only on 'Don't You Want Me', where the male-female duet inspired thoughts of a synth-pop Abba. This track was released as a single in November and became a Christmas chart-topper, while the album also reached Number 1 in the UK.

A successful tour of the UK was followed by tours of Europe, the US and Japan as the Human League broke big all over the world. The originality of their material had finally been harnessed to a first-class production, courtesy of Martin Rushent. The Human League subsequently kept a low profile, putting out only one LP, *Love And Dancing* (basically a dub instrumental version of *Dare* concocted by Rushent), and just two singles – 'Mirror Man' (released in November 1982) and 'Fascination' (April 1983), both of which reached Number 2 in the UK charts.

While Human League were rocketing to success, Martyn Ware and Ian Craig Marsh were hard at work with their first project under the BEF umbrella, Heaven 17. Named after a group in Anthony Burgess' novel *A Clockwork Orange*, it featured Ware, Marsh and vocalist Glenn Gregory, a former photographer and stagehand. The group put out its debut single in March 1981 – the astonishingly assured '(We Don't Need This) Fascist Groove Thang' – which instantly established Heaven 17's musical credentials as well as their political viewpoint. It was followed in May by 'I'm Your Money' and then August's 'Play To Win', but none breached the Top Thirty.

Success came finally with the appearance of a debut LP, *Penthouse And Pave-*

Above: Heaven 17, from left Ware, vocalist Glenn Gregory and Marsh.

ment, which reached Number 14 in the album charts after its release in October 1981. Singles success still eluded the group, however, despite the release of the LP's title track as a single; another 45, 'At The Height Of The Fighting (He La Hu)', released in February 1982, was also ignored by the public.

Heaven can wait
At this point, Heaven 17 was put into cold storage for some months as Marsh and Ware took on the production mantle of the British Electric Foundation in order to produce an extraordinary LP of cover versions, wherein a variety of famous singers gave personal interpretations of classic songs. *Music Of Quality And Distinction* was released in April 1982 to a mixed critical reception. It featured items such as Tina Turner's version of 'Ball Of Confusion', Billy McKenzie of the Associates doing Roy Orbison's 'It's Over' and Gary Glitter's treatment of 'Suspicious Minds'. Although the LP was a somewhat hit-and-miss affair, *Music Of Quality And Distinction* marked a brave departure for Marsh and Ware. The concept was repeated more successfully when their production of Tina Turner singing Al Green's 'Let's Stay Together' became a Number 6 UK hit in late 1983.

A preview of Heaven 17's second album apeared late in August 1982 in the form of the single 'Let Me Go', which once again failed to provide them with a decent-sized hit. Finally in April 1983, the group's efforts were rewarded with the release of

the single 'Temptation' and the LP *The Luxury Gap*. The 'Temptation' single was fuelled by a magnificent guest vocal by Carol Kenyon, a one-time backing singer with Isaac Hayes. It provided Heaven 17 with their first elusive hit, reaching Number 2 in the UK charts. The album was similarly successful, with nine powerful tracks featuring a host of outside talent – notably John Wilson and Ray Russell on guitars, Nick Plytas on piano and the Earth, Wind and Fire horn section. Two further singles from the album made the Top Twenty, 'Come Live With Me' and 'Crushed By The Wheels Of Industry'.

Crash back
1984's *Hysteria* made Number 3 in the UK but was distinctly patchy, while *Crash* (1986) saw the remaining trio of Oakey, Sulley and Catherall in the hands of the crack US soul production/songwriting team of Jimmy Jam and Terry Lewis. 'Human', the single, was a US Number 1. They released a hits collection in 1988. Heaven 17 continued with minimal commercial success, Ware now earning greater reward producing Tina Turner and Terence Trent D'Arby.   PETER CLARK

Human League
Recommended Listening
Dare (Virgin V2192) (Includes: I Am The Law, Don't You Want Me, Love Action, Seconds, Sound Of The Crowd, Get Carter).
Heaven 17
Recommended Listening
Penthouse And Pavement (Virgin V2208) (Includes: (We Don't Need This) Fascist Groove Thang, Penthouse And Pavement, Play To Win, The Height Of The Fighting (He La Hu), Geisha Boys And Temple Girls, Lets All Make A Bomb).

KRAFT

Locked in the lab with rock's new technocrats

OF ALL THE BANDS to use synthesisers in the early Seventies, perhaps the most influential and innovative proved to be the German band Kraftwerk. While 'progressive' rock musicians like Rick Wakeman and Emerson, Lake and Palmer used the new electronic instrumentation to re-create the sound of a nineteenth-century orchestra, and the Who and Pink Floyd used it to enrich the textures of traditional rock, Kraftwerk pioneered a totally new, overtly electronic sound.

Kraftwerk was formed by Ralf Hütter and Florian Schneider, who broke away from the five-piece band Organisation. The duo's first two albums – released in the UK as a double LP called *Kraftwerk* in 1973 – were recorded in Connie Plank's studio in Dusseldorf, with Plank, Hütter and Schneider co-producing. They showed

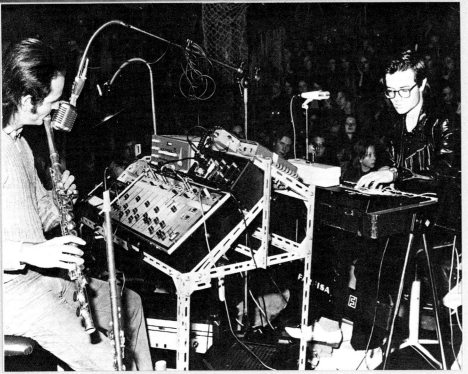

Left: Florian Schneider (left) and Ralf Hütter in an early Kraftwerk incarnation. Above: Now we are four . . .

WERK

Hütter and Schneider casting around in various directions, exploring the different electronic means at their disposal and making adventurous use of the studio, with both electronic and acoustic instruments – such as woodwind and violin – coming in for highly unorthodox treatment. All sorts of influences were being assimilated, from avant-garde musicians like Cage and Stockhausen through to Pink Floyd and Tangerine Dream. There was even a hint of Can in the albums' hard-driven, poundingly rhythmic passages such as 'Ruckzack' and 'Stratovarius'.

Given Dusseldorf's location deep in German industry's heartland and the fact that the band's name translates as 'power plant', it became commonplace for reviewers to label this set as 'industrial music', but this assessment stressed only its harsher aspects. While tracks like the powerfully atmospheric 'Vom Himmel Hoch' almost seemed to look forward to Throbbing Gristle or Cabaret Voltaire at their bleakest, the influence of Pink Floyd and Tangerine Dream were very much to the fore on 'Megaherz' and throughout the quieter, second record, on which the

melodic 'Klingklang' provided the clearest indication of Kraftwerk's future direction.

Hütter and Schneider produced their next album, *Ralf And Florian* (1974), themselves, but retained Connie Plank as engineer. Made partly in their own Kraftwerk studio, it was considerably more unified than its predecessors: the numbers were shorter and more homogeneous, and there was a lot less dissonance and spaciness; instead there was a springy, danceable beat and a fresh, almost open-air feeling. Particularly attractive were the sparkling, 'Kristallo', the album's one long track, 'Ananas Symphonie', which featured an electronically treated voice, very much a harbinger of the future, and the peaceful 'Heimatklange'.

Road werk

It was later that same year that Kraftwerk really established their own personal musical style and also came to wide public notice through the hit single 'Autobahn', taken from the album of the same name. Produced by Hütter and Schneider at Connie Plank's studio, *Autobahn* marked the addition to the group of Klaus Roeder

(violin and guitar) and Wolfgang Flur on electronic percussion. Rather like the previous year's *Tubular Bells*, this was one of those rare records which seemed to be accepted by easy listening, AOR and more 'progressive' audiences alike.

Kraftwerk, however, made nothing from the massive sales, having sold complete rights in the album to Phonogram for 2000 dollars. Most of all, though, *Autobahn*'s title track, like Bowie's *Young Americans*, appealed to the growing disco market – Wolfgang and Ralf were habitual disco-goers. As Steve Taylor pointed out in the *Face* in 1982, 'Kraftwerk pulled off a trick that has never been equalled or imitated yet – to make synthetic and *obviously* synthetic percussion sound warm and dynamic enough to be irresistibly danceable.'

But *Autobahn* was also important for its German lyrics at a time when most German, indeed most European, pop music relied solely on the English – or rather the American – language. 'Everybody said that singing German lyrics was crazy,' Ralf recalled. 'Can you imagine that 75 per cent of our radio programmes were in

2311

To keep pace with recent technological developments, Kraftwerk decided to re-build and computerise their studio, a process that was to take three years. The result was *Computerworld* (1981), an album with computers as its central theme; it received a Grammy nomination, while the single 'Numbers' was so dance-able it even became a hit on the *Billboard* soul charts. Interest in the band was higher than ever, generated partly by the synth-pop boom which they had influenced in the first place. They undertook a highly successful European tour, quite literally taking their new studio out on the road with them, and had a UK Number 1 with 'Computer Love'/'The Model' – their biggest hit since 'Autobahn' had made Number 11 six years previously.

English? In the clubs when we first started playing you *never* heard a German record, you switched on the radio and all you heard was Anglo-American music, you went to the cinema and all the films were Italian or French. We needed our own cultural identity.'

Ohm sweet ohm
Autobahn was followed by *Radioactivity* (1975), on which Klaus Roeder was re-placed by Karl Bartos, another electronic percussionist, to form the guitarless line-up that survived into the Eighties. Pro-duced at the group's own Kling Klang studio, it was less immediately danceable than its predecessor, although its title track contained one of the most glorious melodies Kraftwerk ever produced. Direc-tor Chris Petit made effective use of the track 'Ohm Sweet Ohm' in his 1979 film *Radio On*.

Radioactivity was the first of Kraft-werk's albums to be unified around a theme (in this case, radio waves of various kinds), although they managed to avoid the pretentious philosophising of many pomp-rock 'concept albums'. 'It's not really songwriting,' Ralf explained, 'it's more symphonic the way we write, part of our German musical culture, the orchestral tradition. That's why we use our voices as sound, not really as singing. The words just slipped into the music. We always try to plant lyrics like clues, use them as codes.' Particularly interesting was Kraftwerk's extensive use of 'found' radio material (briefly prefigured on *Autobahn*), pre-dating better-known examples by people like Eno and Cabaret Voltaire.

Trans Europe Express (1977) took up the theme of travel, and also contained 'Show-room Dummies', a track that enjoyed a long and successful life as a single. As an album, however, the project was far less innovative and interesting than its succes-sor, *Man Machine* (1978). With its overall theme of robotics and its utterly contempo-rary electronic sound, *Man Machine* was Kraftwerk's most thoroughly 'techno-logical' album to date. Their music did not, however, represent a simple-minded

Top: Kraftwerk – humans or showroom dummies? Above: Their 1977 album.

fetishisation of machinery: Kraftwerk were very much the masters, not the servants, of technology, and *Man Machine* posited not the domination of man by machine but, as Chris Bohn wrote in *New Musical Express* in 1981, 'a proper working relationship between man and his urban environment, perhaps recognising for the first time the splendid, brittle beauties of new cities and industrial scenery.'

The werk ethic
Kraftwerk saw themselves more as studio technicians than as musicians in the con-ventional sense. They referred to their studio as a laboratory, rejecting the whole notion of individual artistry and the star system. They even utilised uncannily realistic dummies for photo sessions, free-ing them to get on with their work. (These dummies were also used to première *Man Machine* in New York and Paris in 1978.)

Kraftwerk regarded themselves less as creative artists than as a mouthpiece for the spirit of the age: 'It's not really us who make the music, because it's not me personally, or Karl or Florian or Wolf-gang,' Ralf told *Melody Maker* in 1981. 'It's just coming through to us. It is a result of research. I think it is a more scientific attitude.'

> 'Music? I don't think its that import-ant, honestly speaking. We concentrate on our day to day work; we don't feel a part of the traditional music scene. We go to the studios six days a week for eight or ten hours. Music must be work like anything else – that's actually how it is done, like a workshop'.
>
> **Ralf Hütter**

Computerworld, for all its technological brilliance, was no mindless hymn to high technology. The title track, for instance, stressed the sinister ways in which com-puters can be used for surveillance and control by 'Interpol and Deutsche Bank, FBI and Scotland Yard'. Here, as ever, Kraftwerk were quite subtly subversive in intent.

This was to be Kraftwerk's high point of the Eighties; future albums *Trans-Europe Express* (1982) and *Electric Cafe* (1986) failed to catch the public imagination. Yet their decline in commercial success should not obscure their influence.

Kraftwerk saw themselves as bridging the gap between music and technology – they once called their studio the Electronic Garden – emphasising that computers can be used just as much for pleasure as business. 'We're creating a softer attitude, exposing how you can do other things, because computers are like blank tapes.' Kraftwerk's greatest achievement is to have harnessed sophisticated modern technology to essentially popular, dance-able music, paving the way for the synthe-sised pop sounds that were to dominate the charts in the early Eighties. JULIAN PETLEY

Kraftwerk
Recommended Listening

Autobahn (EMI EMC203) (Includes: Autobahn, Kometenmelodie 1, Kometenmelodie 2, Mitternacht, Morgenspaziergang); *Trans-Europe Express* (EMI E-ST 11603) (Includes: Europe Endless, The Hall Of Mirrors, Showroom Dummies, Trans-Europe Express, Metal On Metal, Endless Endless).

REACH FOR THE SKY

Flights of fantasy from Gary Numan

SOMETIMES THE PATH to fame is long and tortuous; sometimes the route is short and direct. Gary Numan took the quick way. When his group's second album was released in April 1979 he was barely known outside (or even within) his record-company offices; by the end of June he had been catapulted to the top echelon of contemporary rock stars. He then sweated in the white-hot glare of superstardom for two years before announcing – at the age of 23 – a retirement that turned out to be as phoney as most other 'retirements' from the popular music stage.

Born on 8 March 1958, Gary Webb had reportedly been an isolated and introspective child, albeit one raised in a middle-class home with strong family bonds. From his early teens, he had

Numan, an enthusiastic pilot, readies himself to become a warrior of the airwaves.

decided to be a pop star when he grew up; at 18, his dismal record of academic achievement had left him few options. As the punk bandwagon careered through London and the provinces in 1976-77, he leapt on board, performing with a group called the Lasers. Gary, like Cliff Richard before him, decided he'd be better off without the plain surname Webb, and so became Numan.

The Lasers' act was totally derivative, but the primary objective of obtaining a recording contract was realised. The band, by then known as Tubeway Army, released its eponymous debut album in 1978. But Numan was already planning ahead, and he used record-company support to further his acquaintance with synthesisers and virtually withdrew from gigging. This may have been hard on fellow group members Paul Gardiner (bass) and Jess Lidyard (drums) but guitarist/keyboardist Numan had never felt comfortable in live performance. He spent much of the next year developing his studio skills, and the resulting *Replicas* was released in April 1979.

Although still credited to Tubeway Army, the album was virtually a Numan solo record. He had written all the material, handled all the crucial synthesiser parts and produced the entire album. It was in this latter respect that his talents seemed at their most precocious; despite his lack of experience, Numan's tyro production was emphatic and assured. 'Are "Friends" Electric?' sounded particularly effective and became the single, reaching Number 1 in the UK charts at the end of June 1979. It stayed there for four weeks, while *Replicas* dominated the album charts in similar fashion.

Numan had worked hard on his image. He had dyed blonde hair and used make-up, which only accentuated his natural pallor. Otherwise, he appeared entirely in

Above: Despite little sign of life from the musicians, Numan's show was a neon spectacular. Opposite: Crooning Numan.

black – black clothes, black eye-liner, even black fingernails. He portrayed himself as the emblem of a bleak, de-personalised future in which machines and monotony had replaced people and passion.

Sci-fi superstar

Numan's pose aroused passionate loyalty in those who overlooked its superficiality, and equally vehement loathing in those who did not. He immediately seemed to gather an army of devoted fans, including many look-alikes, who ensured that his follow-up releases later in 1979 were also well-received. These – the album *The Pleasure Principle* and the single 'Cars' – were ready for early autumn release, and soon topped the UK album and singles charts. By that time, his hair was jet-black and the records were issued under his own name; otherwise little had changed. Numan emphasised the stark, futuristic aspects by giving all the tracks one-word titles. His approach was just right for the time: 'I realised that what the audience needed was a synthesiser star' he explained – so that was what he became.

Numan was a potent phenomenon. Harsh and simplistic though his music was, and however thin his vocals, his production expertise compensated for everything, and the records that he made at this time showed that he understood perfectly how to record synthesisers. His songs may have lacked melody, but they carried a rare punch. He found an adolescent audience which believed in him and claimed him as its own. His image was derived primarily from Bowie, his music from Kraftwerk, Ultravox! and Brian Eno, while a smatter-

ing of science fiction completed the persona. There was an intellectual veneer, but that was all. This was perfect for his audience – it was all they needed. The fact that there was no real depth to his music alienated only the music press.

In fact, press reaction became unremittingly hostile, partly because Numan was essentially an adolescent phenomenon and partly because the press suspected, correctly, that Numan's success had all but invalidated them. As one *Melody Maker* journalist ruefully admitted, Numan's elevation had been an object-lesson in the irrelevance of the music press. Further, Numan, the star, ignored the media as it had once ignored him. Requests for interviews were frequently declined. There was a perfectly good reason for this; his conversation tended to undermine his carefully-created persona, as he talked fondly of his home background and of the assistance his parents had rendered: on tour, his mother acted as his hairdresser, his father as general factotum.

Once his records had established him, Numan – who had not performed at all for 18 months, and then in small venues – was quickly booked for a headlining tour at all the major UK halls. Of his band, only Gardiner had been with him throughout. The others, dubbed Dramatis, were Ced Sharpley (drums), Chris Payne (keyboards), Rrussell (sic) Bell (guitar, keyboards) and Dennis Haines (keyboards). Numan, inevitably, designed the concert sets, which were structured to represent a world in which machines had superseded man. The Touring Principle tour, as it was called, covered the UK in autumn 1979, boosting the next single, 'Complex', to Number 6, and went on to cover the remainder of the globe in stages. By mid 1980, Numan had become an international star, with 'Cars' reaching Number 9 in the US Hot Hundred.

Messages to humanity

By the autumn of 1980, another of his bleak messages to humanity had been unveiled: *Telekon* was the album, and 'I Die, You Die' the single. Neither demonstrated any real development of Numan's technique, though *Telekon* immediately topped the album charts. There were signs, however, that Numan's appeal was on the wane, with empty seats at his Teletour concerts and the single peaking at Number 6 in the UK charts.

Even then, Numan was beginning to refer to the prospect of retirement, and the following spring he undertook what he claimed were positively his final concerts. He intended to concentrate exclusively on films, video and recording, and had already put down a marker in the inchoate video market by putting together a video of the September 1979 Hammersmith Odeon concert, released in May 1980.

The music from this concert was released as a live album in May 1981, as was that from the following year's equivalent date, to coincide with the farewell concerts at Wembley Arena. Available either as a double set, entitled *Living Ornaments 1979-1980*, or separately, they were on sale for only a month – after that, they were deleted. On the one hand, such instant obsolescence was perhaps a fitting metaphor for the future of Numan's imagination; on the other, it represented a crude marketing ploy, the album set reaching Number 2 in the UK charts.

Flying high?

The concerts were breathtakingly staged, with a complicated and expensive set (Numan reckoned that he would finish up £150,000 out of pocket) inspired by the finale of 1977's cinematic epic, *Close Encounters Of The Third Kind*. Numan then quickly completed work on his next recordings before indulging his love for flying, and piloting his own aircraft round the world. In his absence, the album *Dance* reached Number 3, and the single 'She's Got Claws' climbed to Number 6.

The redundant members of Dramatis stayed together after the farewell concerts, signed a contract with Rocket Records and recorded a debut album of their own, *For Future Reference*, released towards the end of the year. Having returned safely from his travels, Numan himself sang lead vocals on 'Love Needs No Disguise', a song the group had written about their stint as his backing band. It became a Number 33 hit as a single.

The Numan devotees remained numerous; the ranks of the press remained solidly critical. Numan continued to attain regular Top Twenty singles success even after the electro-pop field in which he had been so influential had been invaded by so many others, while his 1982 album, *I, Assassin*, made Number 8. By autumn 1983 he seemed to be gathering fresh respect among the music-business fraternity, and recorded his album *Warriors* with contributions from ex-Bebop Deluxe guitarist Bill Nelson and veteran jazz saxophonist Dick Morrissey.

Numan continued into the Eighties, appearing regularly in the lower reaches of the Top Fifty on his own Numa label and, later, on IRS. Although his period of influence had long gone, he still commanded a hard core of support and seemed likely to continue performing and touring as long as this lasted.

The pioneer of synthesised pop music was still in business.   BOB WOFFINDEN

Gary Numan
Recommended Listening

Replicas (Beggars Banquet BEG 50 638) (Includes: You Are In My Vision, I Nearly Married A Human, Down In The Park, Praying To The Aliens, Are 'Friends' Electric?, The Machman); *The Pleasure Principle* (Beggars Banquet BEGA 10) (Includes: Airlane, Cars, Complex, Metal, Films, Observer).

On Manoeuvres

OMD's orchestral journey through the past

WHEN THE LIVERPOOL ROCK SCENE took off in the late Seventies, few people could have expected Orchestral Manoeuvres in the Dark to emerge as the city's most commercially successful group. The prevailing pattern among Merseyside bands was best personified by the likes of Echo and the Bunnymen and the Teardrop Explodes: acid-tinged tunes and doom-laden lyrics inspired by American bands like the Doors and the Velvet Underground.

In stark contrast to the prevailing mood, the two members of OMD, Andy McCluskey and Paul Humphreys, took their inspiration from a different source altogether, namely Germany's Kraftwerk. 'The two of us went to see them when they played the Liverpool Empire in 1975,' McCluskey later recalled. 'I was only 16 and Paul 15. When they dropped in on one of our European dates a couple of years ago it was like meeting our parents.'

Round about the time they first set eyes

on their heroes, Andy and Paul were members of a 'more rock-oriented' group with a drummer, Malcolm Holmes, who was subsequently to rejoin them. Tired of being part of a traditional rock band, they struck out as a duo-plus-tape-recorder. Both confessed to being unable to play an instrument; McCluskey taught himself to play bass as well as sing, while Humphreys bought a Selmer Pianotron for £25.

It was on the latter instrument that Paul Humphreys composed the incredibly catchy 'Electricity', which was released on Manchester's Factory Records in the spring of 1979. Factory's Tony Wilson had been suitably impressed by the band's gigs at Eric's, the now almost-legendary Liverpool club, and offered them a one-off release. Within a couple of weeks 'Electricity' had sold out its initial pressing of 5000. The duo performed for delighted audiences at shows as diverse as the first Futurama Festival in Leeds, headlined by Public Image Ltd, and a Factory Records package tour on which they were sandwiched between Joy Division and A Certain Ratio.

Doubts and discs

Before long, the band were approached by major record companies, and eventually signed to Virgin subsidiary DinDisc. Their first DinDisc releases showed promise: 'Red Frame White Light' could only make Number 67 in the UK charts, but 'Messages' reached Number 13, while the band's self-named debut album appeared in the LP Top Thirty at Number 27. The label's £25,000 advance had enabled them to buy their own studio, the Gramophone Suite, where OMD recorded their first four albums. They spent about six months of each year in this Liverpool hide-out, the rest of the time being taken up by gruelling tours. Realising the musical and visual limitations of using pre-recorded tapes in their live shows, the pair drafted in Holmes on drums and Dave Hughes on keyboards and bass for their first headlining tour in 1980.

The resulting pressures led to the pair experiencing frequent bouts of disillusionment; although outwardly confident and full of blunt northern humour, McCluskey often gave the impression that, artistically, the pair of them were riddled with self-doubt. 'Paul and I constantly wonder if we're doing the right thing, if our integrity's intact. The danger lies in repeating yourself because then you just get bored with what you do.' It was this uncertainty that inspired the radical change in their approach following the band's Number 8 UK hit, 'Enola Gay', the success of which McCluskey ascribed to the fact that 'everything in it was hooks, from the rhythm part out. We were perfectionists with everything on that album [1980's *Organisation*] but the style could very easily have become a formula.'

OMD were also aware that following their second LP, a whole crop of electro-pop bands had sprung up. In the autumn of 1981 McCluskey admitted 'We haven't got that freshness anymore – it belongs to Depeche Mode at the moment.' They still managed to come up with a masterpiece, *Architecture And Morality* (1981) – perhaps the most exquisitely lush study in nostalgia ever released by a rock band. The LP yielded the atmospheric hits 'Souvenir', 'Joan Of Arc' and 'Maid Of Orleans (The Waltz Joan Of Arc)', singles which made Number 3, 5 and 4 respectively in the UK charts. Lyrically, their obsession seemed to be with the past; when on the road, the two had a penchant for visiting museums and castles.

'We've never rabbited on about unemployment or nuclear weapons,' said Andy McCluskey. 'We consider those to be trivia, symptoms of a larger problem . . . the entire mental framework of the human species – genetics.'

Perhaps because of their tendency to view life in a serious light, their fourth LP, *Dazzleships* (1983), came close to being an embarrassing failure. The two 45s taken from it – the witty 'Genetic Engineering' and the raucous rock-out, 'Telegraph', were fine, if nowhere near as commercially successful as former singles; much of the rest of *Dazzleships* was pretentious and disposable.

The pair seemed to have been carried away by the infinite aural possibilities of

Opposite: OMD's Andy McCluskey (left) and Paul Humphreys out on the town. Above: Paul tinkers on synth. Below: Andy pulls out all the stops.

the Emulator synthesiser, a machine into which any sound – from a lawn mower to a banshee – could be programmed and then slowed down or speeded up. By writing lyrics about robots in Czechoslovakian industry and composing another 'song' solely comprising a montage of international clocks ('Time Zones'), OMD concocted a recipe for disaster.

The band's fifth album, *Junk Culture*, was released in late 1983. Recorded on the Caribbean island of Montserrat, it featured saxophonist Martin Cooper who replaced Hughes and introduced a fresh sound into the group's music. The LP and it's follow-up, *Crush* (1984) managed to reaffirm OMD's status in rock history and assure them of continuing commercial success in the Eighties.   MIKE NICHOLLS

Orchestral Manoeuvres in the Dark Recommended Listening
Orchestral Manoeuvres In The Dark (Dindisc DID 2) (Includes: Bunker Soldiers, Almost, Electricity, Messages, Dancing, Red Frame/White Light); *Architecture And Morality* (Dindisc DID 12) (Includes: Joan Of Arc, The New Stone Age, She's Leaving, Georgia, The Beginning And The End).

IN THE MOOG

The whys and wherefores of synthesised sound

THE FIRST MUSICAL instrument that could conceivably be classified as a synthesiser was American inventor Thaddeus Cahill's gargantuan Telharmonium. It took Cahill 10 years from 1896 to 1906 to build the instrument – a relatively modest period when one considers that the device weighed over 200 tons and six railway trucks were required to transport it.

The Telharmonium used rapidly spinning alternators driven by banks of electric motors to produce the required electrical signals; two people were needed to play it and so great was the noise produced by all the motors that the speakers had to be set up in a different room to the main body of the instrument.

Inspired by Cahill's pioneering work, others began to strive for new ways to make music, and over the first half of the twentieth century many novel electrical musical instruments were to appear. The Aetherophone, the Ondes Martinot organ, the Trautonium, the Theremin and the Meissner Piano were among the most successful new devices, but it was not until the mid Fifties that the synthesiser proper emerged as a professional instrument in its own right.

1955 saw the birth of the RCA Music Synthesiser, a monophonic instrument (one that can only play a single note at a time) that was soon to be updated by a Mark II machine which was polyphonic – capable of playing of chords. Several session musicians immediately saw the potential of these instruments and sounds from the RCA machines to grace many a radio advert and sci-fi film of the Fifties. However, the RCA machines were studio tools more than musical instruments as they were so unwieldy and prohibitively expensive. It was not until 1964 when Dr Robert A. Moog developed an electronic musical system that utilised voltages as the method of control that the synthesiser became an acceptable instrument within the financial grasp of most musicians.

Moog's first synthesisers were modular systems, comprising separate units of oscillators, filters, amplifiers and shaping circuits, which had to be linked up together using connector leads. These systems were fairly expensive and cumbersome and often looked more like an old-fashioned telephone exchange than a musical instrument.

Bach to mono
One of Moog's early customers was a young composer named Walter Carlos who, in 1968, used one of Moog's modular synthesisers to produce what was to become the biggest-selling classical album ever – *Switched On Bach*, a selection of the composer's best-known works performed on synthesiser. The modular synthesiser Carlos used was still only monophonic, obliging him to record every part separately using a multi-track tape recorder, but the project's success more than justified the time and effort spent producing it – and it also drew considerable attention to Moog's electronic devices.

Moog was now increasingly pressured to produce an instrument that could be taken on the road and played live, and in 1971 he unveiled a device that was to become the instrument of the Seventies – the Minimoog. Compact and portable, the Minimoog had a warm, rich and full sound which slotted in admirably with the techno-rock requirements of the day.

Many companies now moved in on the monophonic synthesiser market, but Moog had been in there first and had got it right first time – most other instruments that were to come along were pale imitations of Moog's brainchild. But the Minimoog (and its imitators) had two shortcomings: it could still only play a single note at a time, and it was a time-consuming business altering the controls to get a different sound. One way around this problem was to have a bank of Minimoogs all preset to

Above left: Unveiled in 1971, the Minimoog proved a widely-used monophonic synth. Left: Dr Robert Moog (right) helps keyboard-player Roger Powell unravel his machine. Top right: Switched On Bach.

produce different sounds – Rick Wakeman, at one point, had six Minimoogs on stage.

Two further developments were required in order that the synthesiser might become a versatile, all-round instrument. The most pressing was that of producing a polyphonic synthesiser – one on which chords could be played. Moog Music Inc,

the company that produced the Minimoog was one of the first to come up with such a device (although Dr Moog himself had little to do with the project) when, in 1977, they introduced the Polymoog. This was a fully polyphonic synthesiser – one on which all the notes could be played simultaneously – but in effect it owed more to organ technology than to developments in the synthesiser field.

Poly themes
Yamaha simultaneously released their CS-80, a smaller version of their GX-1; the latter, an enormously expensive instrument, had been used only by a few top players – Keith Emerson played it on ELP's 'Fanfare For The Common Man', and Stevie Wonder, Led Zeppelin's John Paul Jones and a few others had one. The CS-80 itself was a large polyphonic synthesiser that utilised a principle known as voice assignment; inside was the circuitry of eight synthesisers and, as a key was pressed, it was assigned one of these voice circuits. The CS-80 could play just eight notes at once – but this was enough. The

Inside a Synth

A musical note can be defined by three basic parameters – pitch (the quality that makes one sound seem 'higher' or 'lower' than another), timbre (the tone colour of the sound) and loudness. A synthesiser is an instrument that specifies these three parameters to create virtually any sound. By using electrical currents moving in a circuit, the synthesiser simulates the vibrations that form sound; most types use a voltage-controlled oscillator (VCO) to set the pitch, a voltage-controlled filter (VCF) to determine the timbre and a voltage-controlled amplifier (VCA) to set the loudness.

The most usual method of control for producing the voltage is a keyboard. Each key on the board produces a dif-

Tangerine Dream's array of synths include ARP and Moog instruments.

ferent voltage, which is fed to the VCO – the higher the voltage, the higher the resulting note pitch. In addition, when each key is pressed, a trigger pulse is produced as a signal to the VCF and VCA.

Another important feature of the synthesiser is the performance controls. These enable a player to change certain characteristics of the sound while he is playing a note. The most widely used performance control is the pitchbender which enables the player to raise or lower the pitch of a single note in order to achieve a similar effect to a guitarist bending a string.

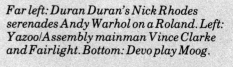

Far left: Duran Duran's Nick Rhodes serenades Andy Warhol on a Roland. Left: Yazoo/Assembly mainman Vince Clarke and Fairlight. Bottom: Devo play Moog.

instrument was a great success, and was featured on many records of the time, most notably Andrew Lloyd Webber's *Variations* (1977) and 'Argentinian Melody', the theme for the 1978 World Cup football tournament.

Having perfected polyphonic systems, manufacturers set about the problem of how to alter controls quickly and easily. One method that had been used for some years was to have a set of 'patches' (prearranged settings) programmed into the instrument at the factory so that the player just had to touch a button to obtain a required sound, but this restricted the number of sounds the instrument could produce. Eventually, with the aid of microprocessors, manufacturers developed programmable synthesisers which could store a collection of sounds in its computerised memory, to be recalled by the user/programmer as and when necessary.

Prophets of the future

The best example of this type of instrument was the Prophet 5, launched by Sequential Circuits Inc in 1978. This, like the Minimoog, became a classic instrument, and soon almost every rock band with a keyboard player had a Prophet 5 tucked away somewhere. Following the appearance of the Prophet, the only major development in the synthesiser field was in terms of cost – better instruments at lower prices. Microprocessors made electronic instruments cheaper and more reliable than they would otherwise have been.

With the boom in computer technology during the late Seventies and early Eighties, computer-based musical instruments themselves started to come into their own. The Fairlight CMI, an Australian product based on a business computer, was used by many studio players, as well as by such notable musicians as Geoff Downes of Asia and Larry Fast of Peter Gabriel's band. One of the more useful facilities that such an instrument allowed the performer was the ability to 'sample' a sound and have that sound made available over the entire span of the keyboard – pitched accordingly. So if one were to sample the sound of a girl singing a note (via a microphone), the instrument would automatically transpose the sound to all pitches of the keyboard, and allow the player to play her voice polyphonically. Machines such as E-mu Inc's Emulator were specifically designed for just such a task, and have been featured on many recordings.

With devices such as these on the market, there seemed to be little left to 'discover' or 'revolutionise' within the field of synthetic music. Yet there was little doubt that further advancements in musical technology were still to come.

DAVE CROMBIE

Seeing is Believing?

How the video age took the romance out of rock

HAVING BEEN SORELY strained by the likes of the Sex Pistols and their unruly antics, the bonds between rock and the stage, television and cinema were to be forged anew in the aftermath of the turbulent mid Seventies. As the anti-fashions of punk became punk chic, the emphasis in rock turned once more to the visual.

The punk movie *Jubilee* (1978) yielded two new stars who later employed different means by which to impress their image on an expectant public. Adam Ant became one of the first rock stars to master the pop promo video, while the significance of Toyah Willcox was not so much in her use of mime and stage moves in the context of a rock show – Kate Bush was clearly superior in that field – but in proving that a stage and film career could legitimately co-exist with that of a pop star. Where Adam Faith, Tommy Steele and others had disowned their musical antecedents, rock had now won grudging respect from the showbiz establishment – largely due to the box-office success of such unthreatening multi-media productions as *Jesus Christ Superstar* and *Evita*.

Famous names

Acclaimed as a cost-effective breakthrough in record marketing in the late Seventies, video took only a few years to overreach itself. With directors plundering the cinema for familiar scenes and images, such famous names as photographer David Bailey and cinematographer Nic Roeg were quick to see opportunities (and cash) in elevating pop videos into an art form. Rock's golden era in the United States had been linked inextricably with the car radio, with the automobile hymns of Chuck Berry and Bruce Springsteen providing a soundtrack to the adolescence of Sixties and Seventies youth. Teenagers of the Eighties, however, were presented with the pre-packaged, second-hand spectacle of 24-hour rock television courtesy of the MTV cable channel. Rock was no longer an integral part of their life, but was served up like fast-food, to be consumed and forgotten. The romance of radio was history – video had indeed killed the radio star.

Rock films of the Seventies had provided a mixture of nostalgia and performance movies, with few really innovative individuals at work. Supergroups like Led Zeppelin and the Rolling Stones traded on their unavailability by releasing turgid concert footage, 'enlivened' in Zeppelin's case by horrifyingly self-important fantasy clips. The latter group's 1975 concerts at London's Earls Court, however, set the style for arena gigs by mounting a video screen over the stage to give even the cheapest seat a front-row view. How long, one wondered, would it be before live concerts were a thing of the past?

If rock in the post-punk years was once more putting on the style in time-honoured fashion, it also ran the risk of over-exposure. While Bill Haley had caused riots with his music for 1955's *Blackboard Jungle* without appearing on screen himself, the infinitely more charismatic Elvis Presley had been progressively emasculated by the Hollywood film machine after the sensation of his initial TV breakthrough. In the same way, the video revolution and the ever-increasing demands of the visual media in the Eighties threatened to rob rock of its spontaneity, its power to surprise and thrill.

MICHAEL HEATLEY

Toyah Willcox takes on all-comers in the London stage production of 'Trafford Tanzi' in 1983. Her success in combining a career as a serious actress with that of a rock singer reflected the music's new-found respectability, acquired through a decade of lucrative 'rock opera' productions.

ANTMUSIC!

Adam Ant: from punk reject to Prince Charming

As THE SEVENTIES drew to a close, the British pop scene seemed distinctly lacking in glamour. Punk rock had made way for a 'new wave' of grim-sounding electronic bands that vied with tired disco acts for chart success. Just as in the early Seventies, when glitter and glam-rock had arrived to enliven a slumbering pop market, the time was ripe for artists offering colour, bravado and pure escapism. And late in 1980, the first signs of a pop revival began to show themselves when Adam and the Ants, sporting face-paint and gaudy threads and whooping exuberantly, sauntered into the UK Top Ten with 'Dog Eat Dog'. Few, if any, could have predicted the sudden ascent to star status of Adam Ant who had, long before, been written off as a washed-up, talentless, third division punk has-been.

Adam Ant was born Stuart Goddard in London on 3 November 1954. After leaving Marylebone Grammar School in 1973, he studied graphic design at Hornsey Art College where he fronted a couple of Roxy Music-influenced bands, Bazooka Joe and the B-Sides. But, as with many of his contemporaries, it was after witnessing the Sex Pistols in action in 1976 that he was inspired to make a career of music. Having dropped out of college, he turned punk, changed his name to Adam Ant and formed the Ants with Lester Square (guitar), Andy Warren (bass) and Paul Flanagan (drums). In April 1977, Adam and the Ants made their first live appearance at London's prime punk niterie, the Roxy Club in Covent Garden.

S-M jubilee
From the first, Adam Ant adopted the most outrageous aspects of punk, dressing in S-M and bondage garb, wielding leather whips and writing tasteless songs like 'I Wanna Be Your Lavatory' and 'Plastic Surgery' (which, he stated at the time, was based on 'Liz Taylor and people like that. Like there was this surgeon who rebuilt his wife and replaced all her old bits with new bits in plastic.') The singer's unappealing stage presence – one critic described him as 'a pudgy reprobate, as sinister as Billy Bunter in biker drag', another as a 'tubby buffoon who can't sing for toffee' – coupled with the band's quite deplorable sound, rapidly turned Adam and the Ants into the music press's most despised and derided punk act of the period.

But under the management of punk icon Jordan, who had once worked in Malcolm McLaren's sex boutique, the band gigged regularly throughout 1977, picking up a hard-core cult following, and in the summer recorded two songs, 'Plastic Surgery' and 'Deutscher Girls', for the soundtrack of Derek Jarman's punk-exploitation film *Jubilee*. Jordan had a starring role in the movie and persuaded Jarman to offer Adam a small acting part.

Adam's subsequent performance was savaged by the critics, while 'Deutscher Girls', with its Nazi references, gained the group an unsavoury reputation for flirting with fascism. By mid-1978, Adam and the Ants had become so unpopular within the music business that it came as a surprise to all when, in July, the band were signed up by Decca. Less of a surprise was the termination of their contract four months later after just one flop single, a self-conscious pastiche called 'Young Parisians'.

The following year, the group managed to secure a deal with the independent label Do It and released a single, 'Zerox'/'Whip In My Valise', and an album, *Dirk Wears White Sox*, both of which sold reasonably well to those who still believed in the spirit of punk rock. But it was in October that Adam Ant's fortunes began to change; at a party in Pimlico, London, he bumped into Malcolm McLaren and offered the former Sex Pistols manager £1000 to re-shape the Ants' sound and inject some fresh ideas. Re-shape the Ants McLaren duly did – the following January, he persuaded the backing group (which now consisted of bassist Lee Gorman, drummer Dave Barbe and guitarist Matthew Ashman) to part company with their singer and become Bow Wow Wow. The press sneered at Adam's plight and pronounced him dead.

Above: Bazooka Joe, the Roxy Music-influenced group fronted by Stuart Goddard (in spectacles) during his days as an art student. After dropping out of college in 1976, Goddard transformed himself into Adam Ant, sleazy punk singer. Opposite: 1980 brought a further change of image for Adam Ant; as a 'noble warrior', the singer became the first teen idol of the new decade.

Euphoric jungle sounds
The short and sour association with Malcolm McLaren proved to be the turning point in Adam's career, however. McLaren had introduced the singer to the African drum beat of the Burundi tribe – a noise that would soon surface in the music of Bow Wow Wow – and Adam, although he now had no band, was determined to introduce tribal rhythms to future projects. In February 1980, he contacted guitarist Marco Pirroni, an old friend who had played with Siouxsie and the Banshees, the Beastly Cads, the Models and Rema Rema; the pair formed a songwriting partnership and began to assemble a new band. With drummer Merrick (Chris Hughes), they released another Do It single, 'Car Trouble', which offered a taste of things to come. A second drummer, Terry Lee Miall, was recruited to take care of the pounding beat that was to become an

essential element of 'Antmusic' from now on, and bassist Kevin Mooney was brought in, although he was later replaced by former Vibrator Gary Tibbs.

A cleverly conceived fantasy image was constructed around Adam's swashbuckling togs (which now clothed a rather slimmer figure) and Red Indian warrior warpaint on his undeniably striking face. Combined with the new euphoric jungle sound, it impressed CBS Records enough to offer the re-styled group a contract.

In July 1980, a new single, 'Kings Of The Wild Frontier', was released. The record's rapturous whooping and pounding – a curious hybrid of a Zulu battle party and the Glitter Band – was a triumphant departure from previous Ant efforts, and scraped into the UK Top Fifty.

Marco and Adam repeated the formula on the follow-up, 'Dog Eat Dog', and this time the tribal drums and warrior imagery – helped by a 'Top Of The Pops' TV appearance – captured the public imagination. In October, 'Dog Eat Dog' reached Number 4; another single 'Antmusic', released the following month, made Number 2 and by February, Antmania was rampant. Adam and the Ants had five singles in the Top Forty – 'Antmusic', 'Car Trouble', re-issues of 'Young Parisians' and 'Zerox', and a re-promoted 'Kings Of The Wild Frontier'. Their new LP, *Kings Of The Wild Frontier*, stood at Number 1 in the album charts, and *Dirk Wears White Sox* reached the Top Twenty.

Licking Hitler

1981 belonged to Adam Ant; a series of cleverly crafted pop singles were promoted by visually stunning videos – directed by Mike Mansfield and devised by Adam himself – in which the singer adopted various enticing looks. For 'Stand And Deliver', he became a jaunty highwayman in three-cornered hat, for 'Prince Charming', he turned into a nineteenth-century dandy (as well as impersonating heroes Clint Eastwood, Marlon Brando and Alice Cooper with uncanny accuracy), while for 'Ant Rap', he transformed himself into a knight in shining armour and a beefy American football player. 'Stand And Deliver' and 'Prince Charming' both made the top of the UK charts, while 'Ant Rap' reached Number 3.

By the end of the year, Adam Ant had become the biggest pop phenomenon since the Bay City Rollers. Poster magazines and Ant highwayman kits for tiny tots abounded, the Ant features were plastered across the covers of colour magazines and other glossies. *Tops* ('A Great New Mag For Boys And Girls') was running a cartoon strip in which Adam was cast as a

Left: A bare-chested Adam raises the roof during 1981's rafter-rattling rout of recoiling rock venues. Right: Adam and the Ants on stage, from left Marco Pirroni, Terry Lee Miall, Adam, Merrick and Gary Tibbs. Above right: Ant action.

ime-travelling super-hero, licking Hitler and other fiends. This was fame indeed.

'I'd done a lot of research on tribal vocals which involved hours of listening to quite dull vocal sounds,' Adam had said of the musical style which had brought him success. 'I wanted influences that were not commonplace, and a different vocal delivery – chanting, growling, grunting and yodelling.' But by 1982, he believed he had taken his sound as far as he could and decided upon a change.

Insect disposal

In the spring, he dispensed with the services of the Ants – although Marco was retained as musical partner – and his first solo single emerged in May. A rather meaningless stab at rock'n'roll, 'Goody Two Shoes' gave Adam his third Number 1, but the panache of old seemed lacking. The autumn's album, *Friend Or Foe*, and single of the same name, were lacklustre efforts, sadly short on drive or ideas; a further single, 'Desperate But Not Serious', failed to make the Top Thirty and Adam's bubble appeared to have burst.

By the end of 1982, the pop revival that Adam had instigated was in full swing. New teen idols – Duran Duran, the Human League, Haircut 100, Culture Club, Kajagoogoo and Wham! – were mincing onto the scene to exploit the market Adam had prised open and, having temporarily turned his back on Britain to concentrate on winning foreign audiences, the singer seemed unlikely to regain his pop crown. But then, in the autumn of 1983, he came bouncing back with a new album, *Strip*, and single, 'Puss'n'Boots'.

On 'Puss'n'Boots', the accent was firmly back on a dominant drum sound (courtesy of producer and Genesis drummer Phil Collins) and joyous howling, while the album – which confirmed Adam's obsession with 'pure sex for Ant people' ('sex is the last great adventure left to mankind,' he had once remarked) – was a vibrant collection of rhythmic intrigue and party tunes. The single climbed to Number 4 in the UK and the LP sold healthily.

'The first time we did "Top Of The Pops", we were a foretaste of things to come,' Adam had said in 1981. 'We did it before Spandau Ballet or any of the "look" bands.' That he had spearheaded a renaissance in colourful, escapist pop music was testament to Adam's energy and unshakeable self-belief; that he managed to survive in the face of all the pop opposition that followed attested to his (and Marco's) enormous talent for the creation of vital pop sounds and images. There had been nothing particularly *new* about Adam and the Ants – the various styles and noises had all been used in pop before – but the inspired mixture of borrowed elements had arrived in the right place at the right time, enlivening a stagnating rock scene.

Adam Ant's inclusion on the Live Aid bill in July 1985 was to prove a final flourish. After an album, *Vive Le Rock,* was poorly received, he turned to an acting career

music temporarily forgotten. It was somehow fitting that the master showman of Seventies punk had not deserted the stage entirely.   TOM HIBBERT

Adam and the Ants Recommended Listening

Kings Of The Wild Frontier (CBS 84549) (Includes: Dog Eat Dog, Kings Of The Wild Frontier, 'Antmusic', Jolly Roger, The Human Beings, Ants Invasion); *Strip* (CBS 25705) (Includes: Strip, Puss 'n' Boots, Navel To Neck, Amazon, Playboy, Libertine).

How rock cinema fared in the wake of Woodstock

IN MANY WAYS, the first half of the Seventies was a drab time for rock music and, to some extent, this was reflected in the movies of the era.

Michael Wadleigh's *Woodstock* was the rock film event of 1970; it was visually and aurally stunning and perceptively directed, but before the film was released, the dreams of the Woodstock Nation had been shattered. The murder of Meredith Hunter by Hell's Angels at Altamont, while Mick Jagger looked on from the stage, ensured that *Woodstock*, the movie, could never be a celebration of a new era of peace and love. Instead, it stood as its glorious wake.

Similarly, the deaths of Brian Jones, Janis Joplin, Jimi Hendrix and Jim Morrison cast a giant shadow over the memory of Sixties music, while many surviving musicians seemed to have lost their energy and direction. The Beatles had split, and their agonising disintegration was preserved for all to see in the movie *Let It Be* (1970).

Memo from Turner
There were two movies starring Mick Jagger in 1970; *Ned Kelly*, which featured his extremely limp-wristed and exasperatingly English interpretation of the Australian outlaw, is best forgotten. The other was *Performance*, in which he was given the tricky task of playing a retired pop star (which, perhaps, he should have been by then). Jagger handled the role perfectly – hardly surprising because the character was little more than an exaggeration of his own bisexual public persona.

Nevertheless, *Performance* was unquestionably the most satisfying rock movie of that year. Starring James Fox as a mobster on the run from his own gang who hides out in a flat owned by the decadent, mysterious Turner (Mick Jagger), the movie not only featured an excellent soundtrack with music by Jagger, Randy Newman and Ry Cooder, but marked the first of a string of films in which cinematographer/director Nicolas Roeg successfully coaxed decent performances out of pop stars.

By the following year, the Seventies were really scraping the Sixties barrel and the only rock offerings on the big screen were sub-Woodstock festival movies (such as *Celebration At Big Sur* starring the inevitable Crosby Stills Nash and Young, John Sebastian and Joan Baez) and on-the-road epics (like *Mad Dogs And Englishmen* with Joe Cocker). As a result, Pink Floyd's *Live At Pompeii*, filmed in a crumbling, deserted amphitheatre, stood out as the only innovative rock film of the year, although it was overshadowed, commercially, by *Gimme Shelter*, the Rolling

David Bowie graces the poster for Nicolas Roeg's The Man Who Fell To Earth *(1976). In the film, Bowie played the part of a homesick alien.*

Stones' documentary which dealt in part with their ill-fated Altamont concert.

By 1972, glitter and glam-rock had arrived to provide loud, meaningless entertainment in an understandable reaction to the 'meaningful' lyrics and cosmic/political awareness of progressive and hippie music. Marc Bolan strutted his stuff effectively enough in *Born To Boogie* (directed by Ringo Starr), but the old school was still represented in *Concert For Bangladesh*, documentry footage of George Harrison's benefit concert in which he appeared with Bob Dylan, Eric Clapton and others of that ilk.

Dust to dust

The passing of the Fillmore West, the most important of the legendary West Coast acid rock ballrooms was recorded in *Fillmore*, and reggae bowed onto the big screen with Jimmy Cliff starring in *The Harder They Come*. Although reggae was later to be more identified with Rasta and black roots, *The Harder They Come* was a powerful political – rather than religious or social – statement, and Cliff made a very effective pop star-cum-cultural guerrilla.

The commercial success of 1973 proved to be *American Graffiti*, directed by George Lucas (who would go on to make *Star Wars*), which humorously and nostalgically evoked teen-life in pre-Beatles America with the aid of a brilliantly selected soundtrack of doowop and pop hits. The British film *That'll Be The Day*, meanwhile, explored similar territory; written by music journalist Ray Connolly, the film was the first attempt at a fictionalised, but reasonably realistic, interpretation of the life of a would-be pop star in the Beatles era of the early Sixties. Like *American Graffiti*, it used period music to great effect, but went further by also having original rock songs composed for the film by Essex and Dave Edmunds.

Although background music had been used to considerable effect in *Easy Rider* (1969), both *American Graffiti* and *That'll Be The Day* moved the process a stage further, so that the film and the soundtrack were inextricably bound up together. Without the powerful nostalgic effect of the music, the films simply could not exist. *That'll Be The Day* was sufficiently successful to warrant a sequel, and *Stardust* emerged in 1974; the new film was glossier but not better than the original – and, although Essex proved himself a competent actor, he was totally outclassed by former Sixties singer Adam Faith's portrayal of his manager.

1975 saw the appearance of the first filmed 'rock opera'; this horrific term had been bandied about since the mid-Sixties when showbiz curiosities like *Hair* and *Jesus Christ Superstar* misappropriated, sanitised and castrated rock music for the amusement of would-be hip theatre-goers. It was perhaps fortunate then, that the first rock opera to reach the screen was Ken Russell's adaptation of the Who's *Tommy*. Unlike most rock operas, *Tommy*

The Harder They Come *brought the sound of reggae music to the big screen in 1972.*

featured real rock music played by real rock musicians. Russell's bombastic, nightmarish vision perfectly complemented Pete Townshend's music and, for once, the lack of a coherent storyline in a rock film barely seemed to matter.

The Who's Roger Daltrey teamed up with Russell again later in the year to make *Lisztomania*, but the combination proved much less effective. Apart from *Tommy*, the only other notable rock film of 1975 was *The Rocky Horror Picture Show*, a successful stage show transferred after some years to the screen. The show's blend of camp horror, stagey rock and transvestism ensured it cult status, although its level of humour rarely rose above the *Carry On* level. Nevertheless, it was clearly a forerunner of many of the more outrageous punk styles which evolved in the succeeding couple of years.

In 1976, Nicolas Roeg continued his flirtation with pop stars by casting David Bowie as *The Man Who Fell To Earth*. Despite (or possibly because of) his reportedly large cocaine intake at that time, Bowie's representation of the homesick alien was suitably devoid of normal human emotions and was to remain his best screen appearance.

The great escape

In 1977, the rock film industry came to life at last. What might otherwise have been pop film of the year, *Abba: The Movie*, was reduced to insignificance by *Saturday Night Fever*, which created a new teen heart-throb, John Travolta, and revitalised the flagging career of the Bee Gees, who provided the bulk of the soundtrack. It was the first film to recognise that a new breed of pop fan existed – the disco kid. Instead of evoking nostalgia for the pop of

the past, *Saturday Night Fever* was about the present. It was idealised but sufficiently gritty to seem real, especially to kids beginning to feel the effects of the new economic slump. For them, the disco was a place to escape the tedium of daily life, and the film accordingly became the highest-grossing rock film ever.

Jubilee fever

Saturday Night Fever opened the floodgates, and the following year saw the release of such diverse rock-oriented films as *The Buddy Holly Story*, *FM* (about a US radio station), *The Last Waltz* (a farewell concert by the Band), *The Wiz* (a disco *Wizard Of Oz* with Diana Ross and Michael Jackson), *Thank God It's Friday* (a blatant attempt to copy the formula of *Saturday Night Fever*) and *Renaldo And Clara* (Dylan's incomprehensible epic).

The Robert Stigwood Organisation, which had backed *Saturday Night Fever*, stayed ahead of the field with *Grease*, which boosted Travolta to superstardom and totally revamped the image of Olivia Newton-John. The cute, virginal country-rocker became a vampish (if not totally convincing) sex siren overnight.

There were even two Beatle-based movies in 1978. The Steven Spielberg-produced *I Wanna Hold Your Hand* told the story of four fans attempting to gate-crash a Beatles TV show, while the Stigwood Organisation offered a lavish fantasy based on *Sgt Pepper's Lonely Hearts Club Band*. This starred the Bee Gees with Peter Frampton and featured universally dismal treatments of Beatles classics by everyone from veteran comic George Burns to soul stars Earth Wind and Fire. The film flopped, ending Stigwood's run of good fortune.

It is interesting to note that Stigwood probably never really understood why *Saturday Night Fever* had succeeded. Each of his subsequent movies evoked the music of a lost period, and returned less cash to his coffers. *Saturday Night Fever* was the cheapest to make, but earned the most because it reflected the dreams of the audience by dealing with a modern lifestyle with which they could identify.

More in tune with the British audience was Derek Jarman's *Jubilee*, the first punk fantasy which featured such (then) little-known names as Adam Ant and Toyah and caricatured the punk lifestyle in entertaining fashion.

Candid cameras

Although 1979 showered a similar volume of movies on the fans, their quality was generally poor. The stage musical 'Hair' finally limped into the cinemas 10 years too late, while *More American Graffiti* totally lacked the charm and style of the original. The master of cheap movies, Roger Corman, pumped out *Rock'n'Roll High School* simply as a vehicle for the Ramones – and, like them, it was loveably dumb, tacky and not too demanding.

Even so, there were some honourable entries. The Who's *Quadrophenia* succeeded, like *Tommy*, in mirroring the music that had inspired it and was, by focussing its story on the life and death of a Sixties Mod, largely responsible for a short-lived Mod revival.

But with the Seventies drawing to a close, an unlikely contender for best rock movie of 1979 arrived in the shape of film critic Chris Petit's powerful contemporary road film, *Radio On*. A muddy plotline followed a London DJ as he drives north to investigate his brother's death, but what the film captured best was the feeling of futility and alientation in post-punk Britain. There was a brief cameo role from Sting of the Police for star spotters, but the actors were less important than the concrete landscapes and the industrial beat of Kraftwerk's 'Trans-Europe Express', which lent the film much of its atmosphere.

It was only in the Seventies that the music business finally latched on to how much vinyl could be shifted in the form of film soundtrack compilations – a vital realisation in a period when total record sales were falling .dramatically. (The astronomical sums involved can be judged by the fact that in 1980, the Bee Gees filed suit against the Robert Stigwood Organisation, claiming lost royalties of 125 million dollars, largely based on sales generated by their success with *Saturday Night Fever*.) As a result, many movies of the late Seventies were little more than marketing exercises, carefully devised to part fans from their cash twice – once in the cinema, then again in the record store.

During the early Eighties, rock films

Right: Punk starlet Jordan as a rather chubby Britannia in 1978's futuristic fantasy Jubilee. *Inset top: John Travolta and chums enjoy a swinging romp in* Grease *in the same year.*

cornered an even bigger share of the cinema market, although quality remained generally poor. The British *Party, Party* (1983), featuring music by Altered Images, Madness, Dave Edmunds and others, attempted to blend the spirit of *American Graffiti* with *Carry On* vulgarity to pitiful effect; the American *Fast Times At Ridgemont High* (1982), with music from Joe Walsh, Jackson Browne and more, explored similar territory. *The Music Machine* (1979), *Car Wash* (1978) and *Staying Alive* (1983) had tried to recreate *Saturday Night Fever*, while 1979's *The Rose* (with Bette Midler) and the following year's *Breaking Glass* (with Hazel O'Connor) were a pair of predictable showbiz yarns about the rise and fall of tired and emotional singing stars.

Other misguided cinematic efforts of the era included 1981's *No Nukes*, with its dull footage of James Taylor, Bruce Springsteen, the Doobie Brothers and other stalwarts of US rock performing at a benefit concert, *Roadie* (1980), a weak, jokey item starring Meat Loaf and featuring Blondie, Roy Orbison and Alice Cooper, *American Pop* (1981), a celebration of bombastic US rock in cartoon form, and the screen version of Pink Floyd's *The Wall*, which proved to be as tiresome as it was depressing.

Shooting the Pistols
The best rock films of the early Eighties were, arguably, *The Great Rock'n'Roll Swindle* and *Rude Boy*, both 1980 releases which were inspired by punk but which tackled the subject in entirely different ways. Julien Temple's *Rock'n'Roll Swindle* featured the Sex Pistols and told the story of the band's short, turbulent career; part documentary, part animated cartoon, part ridiculous japery, the film was wildly entertaining, with cameo roles from such diverse talents as Irene Handl, Jess Conrad, Tenpole Tudor and Dave Dee adding to the fun. Jack Hazan and David Mingay's *Rude Boy*, on the other hand, painted a grim portrait of life in contemporary Britain through the eyes of a fan of punk-rockers the Clash.

Although the overall quality of rock-related films in the Seventies and Eighties remained poor, the best examples, from *Performance* to *Jubilee, Saturday Night Fever, Radio On* and *The Great Rock 'n'Roll Swindle*, were in many ways better conceived and executed than the movies of the two preceding decades. The raw excitement of 1955's *Blackboard Jungle* and the cocky irreverence of 1964's *A Hard Day's Night* might never be recaptured, but the real innovators of the Seventies didn't even try. Instead, they created something fresh, something as forward-looking as the best rock music itself.   JOHNNY BLACK

Top: Bathtime fun for Jagger in Performance *(1970). Above right: Gary Busey's 1978 portrayal of Buddy Holly. Far right: 1973's* Jesus Christ Superstar. *Right: Sting strums in* Radio On *(1979).*

The Kick Inside

SINCE HER CAREER BEGAN in the late Seventies, a great deal has been written and said about Kate Bush. Although her varied and unusual talents resulted in some critics ridiculing and dismissing her as a 'weirdo', to others she was a truly gifted singer/songwriter/dancer. Such was the air of mystery that surrounded arguably one of the most distinctive artists to come out of British rock music.

'Heathcliff, it's me!'

For most people, Kate came seemingly from nowhere in January 1978, wailing her debut single 'Wuthering Heights' across the radio airwaves like, as one reviewer subtly put it, 'a female turkey having its neck wrung'. However, within six weeks of the record's release, Kate Bush had ousted Abba from the UK Number 1 spot. Many were of the opinion that she was a 'one-hit wonder' and believed she would disappear as quickly as she had arrived; others wondered from where this enigmatic, precocious talent, this 'overnight discovery' had come.

In reality, Kate was no 'overnight discovery' at all – indeed, her rapid rise to fame was the fruit of careful calculation. Born on 30 July 1958 in Welling, Kent, Catherine (as she was christened) was the third and last child of Robert, a practising doctor, and Hannah Bush. Hannah's background – she was born in County Waterford, Ireland, and was an accomplished folk dancer in her youth – was to become an influence on her daughter's career. Kate and her brothers, Jay and Paddy were brought up in a 350-year-old sprawling farmhouse called East Wickham Farm, situated on the Kent/London border.

There always seemed to be music around

Kate Bush: the birth of a rare talent

the farm, especially with her two elder brothers' interest in folk music; Kate studied the violin for a short while before developing a keen interest in the piano. After a brief introduction to the instrument from her father, Kate set about teaching herself and, by the age of 11, when she began to attend St Joseph's Convent Grammar School in Abbey Wood, she was already quite a proficient pianist. During this time Kate would create her own interpretations of personal favourites like the Beatles' 'Eleanor Rigby' until, aged 14, she began to compose her own material.

Some time later a friend of the family, Ricky Hopper, heard a few of her crudely-recorded home demo tapes and offered to play them to his contacts in the record business. He remembered in particular an old friend, David Gilmour, guitarist with Pink Floyd. Gilmour was immediately struck by the girl's talent and soon afterwards, in June 1975, brought Kate to AIR London studios to personally supervise and finance a professional recording, produced by Andrew Powell, of three of her original compositions. (Two of these, the haunting 'Man With A Child In His Eyes' and 'Saxophone Song' appeared three years later on Kate's debut album, *The Kick Inside*.)

Shortly afterwards, the session tapes were

brought to the attention of both the record and music publishing divisions of EMI and, at the age of just 17, Kate Bush was signed up. Perhaps unusually for the record industry, EMI were in no particular hurry to launch her career, and instead gave Kate an advance of £3500 'to go away and grow up with'. Her scrupulously fair contract gave her the freedom to experiment in any way, without obligation, provided she periodically show her songs to EMI.

Having left school at 16 with a cache of 10 GCE 'O' levels, she quickly formed the KT Bush Band who, for a short while, gigged around the Lewisham area with a repertoire ranging from 'Heard It Through The Grapevine' to 'Honky Tonk Women'. Around this time, Kate also became engrossed in a passion for dance which was to have a dramatic and important effect on her

career. At the Collegiate Theatre in London she saw the British master of mime, Lindsay Kemp in his show *Flowers*, and was so stunned that she reputedly returned 21 times during the following month. She soon enrolled for Kemp's informal teaching sessions, held in a church hall in Fulham.

EMI finally gave her career the green light in the summer of 1977. With Andrew Powell again producing, Kate plunged into the recording of her first album. Six weeks in the making, *The Kick Inside*, released in February 1978, was a truly remarkable achievement and one of the best debut LPs from any rock artist. The 13 original compositions, most of which had been written over the previous year, but all of which fulfilled Kate's desire 'to paint beautiful pictures in sound', were compelling but complex, adult in construction yet delivered with girlish enthusiasm. They dealt candidly with taboo subjects, yet were somehow still vulnerable.

The LP's most distinctive feature was Kate's caterwauling vocal style, and among its best tracks were 'Feel It', a gorgeously erotic yet somehow innocent spine-tingler which most other 19-year-olds would have been far too embarrassed to perform; 'Them Heavy People', dedicated to those, like Lindsay Kemp, who had pushed her career; the title track about a girl, impregnated by her brother, who is about to commit suicide; and 'Wuthering Heights', inspired by Emily Bronte's novel. When released as a single, the song set the pattern for Kate's future career, with half of Britain's pop fans dashing out to buy it while the other half just could not bear to listen to it. When she sang the song on BBC-TV's 'Top Of The Pops' she stood alone, a little girl with an ethereal beauty, bewitching eyes never leaving the camera, arms flailing, voice ululating banshee-style.

A terrible beauty is born

Sincere, demure and charmingly shy off stage, Kate Bush in performance was, in her own words, 'a horrible creature, a biting, shouting, cruel thing'. This frightening persona was further unmasked in Kate's songwriting, which displayed a clear attempt to conquer her off-stage inhibitions. This apparently schizoid behavioural pattern was probably the root cause of her frequently negative media coverage. The UK music press in particular, having failed to understand what Kate Bush was about, opted to deride, rather childishly, her off-stage 'niceness' and her abundant usage of what they felt to be outdated and unfashionable clichés like 'groovy', 'amazing' and 'wow'. Kate's quick answer to this amusing though trite criticism was to include on her follow-up album, *Lionheart*, a track called 'Wow', the lyrics of which consisted of a profusion of all these words.

Although *Lionheart* – recorded over 10 weeks in the autumn of 1978 and released that December – indicated a progression in

Away from the spotlight, Kate Bush is easy-going and unpretentious (above). But anything can happen when the cameras start rolling (opposite) . . .

Kate's career, it was undoubtedly recorded too quickly after *The Kick Inside* to offer clear indications of any musical development. After *Lionheart*, EMI allowed Kate almost total control over her pace of work and the release of new material.

Nonetheless, the album consolidated Kate's right to the top newcomer, female singer and songwriter awards for 1978, and it included a number of fine tracks like 'Symphony In Blue', 'Don't Push Your Foot On The Heartbrake' and 'Oh England My Lionheart', the latter a beautifully crafted tribute to the mother country complete with mandolin from brother Paddy. The song encapsulated Kate's *Englishness* and went some way to explaining why, by the mid Eighties, she had yet to break big in the US. Her appearances on American TV were rare, and only two of her four albums – the first and fourth – saw US release.

Almost immediately following the recording of *Lionheart*, Kate began preparations for her first British tour. Preceded by six months of exhaustive rehearsals, the show – an ambitious, expensive, dramatic extravaganza – was a gruelling test of stamina and talent: two-and-a-half hours of almost non-stop singing, dancing and mime, with 17 lightning-quick changes of costume between songs. Kate conceived, wrote, produced and choreographed the entire show, describing it as an 'embryo circus'. Critics hailed it as a visually breathtaking theatre of music and movement, and it played to sell-out audiences everywhere.

Having rapidly reached the pinnacle of her profession, it was time for Kate to sit back and look to the future. In 1978, when 'Wuthering Heights' had been charting all over the world, she had said: 'I hope people will begin to realise that I'm going to be

changing; I don't want to be stuck in a strait-jacket all my life'. It seemed likely that the next stage in her career would be one of serious, concentrated recording, with fewer public appearances.

Thinking all the time

On her next album, *Never For Ever*, this objective was reflected not only in meticulously constructed compositions but also in the LP's production (for the first time Kate co-produced the sessions) and in the inordinate length of time – almost a year – taken to put the project together. The record, released in September 1980, was by no means flawless, though it did give Kate her first UK Number 1 album and yield three outstanding hit singles in 'Breathing', 'Babooshka' and 'Army Dreamers'. Songs like 'Breathing', which recounted the story of an unborn child who witnesses the nuclear holocaust through the wall of her mother's womb, and 'The Infant Kiss', which concerned a governess who falls for a young boy, illustrated Kate's ability to write convincingly about situations borne solely out of her fertile imagination. 'Army Dreamers', however, was perhaps Kate's finest achievement: a powerful anti-war song skilfully delivered in a gentle, Irish lilt. The forceful lyrics were rammed home in a moving video directed by Keef (Keith MacMillan) that accompanied the release.

The Dreaming, an experimental, courageous, though arguably over-serious album, followed *Never For Ever* in September 1982. Just under two years in the making, the album was produced by

Much of Kate Bush's appeal lies in her elastic ability to swing from romantic softness, stillness and silliness (opposite) into a loopy, wild-eyed harpy, snaking about the stage in exotic mime (above) or energetic dance routines (below).

Kate herself, a role she had been moving toward since *Lionheart*. 'Sat In Your Lap', inspired by a Stevie Wonder gig, and trailed as a single as early as July 1981,

was indicative of what was to follow: complex lyrics; a deepening of Kate's vocal timbre; a heavy use of polyphonic synthesisers, and an oppressive, almost claustrophobic production. The album, recorded in three separate studios, each carefully chosen not only for acoustic quality but for ambience and 'vibe', featured some unusual guest artists. Rolf Harris and animal-impressionist Percy Edwards appeared on the title track, which delineated the plight of the Australian aborigine. Four members of the Irish band Planxty were recruited for 'Night Of The Swallow', while German bassist Eberhard Weber appeared on the eerie 'Houdini'.

The Dreaming was Kate Bush's least accessible album – a fact reflected in sharply decreased record sales. Although the album entered the UK charts at Number 3, it dropped from the Top Hundred in just nine further weeks, while a single 'There Goes A Tenner', could not win a chart placing, her first such failure.

Kate was back with a successful musical offering in 1985, however, with her well-received album *Hounds Of Love* and a single 'Running Up That Hill' which made the UK Top Ten.

It was evident by the mid Eighties that Kate Bush had come a long way since 'Wuthering Heights', and that her audience, though small, had grown up with her. She may not have directly influenced any new sphere of music, but Kate Bush was certainly unique – the leader in a field of one. MARK LEWISOHN

Kate Bush Recommended Listening

The Kick Inside (EMI EMC 3223) (Includes: Moving, Wuthering Heights, The Man With The Child In His Eyes, The Kick Inside, Them Heavy People, Room For The Life); *The Dreaming* (EMI EMC 3419) (Includes: Sat In Your Lap, The Dreaming, Night Of The Swallow, Leave It Open, Houdini, There Goes A Tenner).

TOYAH

music and formed her own rock group, called simply Toyah; the band's early stage work was characterised by an enthusiastic rapport with the audience and a handful of acceptable songs. Toyah was soon signed to the independent label, Safari, and in the summer of 1979, released a single, 'Victims Of The Riddle', and a gimmicky 6-track EP, *Sheep Farming In Barnet*. These featured a crude amalgamation of Toyah's soaring vocals and fanciful lyrics with her band's workmanlike rock backing; rather unremarkable stuff, perhaps, but there was obvious potential nonetheless.

This was soon realised in the form of her debut album *The Blue Meaning*, released in mid-1980, which featured the single 'Ieya'. 'Ieya' was a typical Toyah song, displaying both the irresistible strengths and infuriating weaknesses; it was too long, it had a sing-song simplicity that bordered on the realm of nursery rhymes, and musically it was repetitive and clichéd. Yet Toyah's vocal inflections (her natural voice, with its lisp, often sounded quite childish) flitted around the melody line, sustaining interest, while the incessant pounding of drums gave the song a forceful, almost addictive, momentum. As ever, the five foot two, waif-like figure of Toyah Willcox employed her sense of drama, humour and infectious *joie de vivre* to

The winning ways of Ms Willcox

UNLIKE OTHER ROCK stars who become recognised as stage or screen figures, Toyah Willcox's first love was always acting rather than music: throughout her ascent to rock stardom during the late Seventies, she never lost sight of her other profession, and the fact that she was able to sustain two separate and highly successful careers so well was a tribute to her natural buoyancy, effervescence and talent.

Sheep on safari

Toyah Willcox was born in Birmingham on 18 May 1958. After leaving school with just one GCE 'O' level – in music – she attended Birmingham Old Rep Drama

School. Here, in 1976, she was spotted by a BBC producer who offered her a part alongside DJ Noel Edmunds in a TV play called 'Glitter'. Her appearance brought her to the attention of the National Theatre; they offered her a place which she eagerly accepted.

By the age of ninteen, before she had even released a record, Toyah had come to the public's attention through such ventures as Derek Jarman's futuristic punk movie *Jubilee* (1978) and playing opposite Katharine Hepburn in the film *The Corn Is Green* (1978). In 1979, she became a Mod for the highly-acclaimed *Quadrophenia* and played Miranda in Jarman's film *The Tempest*, and later made numerous television appearances on pop programmes and chat shows.

In 1978, she turned her attentions to

Top left: Toyah Willcox – 'You can feel the energy from my hair flying all over the place!' Above and opposite: Toyah expresses herself.

transform basically ordinary music into a celebratory anthem.

By now, Toyah had become hard for the public to ignore; she appeared as punk singer Toola in an episode of the highly popular BBC-TV series 'Shoestring', the band not only contributing background music to the show but playing two numbers live. As if this exposure was not enough, ATV devoted a one-hour documentary to the actress/singer; an accompanying soundtrack album was released under the title *Toyah! Toyah! Toyah!* and reached Number 22 in the UK album charts.

1980 also saw Toyah enjoying a successful run in the play 'Sugar And Spice' at London's Royal Court Theatre; because of Toyah's continual acting commitments her group could never maintain a stable line-up. On 3 September the original band played its final concert at London's ICA, the event being filmed for inclusion in Michael White's movie *Urgh! A Music War*. In early 1981, however, with the stage run out of the way, Toyah pieced together a new band; guitarist Joel Bogen was retained from the old one and Phil Spalding was brought in on bass, Adrian Lee on keyboards and Nigel Glotker on drums. The new Toyah quickly found commercial success when the Nick Tauber-produced EP *Four From Toyah* shot into the singles charts to reach Number 4 in March.

An air of mystery
The record's success was due to the insistent charm of 'It's A Mystery', a teasing, playful ditty of a song with an infuriatingly catchy keyboard refrain and chorus. 'It's A Mystery' was the very essence of Toyah, with its childlike/childish simplicity and clear, repetitive tune, while 'I Want To Be Free', a Number 8 hit single which followed in May, was both naively petulant and marvellous commercial pop music. Toyah's preoccupation with fables, fairies and the supernatural was continued with the 'Thunder In The Mountains' single (which reached Number 4 in October) and her third LP *Anthem*, whose cover showed her as a strange, winged creature.

Despite her love of the theatre, however, Toyah shied away from making her stage shows with the band overly 'theatrical'. For instance, she never used the elaborate costumery of Peter Gabriel-era Genesis, nor attempted to present a conceptual show like the Residents or Devo. Where Toyah *did* employ her dramatic talents was in makeup that enhanced her looks and expressions, in clothes that lent an air of mystery to her naturally skinny form, and in exaggerated movements that were part-mime, part-modern dance.

Her use of stage effects was restricted to occasional dry ice or smoke, perhaps with an odd thunderflash to highlight the evening's crescendo. Other than that, her success and appeal was due solely to her own instinctive talents. 'People always

expect to see a six-foot amazon on stage, some kind of sex goddess . . . and I'm not like that at all,' Toyah once commented. 'Because I'm so small and people at the back of the hall might not be able to see too well, I take care that my makeup and my hair accentuate my movements and expressions.'

Proud to be a pixie
Having become a top pop attraction, Toyah seemed to use 1982 as a year for consolidation. Both of her UK hit singles – 'Brave New World' (Number 21) and 'Be Proud, Be Loud, Be Heard' (Number 30) – were brash anthems for teenagers, while the cover of *The Changleing* LP showed her as a cute little pixie. The year ended with an excellent live double album, *Warrior Rock-Toyah On Tour*.

The following year, Toyah returned to acting with two gruelling – but utterly different – roles. The stage play 'Trafford Tanzi' at London's Mermaid Theatre required her to learn genuine fighting skills for her part as a lady wrestler, while she also played opposite Sir Laurence Olivier in a film adaptation of John Fowles' book *The Ebony Tower*.

Fresh from that dual challenge, Toyah released *Love Is The Law* (1983), an album which began to show distinct progression towards a more electronic, atmospheric overall sound, without sacrificing the unique traits that made Toyah instantly recognisable. Co-written by the singer with Joel Bogen and new keyboardist Simon Darlow, tracks such as 'Martian Cowboy', 'Time Is Ours' and 'The Vow' hinted at a greater degree of maturity.

After a break of nearly a year, during which Toyah was busy with her acting career, she returned in 1985 with a new LP, *Minx*, on the Portrait label. Marriage to King Crimson guitarist Robert Fripp slowed down her recorded output, though her acting career continued to demonstrate her dramatic flair and great determination.   JOHNNY WALLER

> **Toyah**
> **Recommended Listening**
>
> *Warrior Rock – Toyah On Tour* (Safari TNT 1)
> (Includes: Good Morning Universe, It's A Mystery, Angel And Me, Thunder In The Mountains, I Want To Be Free, Ieya).

SONG & DANCE

The very special magic of Rice and Lloyd Webber

To WRITE FOR the musical theatre had long been the traditional ambition of pop-based professional songwriters, but few made the transition with ease. Stalwarts of British pop like Tony Macaulay, Geoff Stephens and David Essex all composed for the stage with largely unspectacular success, while even Lionel Bart – composer of early hits for Cliff Richard and Tommy Steele – was never forgiven by the critics for failing to produce another *Oliver!*, his widely acclaimed musical adaptation of Dickens' *Oliver Twist*.

The only British songwriting team of the rock era to make an international impression on the musical theatre were Tim Rice and Andrew Lloyd Webber, whose track record demonstrates the value of having true commitment to and understanding of the musical play as a theatrical form. Their great strength, individually and collectively, was to see themselves as much more than just providers of songs: each of

With a record-breaking run at London's Palace Theatre (top), Jesus Christ Superstar *was the show that made lyricist Tim Rice and composer Andrew Lloyd Webber (above left and right respectively) world supremos of the rock musical.*

their shows was a complete dramatic entity, originated, developed and overseen by them. No other pop writers used the conventions of the musical stage with such skill and commercial acumen.

The likes of us
Rice (born in Harpenden, Hertfordshire, on 10 November 1944) and Lloyd Webber (born in London on 22 March 1948) first met in 1965. Rice was a public school-educated law student with undefined pop ambitions; he had fronted a group called the Aardvarks while at school, had auditioned unsuccessfully for Decca and had written the occasional song. Lloyd Webber, though a pop fan from his teens, was classically trained and passionately interested in the theatre. Their first musical together, based on the story of philanthropist Dr Barnardo and called *The Likes Of Us*, was published but never professionally performed; it was, as they later admitted, rather too much of a poor man's *Oliver!*.

In 1967, Rice joined EMI as a management trainee and worked closely with producer Norrie Paramor, whom he joined

as personal assistant when Paramor set up his own company a year later. Also that year, Lloyd Webber was approached by Alan Doggett, teacher at the Colet Court School in the City of London, to write a piece for an end-of-term concert on any theme that he or Rice chose. What finally emerged was an inventive, skilfully conceived 20-minute 'oratorio' called *Joesph And The Amazing Technicolor Dreamcoat.*

Joseph brought Rice and Lloyd Webber to the attention of David Land, a property tycoon with interests in entertainment and leisure, who offered them a three-year contract in return for a share in future royalties. The timing was opportune: Paramor had wanted Rice to become a virtual junior partner in his company, while Lloyd Webber was about to graduate from music college.

Their express task, as employees of the Land organisation, was to write a musical built around the last week in the life of Christ and told through the eyes of Judas Iscariot – Rice's own idea, inspired by Bob Dylan's famous lines, 'I can't think for you – you'll have to decide/Did Judas Iscariot have God on his side?'.

'Superstar', from *Jesus Christ Superstar*, was eventually released in late 1969, on the MCA label. It sold well and attracted much interest, some predictably hostile, from the press, but failed to reach the Top Fifty. In the United States, however, the record was picked up by FM radio stations despite scant promotion and became enough of a hit, peaking at Number 14, to persuade MCA in the UK to give the go-ahead to record the score on an LP.

Men in a suitcase

With its success in America, there was no shortage of backers willing to finance a Broadway production of *Jesus Christ Superstar*, but a deal was quickly signed with Robert Stigwood's rapidly expanding RSO company. The show opened in New York on 20 October 1971 and in London on 9 August 1972, each time to somewhat mixed critical reaction but enormous public interest. The British production went on to break all previous box-office

Above left: Bonnie Langford, Elaine Paige and Finola Hughes in Cats. *Above right: Joss Ackland and Paige in* Evita.

records for a London show, remaining at the Palace Theatre for over eight years, although a film version made in Israel during 1972 by director Norman Jewison was markedly less successful.

Jesus Christ Superstar became almost an industry in itself, and much of Rice and Lloyd Webber's time between 1972 and 1976 was taken up with planning new productions in different countries. Lloyd Webber's one attempt to go it alone, combining with playwright Alan Ayckbourn in a comedy with music called 'Jeeves' (based on the P. G Wodehouse stories), was a flop, while Rice indulged his passion for rock'n'roll and early-Sixties pop in a regular show on Capital Radio.

After toying with numerous ideas for a follow-up to *Superstar*, Rice suggested adapting the life of the controversial Eva Peron, charismatic wife of the former Argentinian dictator Juan Peron, into a musical. Again the project was conceived initially in album form, with Julie Covington taking the singing role of Eva and Tony Christie, Paul Jones and Barbara Dickson also appearing. Titled *Evita*, the score was released as a double album in October 1976; two singles taken from it, Julie Covington's 'Don't Cry For Me, Argentina' and Barbara Dickson's 'Another Suitcase In Another Hall', became major UK hits at Numbers 1 and 18 respectively, and this helped generate the requisite interest.

Evita opened on stage in London on 21 June 1978 and was well received. As a stage spectacle it was indeed a much less garish, more imaginatively mounted affair than *Jesus Christ Superstar* had been, thanks mostly to the skilled direction of Broadway veteran Hal Prince. The cast included Elaine Paige in the title role, Joss Ackland as Peron and David Essex as the revolutionary Che Guevara, while Tim Rice's libretto was considerably faster-paced and less ponderous than his previous efforts had been.

Evita was to be Rice and Lloyd Webber's

last major work together, however. Musically, they were already moving apart, Rice into the pop world that had always been his first love, Lloyd Webber deeper into the theatrical environment that had always inspired him. Rice collaborated with his brother Jo and disc jockeys Mike Read and Paul Gambaccini on the best-selling *Guinness Book Of Hit Singles* series, launched his own publishing company, Pavilion Books, and began writing on a one-off basis with the likes of Paul McCartney, Rick Wakeman, Mike Batt and Elton John. He returned to musicals in 1985 with *Chess,* a collaboration with Bjorn and Benny from Abba.

Cats people

Lloyd Webber, meanwhile, devised and wrote the show *Cats*, inspired by the cat poems of T. S. Eliot, which enjoyed a phenomenal run in both the West End and Broadway, and provided a UK hit twice over for original singer Elaine Paige (Number 6) and Barbra Streisand (Number 34). He produced the somewhat self-celebratory *Song And Dance*, a revue-type entertainment consisting entirely of dance and vocal interpretations of his music: it also featured the entire suite of songs from his album vehicle for singer Marti Webb, *Tell Me On A Sunday* (1980), written with lyricist Don Black. In 1983, he produced the play 'Daisy Pulls It Off' in London's West End, and realised a lifetime ambition by buying the Palace Theatre to refurbish as a home for British musicals.

In pop terms, both Rice and Lloyd Webber were essentially peripheral figures, though they did much to spread the use of pop music in a theatrical context. The strength of their legacy could be seen in enterprises like Jeff Wayne's *War of the Worlds*, launched in 1978 as a double album with an all-star cast and later mounted (unsuccessfully) on stage, and in David Essex's 1984 production of *Mutiny!*. More than anything, the partnership proved the marketing value of using the pop world as a platform for promoting a separate, but complementary, kind of entertainment.   STEPHEN BARNARD

CATCH MY SOUL

Religion and nostalgia shaped the rock musical

BILLED AS 'The American Tribal Love-Rock Musical', *Hair* appeared to be propaganda for the hippie counter-culture; nevertheless, this didn't prevent the producers firing at least one actor from the London production for smoking a joint backstage! For all its superficial radicalism, *Hair* – as George Melly pointed out in 1969 – was 'a completely traditional theatrical presentation sailing under false colours'. So, too, were many of the successful so-called 'rock operas' or 'rock musicals' that followed in its wake.

God sell
With young people wandering around long-haired and bare-footed, eschewing the materialistic values of the society to which they belonged, it wasn't long before someone came up with the tasteless notion of putting Christ on stage with music. The American *Salvation* (1969) was the first of the 'Jesus Rock' stage shows and, as opposed to those that followed, it took an anti-religious stand, proposing redemption only through sex and drugs. Such iconoclasm, however, did not prove a good crowd-puller and *Salvation* failed to save itself.

Godspell (1971) depicted Christ as a clown facing the world's intellectuals in the Tower of Babel in an attempt to 'bring celebration back into religion'. David Essex played the lead in London and despite (or possibly because of) critic Robert Cushman's declaration that it was 'the blandest thing since *The Sound Of Music*', the show was a huge hit. Musically, *Godspell* was a mish-mash of gospel, folk and Tin Pan Alley tunes, with a touch of electric rock; it was certainly not the rock musical the producers proclaimed it.

The same year saw the opening of Tim Rice and Andrew Lloyd Webber's *Jesus Christ Superstar*. The plot concentrated on the Jesus/Judas relationship and again, musically, it was a hybrid that belonged to neither the theatre nor the rock world. Following this success, a 20-minute show Rice and Lloyd Webber had been commissioned to write in 1967 for a London school – *Joseph And The Amazing Technicolor Dreamcoat* – was lengthened and hit the London stage in 1973, later touring extensively with former Manfred Mann singer Paul Jones, among others, in the lead. The final show to be based on St Matthew's Gospel was *Your Arm's Too Short To Box With God* (1976) – a good enough title, perhaps, but by this time theatre audiences had had enough of religion.

In the Seventies, producers saw the box-office potential of grafting a brand of rock

Above left: Othello strangles Desdemona in Catch My Soul. *Left: The three Presleys in* Elvis, *from left James (P.J.) Proby, Timothy Whitnall and Shakin' Stevens.*

music on to all kinds of plays and musicals. *Catch My Soul* (1970), based on 'Othello', was probably the best adaptation of Shakespeare; *The Black Mikado* (1975) was the first pop version of Gilbert and Sullivan, and was followed by *The Pirates Of Penzance* (1981), which featured popular singers such as Linda Ronstadt and Peter 'Herman' Noone in leading roles. Not only did the music of these shows bear little resemblance to what rock fans were actually listening to, but their content lacked any genuine 'rock' sentiment – there was little sense of youthful revolt or outrage. Both plot and music were sanitised for a mainly middle-class (and often middle-aged) theatre-going audience.

While 'Jesus Rock' was packing them in, the real counter-culture was flowering elsewhere. In the Sixties, rock music achieved cultural respectability and inspired artists in other media. More pop-oriented programmes appeared on TV and modern art briefly became Pop Art. The Liverpool 'pop' poets – Roger McGough, Adrian Henri and Brian Patten – toured on and off with musicians Neil Innes, Zoot Money and Andy Roberts in the early Seventies, mixing poetry and music with clowning around. These poets were, in fact, the precursors of later wordsmiths like John Cooper Clarke, Linton Kwesi Johnson and Mark Miwurdz of Channel 4 TV's 'The Tube'.

In the theatre, actors and directors banded together to form hundreds of small theatre groups. They integrated music and art, mime and improvisation to present what were known as multi-media events. Some of these groups survived into the Eighties – such as the People Show – while others like Principal Edwards Magic Theatre, disappeared after a few years. In general, multi-media shows satisfied neither the theatre-goer nor the pop fan: haphazardly bombarding the senses was no replacement for intelligible entertainment or good music.

Frankenstein in fishnet

The first approximation to a genuine rock-theatre was Richard O'Brien's *The Rocky Horror Show*, which opened in Chelsea, London, in late 1973. O'Brien had knocked off this transvestite/Frankenstein romp while on the dole and was utterly surprised by its success. 'I like rock concerts and *everyone* enjoys sex and having a laugh. And there it was . . .' he said. Although musically the show was nothing original – 'three chords go an awfully long way, don't they?' he commented to one journalist – as an actor and a rock fan O'Brien had a foot in both camps and managed to produce what was called 'one of the most morally subversive shows in town'.

The Rocky Horror Show captured the mood of the moment – not surprisingly when one considers that many of the most fêted rock stars were dressing in unisex fashion, plastering on makeup and admitting to bisexuality. On his 1972 album *The Rise And Fall Of Ziggy Stardust And The*

Spiders From Mars, David Bowie played the part of an androgynous rock star five years before the end of the world. Bowie also had the Astronettes mime troupe led by Lindsay Kemp accompanying his concert performances.

Snake charms

Lou Reed, Roxy Music, Iggy Pop, Alex Harvey and others dramatised themselves in their concerts, but the most outlandish was surely Vincent Furnier, better-known as Alice Cooper. With the help of a few beers, Alice could go right over the top: chopping up baby dolls, decapitating chickens, giving his pet boa-constrictor the come-on, being guillotined and fighting off a giant tooth with a toothbrush! Alice managed to save this appalling display from being truly nasty by his solid sense of the absurd.

By late 1976 the backlash to this often

Above: Helen Mirren lets rip in David Hare's acerbic play-with-music, 'Teeth'n'Smiles'. Below: Godspell was one of the first musicals to put Jesus on stage.

narcissistic theatricality came with punk, which urged a return to less pretentious music and presentation. Two people from Hull, however, Cosey Fanni Tutti and Genesis P. Orridge, did combine music performances (calling themselves Throbbing Gristle) and what has come to be known as 'performance art' (under the name COUM Transmission). The Tubes and others brought art and dramatic techniques into their acts, but the most notable performance artist was Laurie Anderson of 'O Superman' fame, whose highly acclaimed, two-evening show at London's Dominion Theatre in 1983 featured her playing her 'viophonograph', synthesising her voice and, with other

musicians, employing the latest in hi-tech electronic devices.

By the mid Seventies the legitimate theatre was throwing up playwrights reared on Fifties and Sixties sounds who began to use the rock business as a microcosm for larger themes – usually the battle between youth and the establishment and the disillusionment of the former. David Hare's 'Teeth'n'Smiles' (1975) portrayed a female singer performing in the face of privilege at a May Ball at Cambridge and Barrie Keefe's 'Bastard Angel' (1980), later extended into a TV series, 'No Excuses', took up a very similar situation. Stephen Poliakoff presented a disillusioned local radio disc jockey in 'City Sugar' (1976), while his 'American Days' (1979), with Toyah Willcox in the fine cast, set the action in the plush offices of a big record company. Although these plays used rock music, they appealed more to an

Below: Laurie Anderson, one of America's leading performance artists, plays a tune on her 'viophonograph'.

older audience – the writers' peers – than to contemporary youth.

All our yesterdays

Many musicals in the Seventies and Eighties achieved success by evoking a vanished era. Audience nostalgia for the Fifties made *Grease* a smash in the early Seventies, and in 1982 the decade was once more recalled by *Yakety Yak!*. With only the sketchiest of story-lines, *Yakety Yak!* was little more than vehicle for the great songs of Leiber and Stoller, such as 'Hound Dog', 'On Broadway' and 'Stand By Me'; the show's success was due in no small part to the fine singing of the Darts.

Similarly, 1983's *Jukebox* was low on plot but presented hits from the past 30 years, much in the manner that *Bubbling Brown Sugar* (1976) had raided the treasure trove of black blues and jazz. *The Little Shop Of Horrors*, a clever parody of Fifties and Sixties sci-fi movies, enjoyed a successful run in London's West End in the early Eighties.

Basing a show around a single rock hero

or band provided a number of hits and flops. The Beatles and/or their songs were the subjects of no less than four stage shows, beginning with Willy Russell's intelligent *John, Paul, George, Ringo . . . And Bert* in 1973. The twee *Sgt Pepper's Lonely Hearts Club Band* played on Broadway in 1974, *Beatlemania* was a hit on both sides of the Atlantic in 1978-79 and *With A Little Help From My Friends* opened in July 1981 in London, closing eight days later! John Lennon's death also provoked a rash of tributes on the provincial British stage.

Elvis Presley couldn't escape exploitation after his death and *Elvis*, devised by Jack Good, who had produced such early Sixties TV shows as 'Oh Boy!', was a hit in 1978. In the show, three singers played Elvis at various stages in his life, two being the excellent James (P.J.) Proby and Shakin' Stevens. Probably prompted by the success of *Elvis*, the next biographical musical was the disastrous *Let The Good Stones Roll*. Commonsense should have dictated that while it was feasible to portray dead artists on stage, to do the same to a thriving band like the Rolling Stones was tempting fate.

Community chorus line

In the early Eighties, perhaps the greatest hope for the future of the rock musical lay in two comparatively obscure London productions – *Chorus Girls* and *Labelled With Love*. Although universally panned by the critics, Barrie Keeffe's *Chorus Girls*, written in collaboration with Ray Davies of the Kinks, had some good songs and a few good moments. *Labelled With Love* by John Turner, with songs from Squeeze's album *East Side Story* (1981), was altogether more entertaining. Set in a pub, it avoided the dreadful 'cues' for song that dog the musical genre by quite naturalistically having a pub band perform the songs in four separate sets.

Both these shows were about the needs of the ordinary community versus those of commerce and government – in Keeffe's play the theatre was to be turned into a Job Centre (with no jobs to offer) and in Turner's the pub was to be converted into a neon-lit cocktail bar. Unlike the portrayal of mega-myths in *Evita* or *Godspell*, these plots were firmly rooted in the real, contemporary world and had some direct relevance to the everyday concerns of audiences.

These shows underlined the fact that, to appeal to genuine rock fans, writers and musicians needed to create original and relevant forms of entertainment. Much was made of the involvement of non-musical playwrights such as Alan Bleasdale, whose Elvis bio-musical, *Are You Lonesome Tonight,* enjoyed a London run. But in the late Eighties it was the old favourites—*Cats, Chess,* even a revival of *Godspell* that were still making headlines.

RENE TIMMINS

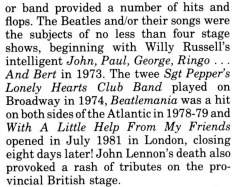

A Fine Romance

**How the new romantic élite rebuilt
the barriers torn down by punk**

*Spandau Ballet, foremost of the
new romantic bands, play to an
attentive audience. Their
television exposure in mid 1980
took the movement out of the
London clubs and into the
national spotlight.*

ANY EXPLANATION OF how a gleaming new species
of white pop music came to dominate mainstream tastes in Britain at the start of the
Eighties is inevitably going to be complex and
fragmentary. The loosely linked gaggle of
groups known as 'new romantics' won an
artistic credibility well beyond that of the
entirely manufactured pop stars that nestled
beside them in the charts. Yet they offered no
convenient revolutionary dogma for rock
critics to cling to, provided few inflatable anti-
establishment values, and demanded no uniform dress code from their followers. They
never aspired to outrage 'decent' society,
craving instead a reaction of confusion mixed
with envy at their extravagant attire and
apparent material well-being.

The insinuation of these new pop values into

the hearts and minds of British youth cannot be
explained in the same terms as, say, the advent
of the Sex Pistols or the Rolling Stones; the new
ideology was far too obedient for that. Instead,
its rise may be attributed to a combination of
factors – the materialistic values of the music-
industry establishment, the predictable tendency of a depressed society to find pleasure in
escapism and a general, possibly permanent,
disillusionment with rock'n'roll's conventional
wisdoms.

Ballet on the box

The new romantic – a term conveniently and
meaninglessly coined to describe a glossier
type of British musical product – was first
packaged for public consumption in mid 1980
when a young London band called Spandau

Left: Ultravox's Midge Ure (left) and Japan's Mick Karn, two erstwhile new romantics who joined forces in 1983 to record the appropriately-titled single 'After A Fashion'. Right: Sheffield's ABC were one of many groups to ride to success on the bandwagon. Below: Steve Strange holds court. Below far right: The Camden Palace, north London.

Ballet became the subject of the youth cultural TV show '20th Century Box' and appeared on the cover of the rock weekly *Sounds*.

The group's members and entourage professed themselves in favour of things that were certain to appal those who had identified punk in the late Seventies as the disenchanted voice of a generation. They spoke enthusiastically of their interest in clothes, of creating an air of uniqueness around themselves. They defined their goals not in terms of a social critique but as the pursuit of a creative type of pleasure-seeking, a desire for self-validation through self-improvement. 'The whole scene attracts people who want to develop, who want to achieve something in any direction, whether it's art, or whether it's money. It's ambition,' said songwriter/guitarist Gary Kemp, 21, soon to become one of a new collection of pin-ups.

Spandau identified the bedrock of their then comparatively small following as an informal crowd of designers, artists, musicians and lovers of dance music who congregated, not in the grimy cellars of the London rock circuit, but in particular West End nightclubs. A mutual admiration society flourished undisturbed to varying proportions of soul and disco music, and Spandau's was to be the sound of this intriguingly concealed scene. They had a manifesto – and a mythology was born.

Deep and meaningless

During the same period, a number of young musicians had at last taken up the synthesiser – by now a cheaper, easier and more accessible instrument – and applied to it the basic rules of pop. Ultravox! – who, in another form, were soon to have a huge hit with the grandiose, meaningless 'Vienna' – had already applied the instrument to a peripheral punk-inspired music and milked its vaguely *Brave New World* connotation for all it was worth. Many of the new groups made their first appearance on 1981's *Some Bizarre Album*, the first release of the independent label Some Bizarre.

From Basildon, the cute, boyish quartet Depeche Mode scored hits with airy, gently melancholic ditties of the modern world played exclusively on synth. Leeds duo Soft Cell emitted a more flamboyant vanity, and after reaching Number 1 in the UK and Number 8 in the US with only their second single, an artful rendition of Gloria Jones' underground soul hit 'Tainted Love', went on to detail an uncompromisingly camp vision of urban degeneracy and sexual ambivalence. Both groups had debuted on the *Some Bizarre Album*, together with Blancmange, The The and sundry others.

But it was Sheffield group the Human League who won the greatest commercial success in this field. After a few years on the post-punk experimental fringes, their *Dare* album of 1981 mined a seam of cosmetic pop perfection, and produced a string of hit 45s. Although they were by no means aligned to the 'clubby' London scene, their music typified the criteria for success in the new environment – instant melody, clinically-defined love tangles, a kind of emotional objectivity and an image pieced together from the whole range of post-war romantic clichés.

The space-age connotations of electronic instruments soon gave rise to a new label to sit alongside 'new romantic' – the 'futurist'. This was an inappropriate title, since what united most shades of the new musical kaleidoscope was their reliance on plundering familiar clichés from the past.

Glam, androgyny, narcissism and stylised alienation were hardly new to British pop. David Bowie is inevitably cited as a precursor of the painstaking presentations of the 'new pop', and it was not difficult to spot echoes of the doomed spaceman of 'Space Oddity', the shimmering grey Europeanisms of his work with Eno and the superficial soul of 1975's *Young Americans*. But although Bowie's successive musical and imagistic phases were always executed with a shrewd commercial awareness, his embrace of each new style generally acted as a device to trigger some more fundamental emotion, or evoke some deeper irony. Few of the 'new pop' people shared, or even cared to share, such complex achievements.

The readiness with which purveyors and impresarios of reborn romanticism espoused values that some would consider reactionary was to prove a mixed blessing. The liberal

notion that radical music could only exist in the penurious garb of 'the street' had been rightly rejected for its basic condescension, and theorists of the clean new music made play of the need of the dispossessed for self-respect via the respect of a wider, richer world where affluence and ease are the keystones of existence. Punk refugee turned family showman Adam Ant and club entrepreneur Steve Strange openly recommended the work ethic and conventional entertainment values. Such naked pragmatism could not be derided in the face of ample evidence that rock was not going to catalyse a social revolution of any real significance.

Much has been made of the alleged élitism of the new romantic trendsetters, their initial refusal to play the recognised venues or advertise the whereabouts of gigs to the general public. Yet the apparently obsessive competition for increasingly rarefied garb, as manifested by ambiguously-operated dress codes at the entrance to clubs, further helped reconstruct the barriers between consumers and producers. The mystique of the star, in part destroyed by the crude democracy of punk, had been well and truly re-established thanks to a fascination with image.   DAVE HILL

ROCK '82

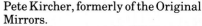

For the UK music scene, 1982 was a year of unprecedented variety; 'serious' rock acts like Dexys Midnight Runners, the Stranglers and the Jam vied with commercial popsters like Bucks Fizz, Tight Fit and Renée and Renato for the top of the singles chart. It was also a year for stylish, arty bands that spanned the gap between rock and showbiz: Soft Cell, Japan and ABC all enjoyed UK Top Ten hits.

The sheer style and scope of the new UK pop acts led to the second 'British Invasion' of the United States, with UK bands like Dexys, Yazoo (or Yaz, as they were called in the US) and A Flock Of Seagulls jostling REO Speedwagon and Styx in the US charts.

The established artists didn't fare too badly either: Roxy Music had the best-selling UK album of the year with *Avalon*, the Rolling Stones enjoyed a successful world tour, while former Motown star Marvin Gaye made a substantial comeback with a worldwide hit single, 'Sexual Healing'.

Meanwhile, a revival of teen-pop was brewing. Haircut 100 enjoyed their brief run of success, future world idols Duran Duran began to make inroads into the UK Top Ten, while the most bizarre new star of all broke onto the scene in October as the androgynous Boy George and his band Culture Club soared to Number 1 in the UK singles chart with 'Do You Really Want To Hurt Me?'.

January

1 Status Quo drummer John Coghlan leaves the band, saying 'I just want to play some different music.' His replacement is Pete Kircher, formerly of the Original Mirrors.

16 Alabama enter the US Top 40 with 'Love In The First Degree', their first crossover single from the country market.

19 Returning from Cannes in his Cessna light aircraft, Gary Numan runs out of fuel and is forced to land on the A3051 Botley to Winchester road. He and his three passengers escape unhurt.

20 Phil Lynott, Charlie Daniels and Rick Derringer appear in a UNICEF benefit concert at the Savoy in New York.

30 'Oh Julie' by Shakin' Stevens tops the UK singles chart, while Daryl Hall and John Oates hold the US Number 1 spot with 'I Can't Go For That (No Can Do)'. Sam 'Lightning' Hopkins dies, aged 70, in Centerville, Texas, from cancer. The blues guitarist and talkin' blues vocalist was best known for his songs 'Bald Headed Woman' and 'Blues Is A Feeling'.

February

3 Glaswegian rocker Alex Harvey dies of a heart attack at the age of 46 while on tour in Belgium.

16 Veteran rockers the J. Geils Band enjoy their first US Number 1 hit with 'Centrefold'.

U2 singer Bono Vox comments on the trends of the day: 'There's too many people hiding behind their haircuts. U2 is not about fashion.'

21 Murray 'The K' Kaufman, the New York DJ who did much to introduce America to the Beatles, dies of cancer at the age of 60.

26 Post-punk doom merchants Killing Joke split in two when singer Jaz and guitarist Geordie flee to Iceland, fearing the Apocalypse.

March

1 Former Rainbow singer Graham Bonnet joins the Michael Schenker Group.

5 Actor/comedian John Belushi dies, age 33, from an accidental drugs overdose.

16 Singer Teddy Pendergrass is critically injured when his Rolls Royce collides with a tree.

19 Randy Rhoads, guitarist with Ozzy Osbourne's Blizzard of Oz, is killed in a flying accident in Orlando, Florida, when a light aircraft in which he was joyriding buzzed the group's tour bus, clipped a wing and crashed into a nearby house.

27 The Goombay Dance Band top the UK chart with their single 'Seven Tears'.

April

24 'Ebony And Ivory', Paul McCartney and Stevie Wonder's hymn to racial harmony, tops the UK singles chart.

26 Joe Strummer of the Clash disappears on the eve of the band's UK tour. According to some reports, he was last seen on the boat train to Paris with his girlfriend.

30 Lester Bangs, one of America's leading rock critics, dies at the age of 33.

Left: US chart-toppers Daryl Hall (left) and John Oates go for it.

May
2 Adam Ant disbands his group to pursue a solo career.
7 Tam Paton, 43-year-old former Bay City Rollers manager, is jailed for three years by an Edinburgh court for behaving in a 'shamelessly indecent' manner towards 10 teenage boys.
22 The Central London Branch of the Musicians' Union call for a ban on synthesisers and drum machines.
24 Joe Strummer returns to the Clash, but drummer Topper Headon then quits. His predecessor, Terry Chimes, is his temporary replacement.

June
5 Roxy Music's *Avalon* tops the British LP chart.
10 Micky Harris of the Shirelles dies of a heart attack. The 42-year-old was performing with the group in Los Angeles.
16 James Honeyman Scott, guitarist and founder member of the Pretenders, dies after taking heroin and cocaine.

July
2 Former Clash drummer Topper Headon is remanded on bail after being charged with stealing a bus stop and receiving stolen property.
3 Captain Sensible of the Damned tops the UK singles chart with his cover of 'Happy Talk', a song from the Rodgers and Hammerstein musical *South Pacific*, while the Human League are Number 1 in the US with 'Don't You Want Me'.
27 Sting of the Police settles out of court after a legal battle with Virgin Music Publishing over a contract he signed before he became famous.

August
7 Dexys Midnight Runners top the UK singles chart with 'Come On Eileen'.
12 Soul star Joe Tex dies of a heart attack at the age of 49.
18 Four streets in Liverpool are named after the Beatles: John Lennon Drive, Paul McCartney Way, George Harrison Close and Ringo Starr Drive.

1982 was the Year of the Haircut, as exemplified by Joe Strummer (top left), Boy George (top right) and Mari Wilson (above).

September
2 Rolling Stones Keith Richards' Sussex mansion, Redlands, burns down for the second time in nine years.
23 WEA Records threatens to withdraw all their advertising from 'any newspaper which supports home taping'.
25 The Steve Miller Band are top of the US singles chart with 'Abracadabra'.

October
2 Musical Youth top the UK singles chart with 'Pass The Dutchie', a cover of the old Mighty Diamonds song 'Pass The Kouchie'. The title and lyrics were changed to avoid the original's reference to marijuana smoking.
Neil Diamond enters the US Top 40 with 'Heartlight'. The song is apparently inspired by the film *ET*, but does not anger the director Steven Spielberg, as have some efforts to cash in on his film. To recoup the losses incurred by his WOMAD (World Of Music And Dance) festival earlier in the year, Peter Gabriel re-unites with Genesis for a one-off benefit at Milton Keynes.
7 Former Led Zeppelin guitarist Jimmy

Page is given a year's conditional discharge and ordered to pay £100 costs for possession of cocaine.
17 The Who play the last show of their farewell tour in Toronto at the Maple Leaf Gardens. This marks the end of the band's career, although they reform briefly for Live Aid in 1985 and the British Phonographic Industry awards in 1988.
23 'Do You Really Want To Hurt Me?' by Culture Club is top of the UK singles chart.
29 Two fans are stabbed, one fatally, and another shot dead at a Peter Frampton concert in Houston, Texas.

November
5 Channel 4 TV's weekly rock show, 'The Tube' is launched with presenters Paula Yates and former Squeeze keyboard-player Jools Holland.
6 Sixties veteran Joe Cocker returns to the charts in the US with his duet with Jennifer Warnes, 'Up Where We Belong', the theme from the film *An Officer And A Gentleman*.
Following the departure of percussionist Mark Fox, Haircut 100 vehemently deny rumours that they are to split.

December
1 The Jam play the first of five farewell gigs at London's Wembley Arena after Paul Weller's decision to disband the group. Their single, 'Beat Surrender', goes straight to Number 1 in the UK chart the same week.
11 US scandal sheet the *Weekly World News* reports that parents are incensed by 'this slinky songbird that drives teen boys wild', Boy George. 'This kind of sexual mix-up could create an entire generation of homosexuals, and where would we be then?' fumed one.
18 'Save Your Love' by Renée and Renato tops the UK singles chart.
Anarchist punk band Crass hold a sit-in at the Rainbow Theatre after dates were cancelled in a row over their single, 'How Does It Feel (To Be Mother Of 1000 Dead)', which criticised Margaret Thatcher over the Falklands conflict.

ANNETTE KENNERLEY, CHRIS SCHÜLER

JOURNEYS·TO·GLORY

Above: Spandau Ballet, from left Gary Kemp,
Tony Hadley, Martin Kemp, Steve Norman and
John Keeble. Right: Gary Kemp, the group's
musical mastermind.

Travelling in style with Spandau Ballet

'OUR AMBITION wasn't to have a hit record; it was to start a whole new chapter in pop culture history,' commented Gary Kemp, guitarist, sole songwriter and main spokesperson for Spandau Ballet. From the outset, the group saw itself as a re-action to the previous prevailing trend in British rock – punk. While punk's various forms of anti-social behaviour – ranging from pogoing and spitting to self-mutilation – might have been vital for street credibility, they weren't necessarily much fun. It is hardly surprising that at the same time American disco music became massively popular with ordinary kids. As Gary Kemp put it: 'In the end, punk wasn't smart enough; it wasn't interesting enough . . . and there weren't enough girls around.'

White soulboys

It was from this soul/funk/disco back-ground that Spandau Ballet derived their style. Five working-class lads from North London, they had been dancing and listen-ing to the likes of Marvin Gaye, the O'Jays, War, the Ohio Players and Kool and the Gang throughout their adolescence. By the winter of 1978, however, a new London club scene had begun to emerge, with Billy's in Soho being the 'in' place. Steve Strange, then one of the regular DJs at the club, recalled that 'One of the great attractions of the soul scene was always the dress, which was always *different*, but by 1978 it was starting to get very bland and the atmosphere wasn't there any more. Billy's offered the chance to get back to the older attitude, more daring dress and a sleazier, more decadent atmosphere.'

Club clientèle wore romantic fantasy clothes; any 'look' was suitable as long as it was outrageous enough, and the only real rule was that you had to make an effort. The club favoured electronic music, but, in Gary's words, 'the reason [it] was played was basically just to prove that we were a different scene.' Another explanation might have been that for people not par-ticularly proficient on any musical instru-ment, playing the synthesiser offered a quick way of making music.

These embryonic 'new romantics', as writer Robert Elms was later to dub them, began to circulate round a nucleus of dif-ferent clubs like the Blitz, St Moritz and Hell on different nights of the week. How-ever, there was something missing from the new scene – suitable live music. John Keeble, Spandau's drummer, recalled: 'We decided to try out a band because there were no bands who reflected the image and the atmosphere of the clubs.' Steve Dagger, the group's old schoolfriend and manager, added: 'In the clubs there were loads of kids who looked great and were well into fashion. All you needed was a band to go on stage wearing those clothes and they'd have it made.'

The fact that Spandau Ballet's line-up remained unchanged reflected a stability unusual in Eighties rock. The group mem-bers had known each other since school-days at Owens Grammar School in Potters Bar and all, with the exception of Martin Kemp, had previously played together as the Makers. John Keeble had been drum-ming since primary school, while Steve Norman had entered the printing trade from school before leaving to devote all his energies to the band. On the group's first LP, *Journeys To Glory* (1981), Steve had his work cut out mastering guitar, but he later progressed to percussion; by the release of *True* (1983), he had become proficient on the saxophone.

Front man Tony Hadley had singing les-sons as a boy, and was inspired by singers like Frank Sinatra, Barbra Streisand and Tom Jones rather than his peers in the rock world. Gary Kemp, with manager Steve Dagger the brains behind the band, developed much of his sense of visual style from the six years he and younger brother Martin spent at the Anna Scher Children's Theatre in Islington. Getting his first guitar at 11, he said of it: 'I wasn't really interested in playing the guitar. I wanted to *write songs*.' His conversation was littered with words like 'style', 'fashion' and, above all, 'pop culture', and he aspired to directing films – 'I want Spandau Ballet to live a shorter life than most bands, and then I can go on to other things.'

Having decided to cash in on the club scene, all the quartet lacked was a bass player. So Gary roped in Martin Kemp, who had played in a school band, the De-fects, but knew nothing of bass guitar until Gary showed him the basics. After all, it wasn't the music that mattered; it was the image, the style, the glory – cynics might add the hype.

Spandau's first gig was carefully planned to boost the band's confidence. About 50 fashionable friends were invited to an Islington studio on a November Saturday morning in 1979 for free drink and to listen to the band; both went down well. The next month they played at Steve Strange's party at Blitz and were offered a record deal by Island Records, which Steve Dagger turned down. 'When we first started playing we didn't like any of the rock scene at all. Every band just seemed to make an album and then do a standard tour of all the Odeons and Dominions.' So Spandau played the clubs where they had formerly been the punters. Their admir-able policy was that 'It's better to support a club scene than a rock venue'. Their gigs were meant to be events, where the audience actually became an integral part of the display rather than merely passive onlookers.

Culture vultures

By May 1980 this developing scene had caught the attention of the media, and Spandau's performance at the Scala Cinema in King's Cross, London, was filmed for Janet Street-Porter's '20th Century Box' television programme. The kids in this peacock phenomenon were called Blitz Kids after the club and Spandau Ballet became the foremost exponents of their 'culture'. In fact, Visage and Ultravox had already released records with the strong electronic hallmark of the new romantics, but neither group was as committed to the projection of the whole 'way of life' package as Spandau Ballet.

What Spandau were propounding was a kind of youthful pride and self-celebration. As opposed to the self-denigration of the punk ethos, the new romantics were primarily young, bold, smart and am-bitious. They criticised the likes of Malcolm McLaren in much the same way

Below: Spandau strut their stuff for their fans in one of the small clubs the band initially favoured.

as past youth-cults had written off their predecessors: 'Bow Wow Wow is completely conceived and contrived by an old shark. With what we're doing, there's no-one over the age of 23 involved.' Furthermore, Spandau advocated having a good time, which in 1980 – when UK unemployment doubled – struck many observers as insensitive to the point of being immoral. 'Our music is about enjoying yourself, looking good and having a laugh. If there's a message, I suppose we are trying to tell kids not to condition themselves into thinking opportunities are slim. What kids do have is their individuality.'

Opportunities, however, were very slim and, in contrast to the powerful, politicised lyrics that Paul Weller of the Jam was writing at the time, Kemp's views and lyrics came across as pretty crass. But, as the Thirties depression had seen Hollywood produce some of its most extravagant and vapid films, so Spandau Ballet and their fellow new romantics now reflected an urge to dress up and pretend all was well with the world.

Show time
During the rest of 1980 Spandau Ballet continued playing unconventional venues and dates, such as a two-week residency in St Tropez – not another London club but the French jet-set resort – odd gigs in provincial cities and, most bizarre of all, a performance on HMS *Belfast*, a World War II warship permanently moored on the Thames. By autumn the group signed to Chrysalis Records, who granted them their own Reformation custom label. Their first single, 'To Cut A Long Story Short', was a catchy electronic number that reached the UK Number 5 position in December. No longer did Spandau Ballet belong exclusively to those in the know.

The band's second single, 'The Freeze', made Number 17 early in 1981; both hits were included on the first album, *Journeys To Glory*, as was the third single, the Slavonic-sounding 'Musclebound', which reached Number 10. The fact that all their singles were issued in both 7-inch and 12-inch remixed dance versions was, at the time, an innovation for a white group. Videos accompanied the singles, but despite the visual emphasis of the group and the Kemps' acting experience, they were never as impressive as those of Ultravox, Visage or, later, Duran Duran.

The group's preference for smaller, more exclusive venues continued in 1981. The band toured a little in Europe and in London moved, like the scene, to the newly fashionable clubs – Le Kilt (the original Sixties Mod club), Le Beat Route and Club for Heroes. In the spring they ventured across the Atlantic to New York; their US debut, at the Underground Club, also featured a fashion show promoted by Axiom, a group of young British clothes designers. A fourth single, 'Chant No.1', was released in July 1981 and was the first white British record to get extensive air-play on black American radio stations. A

Number 3 hit in their home country, its driving percussion borrowed from trendy African rhythms; synthesiser was kept to a minimum and the bonus of the Beggar & Co horn section all added up to a lively, sophisticated new sound.

While *Journeys To Glory* had been greeted by merely lukewarm reviews, *Diamond* (1982), their second album, was panned by critics. The former, produced by Richard James Burgess, was deservedly described as 'ordinary', 'undynamic' and 'superficial'; jerky rhythms and elementary synthesiser had given it a primitive, empty feel. *Diamond*, also produced by Burgess, was a strange mixture. Besides being released as an ordinary LP, *Diamond* also came out in a boxed set of four 12-inch dance mixes – a very unusual packaging ploy. On the LP, side one sported 'Chant No 1' and three other upbeat numbers, but side two was deliberately 'experimental'. Lifting ideas wholesale from the likes of Japan, tracks like 'Innocence And Science' and 'Missionary' mingled Indian and Oriental sounds, with dripping water sounds behind the slow, monotonous vocals.

The band defended their work as being intended to be film music and an attempt 'to get out of the Duran Duran league' by trying out different styles. But adverse critical reaction and the relative failure of two further singles taken from the album – 'Paint Me Down' (Number 30) and 'She Loved Like Diamond' (Number 49) – caused them to change producers. Trevor Horn, who had produced Buggles and Dollar among others, revamped 'Instinction' from the LP, but the association was not productive as 'he was too overpowering, too dogmatic'. Nevertheless, thanks to Horn and the extra publicity surrounding the band's first British tour of rock venues in spring 1982, 'Instinction' reached Number 10 in the UK charts.

Just one of those things
The success of 'Instinction' was consolidated by the next two singles, 'Lifeline' (Number 7 in October 1982) and 'Communication' (Number 12 in March 1983), both of which were catchy pop songs. Indeed, by 1983 Spandau had become more and more pop-oriented. Countering accusations of selling-out, Gary maintained 'There's no distinction now between pop and what used to be called progressive, more credible stuff.' The band's third album, *True* (1983), included both these singles and showed the band approaching a genuine soul feel, with plenty of 'ooh-ooh' and 'hey, hey, hey' backing vocals, rhythmic precision and a more relaxed, smoother sound. The LP was co-produced in Nassau by Steve Jolley and Tony Swain, who had previously worked with Imagination. Gary Kemp was well pleased with the team: 'They're good because they're into black music, they're Londoners . . . they also make good, clean records which sound loud on the radio and everybody wants to sound loud on the radio'. The album's title

track was subsequently released as a single and made Number 1, while a fourth 45 culled from it, 'Gold', went to Number 2.

Music that achieves popular success often has to bear critical derision, and *True* met with both. Rock writer John Gill felt that 'Spandau Ballet have a picture of themselves as being boulevard soulboys, selflessly dedicated to something-or-other but . . . *True* . . . actually sounds like sub-standard Toto.' Nonetheless, their third LP and its successor, *Parade* (1984), while short on experimentation, made enjoyable listening; in addition Gary Kemp's lyrics made some kind of sense, having been mainly pretentious and inane on earlier releases. Spandau's visuals had also changed: in 1981 they went from tartans to Iron Curtain peasant gear to Zoot suits and could justifiably assert that

Singer Tony Hadley led Spandau's change of image from new romantic Cossacks (above) to demure white soul boys (left).

'everything we've ever started has been in the fashion magazines six months later'.

By 1983, however, they were sporting ordinary casual garb and, though Tony Hadley could not bring himself to renounce his suits, he now wore open-necked shirts. In a sense, they hadn't sold out on the fashion side – they were simply reflecting the more conventional tastes of their new, mass audience which was largely composed of teenage girls.

'We're not five musicians, we're just five creative people who happen to be involved in music at the moment.' Comparisons may be odious, but they are also revealing: the pretentiousness of Spandau Ballet was clear when their music was compared to that of witty contemporaries Culture Club, who came up with good pop songs and a unique style, to say nothing of the many groups on independent labels engaged in genuine musical experiment. In the final analysis, there were enough people around who earnestly wanted to make good music in the Eighties to make dilettantes like Spandau Ballet seem redundant.

A long period of inactivity due to record label problems—their lack of US success being a major issue—ended when Spandau signed to CBS and returned to the charts in 1986 with the hits 'Fight For Ourselves' and 'Through The Barricades', title track of a Number 7 album. Ironically Chrysalis's *Singles Collection*, reached Number 3. A 1989 album *Heart Like A Sky* also flopped short of the Top Thirty.   RENE TIMMINS

2349

Palace People

Camden's Strange creatures of the night

WHEN THOSE CUTE POPSTERS WHAM! sang in 1983 about the Club Tropicana, with its cocktails, famous faces and exotic night-life, they could have been singing about their own regular haunt, London's Camden Palace. If the early Eighties were an era of night-clubbing, glamour and heady escapism (in sharp contrast to the almost puritanical fervour of punk), this glossy niterie summed up its slightly desperate glitter.

Strange days

Run by two young entrepreneurs, Steve Strange and Rusty Egan, the Camden Palace opened on 22 April 1982. Situated in an old music hall (which had previously been used as a BBC theatre and, latterly, a seedy punk venue called the Music Machine) opposite Mornington Crescent tube station, it soon became London's hottest night spot. A faultless sound system, a Hollywood-style open staircase and several gallons of gold paint added to the building's existing advantages. It boasted a capacity of 2000, spread over four tiered balconies, each of which, after refurbishment, offered a bird's eye view of the stage, a sprung dancefloor and laser light-show.

Strange – who would hold court in the third-floor cocktail bar on the fashionable Thursday nights – was born Steve Harrington in Wales on 28 May 1959. He

'Step this way...' Steve Strange (left) introduces an array of Palace people (above). Above, second from left, Strange celebrates with Rusty Egan.

had his first taste of nightlife at the age of 14, when he would hitch to Blackpool or the Wigan Casino to dance at Northern Soul all-nighters. During the punk boom of 1976, he spent some time as a roadie for Generation X before forming the short-lived Moors Murderers with future Pretender Chrissie Hynde.

By the end of 1978, punk had all but fizzled out; to cater for audiences bored with both punk and the bland US disco played in many clubs, Steve Strange and his friend Rusty Egan started their 'futurist' nights at Billy's in Soho. With Rusty manning the turntables, electronic sounds were pushed to the fore. At the time, Ultravox!, the Human League and Gary Numan's Tubeway Army were merely cult names, but they provided the soundtrack for the exotic nightlife at Billy's alongside music by David Bowie, Brian Eno and Kraftwerk.

Grades of fey
Around this time, Steve Strange and Rusty Egan formed a band, or rather a recording project, called Visage. With Steve singing, Rusty on drums (he had previously played with former Sex Pistol Glen Matlock's Rich Kids), Midge Ure, Billy Currie from Ultravox! and John McGeoch and Dave Formula of Magazine, they recorded several tracks like 'Tar', 'In The Year 2525' and 'Mind Of A Toy'. Strange's languid, washed-out vocals and lyrics of romantic

despair were set to a pounding Eurodisco beat overlaid with pseudo-classical synthesiser.

The project was then shelved for over a year while the various members pursued other projects, but in 1980, after Midge Ure had joined Ultravox and became a hot commercial property, a single, 'Fade To Grey', was released and made the UK Top Ten. An album, Visage, and a follow-up single 'Mind Of A Toy' (both 1981), were also very successful. Another album, The Anvil, and two Top Twenty singles, 'Damned Don't Cry' and 'Night Train', appeared in 1982, while a compilation album, Fade To Grey – The Singles Collection, was released in late 1983.

From Billy's, the scene moved to Blitz in Covent Garden. The club's decor and preferred dress style was based on the Forties, and Strange would patrol the door, vetting the customers' costume. The capital's bright young things congregated there, from the then unknown Boy George to Spandau Ballet, who played one of their first gigs on the premises.

Strange and Egan's most ambitious project to date, however, was hiring the Rainbow Theatre in Finsbury Park for a massive St Valentine's Day ball in 1981. Several major bands, including Ultravox, who had recently topped the charts with 'Vienna', performed in the seatless auditorium, renamed the People's Palace for the occasion.

The duo went on to host two further clubs that year: Club for Heroes at the Barracuda gentlemen's club in the West End on Thursday nights, and Sunday afternoon tea-parties at the exclusive Gardens night-club in Knightsbridge. The style was changing from youthful gaudiness to

sophisticated affluence and traditional, jet-set élitism.

When the Camden Palace eventually opened, the first guests to arrive were a group of middle-aged men who may or may not have been the backers; the cost of refurbishing the building is estimated to have cost the best part of a million pounds, a sum that – despite the success of Visage – was beyond Strange and Egan's resources.

The smell of money
Over the next few years, the Camden Palace remained the most famous and successful of London night-clubs, despite a horde of other, smaller ventures that sprang up in its wake. For a while, Le Beat Route in Soho's Greek Street was the place to go on Friday nights; the Wag Club, run by Blue Rondo A La Turk singer Chris Sullivan, enjoyed a spell of popularity, as did Cha-Cha's, which was held every Tuesday night in the basement at Heaven. One of the most successful was a Gothic punk mausoleum called the Batcave.

Although this thriving nightlife created an impression of affluence, it was for many young people an expensive but exciting form of escape in the midst of a serious economic depression. Among the stars and future stars were scores of hopefuls, forever talking about 'getting a band together' or 'designing something for someone', and meanwhile living off their parents or the dole. Yet, despite the élitist dress codes of its fashionable nights and its slick emulation of the ways of the rich, the Camden Palace was, in an ironic way, a People's Palace after all. 'You can be yourself here,' said one customer, a pastry chef at Heathrow Airport. 'Well, not yourself, but you can be a fantasy of yourself.'

MIKE NICHOLLS

ULTRAVOX

From vox pop to synth supremos

WHEN DENNIS LEIGH first left his home in Lancashire in the mid Seventies for the bright lights of London, he found virtually nothing going on at all, 'apart from Dr Feelgood and that pub-rock thing, which I wasn't interested in, although I used to go to some of the gigs and enjoy the atmosphere.' He would occasionally bump into people like Mick Jones and Brian James before they formed their bands (the Clash and the Damned, respectively) and claims he was once even asked to audition as a prospective vocalist for the Clash.

Instead he changed his name to John Foxx and formed a group of a different nature altogether. Following an initial recording attempt under the name Tiger Lily (one dismal single, 'Ain't Misbehaving'), the line-up settled down to Londoner Chris Cross on bass, Canadian Warren Cann on drums, one-time experimental theatre artist Billy Currie on keyboards and violin and Dagenham-based Stevie Shears on guitar, and became Ultravox!. Foxx himself was featured vocalist, singing his own intriguing, impenetrable lyrics.

Their self-confessed influences – Bowie, Warhol, the Velvet Underground and Roxy Music – led to them being tagged 'art-school punk', but also helped them to attract a cult following and secure a contract with Island Records. Their debut album, released in 1977, was called simply *Ultravox!* (at this time the exclamation mark was an integral part of the band's name, and was only dropped when the third album was released) and was a stunning melting-pot of pretension, passion and progression while all around them groups like the Clash and the Sex Pistols were seething with pent-up, primal rage.

Ultravox! were the ideal punk band for people who found it hard to tolerate the brute noise of punk rock (though the Stranglers ran them a close second). But the group always cared more about creation than destruction; they even insisted on a lavish gatefold sleeve to *Ultravox!*, although the expense for it was deducted from their own royalties.

The music itself was a wild, jarring hybrid of Bowie-type pop and hard-edged Velvets-influenced rock experimentation that clearly showed the debt they owed to Roxy Music. There was a haunting, almost ethereal quality about songs such as 'Dangerous Rhythm' (their first single), 'Slipaway' and 'The Lonely Hunter', while others like 'Saturday Night In The City Of The Dead' and 'Life At Rainbow's End' had more obvious links with the punk themes of boredom, apathy and nihilism.

The latter song was subtitled 'For All The Tax Exiles On Main Street', a clear reference to the then-despised Rolling Stones, and Foxx confirmed this in an early interview. 'I saw Mick Jagger and Keith Richards down the studios – sad and rich ... one a fading tart and the other a drugged vegetable, that's what I wrote the song about.'

Foxx on the run
1977's *Ha! Ha! Ha!* was a disappointment, despite featuring a couple of outstanding tracks in the perplexing 'Man Who Dies Every Day' and 'Hiroshima Mon Amour'. The latter, named after the acclaimed 1959 film by Alain Resnais, was a subtle yet innovative blend of drum machine, keyboards, saxophone and John Foxx's crooned vocal.

Following *Ha! Ha! Ha!*, a disillusioned Stevie Shears left the group; he was replaced by guitarist Robin Simon, who added his brand of finely-tempered squealing metallics to the superb *Systems Of Romance* (1978), regarded by fans and critics alike as the finest exposition of the Ultravox style and stance so far. From the simplistic black sleeve to the faultless playing and delightful songs, this third album had class, quality, integrity, emotion and boundless commercial appeal. Unfortunately it did not achieve the sales expected of it.

Tracks like 'Slow Motion', 'Quiet Men'

Opposite: John Foxx, Ultravox's early lead singer. Opposite below: The band in the Seventies, from left Billy Currie, Foxx, Robin Simon, Chris Cross and Warren Cann. Below: Ultravox in the Eighties, from left Cann, Midge Ure, Cross and Currie. Above: Their live shows and videos became increasingly grandiose.

and 'Just For A Moment' inspired a whole generation of synthesiser bands and paved the way for Orchestral Manoeuvres in the Dark and Gary Numan to have chart hits. But disappointment at the album's relative lack of success caused internal friction, intensified by an unsuccessful US tour – and, when Island decided against renewing their option, the band effectively disintegrated with their vast potential frustratingly unrealised.

John Foxx closeted himself away in the studio and continued an intermittently successful solo career, producing a string of

Top Fifty singles and three albums for Virgin, which were interesting rather than startling. Perhaps assuming that the others would simply give up without his leadership and guiding talent, Foxx magnanimously allowed them to retain the name Ultravox, although at the time it appeared to be a matter of academic interest. However, all that was to change dramatically.

Old songs, new songs
Billy Currie had been making some experimental tapes with the help of Midge Ure. Formerly a teenybop star with fleeting pop idols Slik, Ure had subsequently earned a reputation as a journeyman jack-of-all-trades after stints with ex-Sex Pistol Glen Matlock in the Rich Kids and as guitarist (briefly) with Thin Lizzy. His pedigree made him an unlikely candidate to replace the enigmatic Foxx as the Ultravox front man, but as it turned out, Ure's recruitment to the band in 1979 was an inspired move. The nucleus of Currie, Cann and Cross refined and streamlined the smooth electronic anthems of *Systems Of Romance* and Ure, with his knack for distilling commercial tastes, fashioned them into pop songs.

The new line-up's first album, *Vienna* (1980), was not an immediate blockbuster, and the first two singles released from it in the second half of 1980 ('Sleepwalk' and 'Passing Strangers') barely dented the charts, peaking at Numbers 29 and 57 respectively.

One of the band's first major outings since Foxx's departure was a UK tour of large cinemas and theatres in December 1980. It was interesting to note how their audiences became a mixture of old die-hards who regarded Midge Ure as an inferior, unwelcome intruder, and hordes of young kids who adored the new line-up as the most desirable pin-ups since the Bay City Rollers.

But night after night, these two factions of followers were united by the grand

synthesiser pomp of the new music. The band were playing the whole of the new album, plus 'Slow Motion' and 'Quiet Men', the only Foxx-era numbers left in the set. In particular, the audiences were captivated by the hypnotic splendour of 'Vienna' itself.

Reportedly conceived as an experiment in writing an overwhelming love opus with only 'artificial' instruments such as a

Left: Midge Ure goes in for a little judicious note-bending.
Above: Ultravox became synonymous with suave professionalism in the early Eighties.

drum-machine and synthesisers, 'Vienna' was a lush, sweeping cinematic triumph of mesmerising proportions. Aided by a clever, evocative video, the single entered the UK charts in January 1981, and lodged at Number 2 for a month.

The album was eventually no less of a triumph, and stayed in the British LP charts for 71 weeks. Apart from the dire 'Mr X' (a failed exercise in synthesised voice and cross-rhythms), *Vienna* was breathtakingly innovative, liberally mixing electro-disco drum tracks with wide sweeps of melodic melodrama, while even a daring seven-minute instrumental, 'Astrodyne', was a conspicuous success.

Having hit on a winning formula, Ultravox showed themselves reluctant to abandon it. While 1981's *Rage In Eden* was in some ways a further refinement of their original concept, the music was becoming noticeably smoother and, in a sense, too predictable.

Quartet (1982) confirmed this trend, still satisfying a huge worldwide audience demand, but featuring increasingly hollow anthems that seemed to prize superficial style over incisive content. Significantly, the set saw

an establishment figure at the controls in former Beatles producer George Martin.

Part of the group's new-found conservatism could, perhaps, be put down to the members' involvement in other projects. Midge Ure and Billy Currie had formed a part of Steve Strange's occasional band Visage, while drummer Warren Cann collaborated with German synthesiser wizard Hans Zimmer to produce film music under the collective name of Helden. In 1982, Midge Ure released a solo single, 'No Regrets', which made the UK Top Ten; the following year he collaborated with Mick Karn on the single 'After A Fashion'.

Their predicament became ironically similar to the impasse reached almost a decade previously by 'progressive' bands such as Jethro Tull, Yes and Pink Floyd.

But perhaps the most valid comparison was with Roxy Music, who also started out as a vital, invigorating group with extreme attitudes and tastes only to split up due to internal clashes and reform with a modified line-up to have huge international success with a smoother style. The one major difference was that while Roxy Music maintained a respectable degree of class and panache, Ultravox ultimately resorted to recycling their own (admittedly spectacular) second-hand ideas, even to the extent of releasing a stop-gap live album, *Monument*, in 1983.

The band split in 1988 after Ure's solo career had taken off with *The Gift* (a UK Number 2 in 1985) and *Answers To Nothing* (1988). Their final two albums *Lament* (1984) and *U-Vox* (1986) had both gone Top Ten, while the hits LP *Collection* (1984) made Number 2. Ure's involvement in Band Aid (he co-wrote the theme tune, 'Do They Know It's Christmas') and as a prime mover in the royal pop charity The Prince's Trust, made him a name to watch.

JOHNNY WALLER

Japan: full of Eastern promise

'I DON'T CONSIDER JAPAN as just a rock band,' singer-songwriter David Sylvian once reflected. 'I consider it as a group of people who are trying different ways of self-expression.'

Unfortunately, although their various individual bids for creative satisfaction eventually pulled apart one of Britain's most distinctive groups at the peak of their success, neither Sylvian, bassist Mick Karn, drummer Steve Jansen or keyboard-player Richard Barbieri were to make as much impact with their solo careers. However, eight years was a long time for any collection of individuals with such a wide diversity of talents to stay together, and many people who latched onto the band's major success in 1981-82 were unaware that Japan's roots went back as far as the early Seventies.

They were originally formed around a nucleus of the brothers David and Steve Batt, who adopted the surnames Sylvian and Jansen respectively. Together with Mick Karn and Richard Barbieri, the Batt brothers went to school in Catford, South London, and the four were soon united by a common distaste for school regimentation. Their response to this was to dress out-rageously and, even in their early teens, apply a little makeup. 'We thought the kids would rebel and follow us,' recalled Sylvian. 'They didn't. It was a violent school and we had a hard time.'

Adolescent sects

A consuming interest in rock music pro-vided the glamorous misfits with a refuge from this unpleasantness. With the excep-tion of Mick Karn, who received some classical training and played bassoon in the London Schools Symphony Orchestra, the schoolfriends were complete musical novices when they decided to form Japan. The name was chosen, according to David, 'to get away from that rubbishy idea that a band's name has to give an idea of its music . . . and because it sounded nice.'

Their repertoire was a mixture of Motown material and David's early, rather uncertain originals, plus songs popu-larised by US bands like Hall and Oates and Foreigner who were, at the time, con-sidered quite inventive. The initial public reaction was not encouraging, so the band retired to the Batt homestead and prac-tised solidly for six months. This not only galvanised their resolve, but also imbued them with a common, idiosyncratic tech-nique, partly as a consequence of their scant musical training. When they were ready to perform again, in 1977, having recruited lead guitarist Rob Dean through a classified ad, they combined a curious style, verging on heavy metal, with a stage

Right: David Sylvian, debonair front man of Japan, remains unruffled in the face of an adoring audience.

VISIONS
OF THE
ORIENT

presence something after the fashion of the New York Dolls.

In that 'summer of punk', their unconventional outfits and makeup deterred any English record company from taking an interest in Japan. But a German company, Ariola-Hansa, were keen to establish themselves in the UK, and signed them, apparently on the strength of their outrageous looks. David, however, averred: 'A lot of people get the wrong idea about us . . . it would be the easiest thing in the world to *stop* wearing makeup, but I can't as it would be too much of a compromise. Personally, I feel confident wearing it.'

Whatever the contentions about their appearance, Ariola quickly put them in the studio, but it took the band a long time to adjust to this new medium, and their early demos were awkward and confused. Their first album *Adolescent Sex* (1978), which an impatient Ariola rushed out, reflected this and was dismissed by reviewers, a typical comment describing it as 'a rude crossover of rock and funk'. The company compounded the confusion of the band's image by releasing a power-chord slaughter of the Barbra Streisand ballad 'Don't Rain On My Parade' as a single, and putting them on tour supporting Blue Oyster Cult. This neither ingratiated them with a devout heavy-metal audience, nor did it win them an audience of their own.

Furniture music
In the meantime, 'The Unconventional', another single from Japan's first album, aroused considerable interest in the country of the same name, and it took little persuasion for the band to flee to the Orient. After a short, stadium-filling tour of Japan, Ariola herded them back into the studio, the result being the 1979 album *Obscure Alternatives*.

Their confidence-building Japanese trip also introduced the band to Talking Heads, whom they saw playing in a Tokyo club. Japan were impressed with the intelligence of both the group's music and their audience. It was an example they too wanted to follow, but while the American band and their peers were starting to assimilate ethnic African influences, Japan were becoming attracted to traditional Eastern music, and the *musique d'ameublement* (literally, 'furniture music') of the French eccentric composer Erik Satie. *Obscure Alternatives* exposed these interests for the first time, and to good effect. An air of Germanic austerity in some of Sylvian's songs, such as 'Suburban Berlin' and 'Deviations', provided a further interesting counterpoint.

'When you're travelling,' he explained, 'there's an immediate atmosphere when you arrive in a new place which is really exhilarating. I try and recreate this through the music.'

Although *Obscure Alternatives* was a great improvement on *Adolescent Sex*, the band were less than enchanted with producer Ray Singer and recording engineer Chris Tsangarides. Indeed the best track

on the LP was a moody instrumental, 'The Tenant', produced by Sylvian himself. But after another atypical single, this time produced by disco king Giorgio Moroder, ('Life In Tokyo'), the group eventually found a sympathetic ear in ex-Roxy Music man John Punter, 'the first person to appreciate our musical ideas', according to David.

Quiet Life (1978) was their first Punter-produced LP, and on it Japan seemed to find their true métier (and discovered a talented saxophonist in Mick Karn). Unfortunately the Punter association was too much for certain critics who had already noted the Brian Ferry influences in David's singing manner ('sucking Roxy Music dry' was how one critic described it), although *Quiet Life* was unlike anything Roxy Music had released and even included a version of the Velvet Underground's 'All Tomorrow's Parties'. When a US magazine voted David 'The World's Most Beautiful Man', the rock press descended, knives sharpened for the kill.

Despite being branded as Roxy Music copyists and attention-seeking transvestites, the band had built up a large following and by 1980 were selling out major venues in the UK, Germany and Japan. Unfortunately, record sales did not reflect their live popularity and Ariola baulked at financing a fourth album. Ex-Yardbirds manager Simon Napier-Bell immediately took the band to Virgin, a move that caused a legal fracas that removed them from public attention for a year. Their next vinyl offering, *Gentlemen Take Polaroids*, was released in late 1980 and finally turned the critical tide; it proved a strong seller although, ironically, it was a rather patchy affair. It also heralded the first of many solo collaborations; one track, 'Taking Islands In Africa', was a joint effort between David and Yellow Magic Orchestra keyboardist Riuichi Sakamoto. The latter eventually returned the compliment when Sylvian contributed vocals to 'Forbidden Colours', a track on 1983's soundtrack album *Merry Christmas Mr Lawrence*.

Rising sons
However, it was becoming increasingly obvious that Rob Dean's guitar contributions were now out of keeping with Japan's new synthesiser-laden sounds – he featured on only four tracks on *Gentlemen Take Polaroids*. It therefore came as no surprise when he subsequently left the band and moved to Los Angeles (later to resurface as a Gary Numan sideman). As Sylvian explained: 'It was really us holding him back. He'd have ideas but I wouldn't give them room to grow.'

Hansa, taking advantage of the upswing in Japan's fortunes, re-released a string of singles – commencing with 'Quiet Life', which provided the band with their first UK Top Twenty hit in the autumn of 1981 – and a compilation album, *Assemblage* (1981), which made the Top Thirty.

Tin Drum, their new Virgin release in

1981, went gold, confirming the band's best-selling status, and in 1982 they enjoyed two Top Ten singles, 'Ghosts' and another Ariola re-release, their version of the old Motown classic 'I Second That Emotion'.

Tin Drum was also their most successful album musically, and, with its Maoist-inspired cover, emphasised their oriental influences. By the time it was released, though, rumours of a split were rife throughout the pop world. Based initially on an unguarded comment by David prior to a triumphant *Tin Drum* promotional tour ('If I don't enjoy this, I shall possibly give up touring. That would possibly cause a split'), they were compounded by the band's solo projects.

The art of parting
Mick Karn had become a noted sculptor, with exhibitions in London and Tokyo. He was also much in demand as a session player, his fluid fretless bass style being sought by such notables as Robert Palmer and Gary Numan. Karn's loyalties were further stretched, on a personal level, when Sylvian 'stole' his girlfriend on the eve of a tour, causing a long and bitter rift which further destabilised the band.

Sylvian, for his part, began recording with Riuichi Sakamoto, (the duo released a single, 'Bamboo Houses') and was in any case becoming increasingly reclusive. Steve Jansen developed his photographic talents (he had taken the sleeve pic for 'The Art Of Parties' single), while keyboard-player Richard Barbieri produced an LP by Swedish group Lustans Lackejar and became involved with Ballet Rambert. As the originator of Japan's mellifluous, layered sound, it was particularly telling that Barbieri should publicly profess a growing disinclination for the Eastern affectation, expressing a preference instead for the influences of Spanish and Turkish cultures.

Although vigorous denials were issued both by Virgin and by individual members of the band, by the start of 1983 the cracks were too obvious to paper over. The spring release of a double live album and accompanying video, *Oil On Canvas*, provided a fine, if sad, epitaph for Japan.

Despite their many years together, Japan would be remembered chiefly for the evocative keyboard-dominated music of their later work, and the flamboyant, androgynous image, particularly of David Sylvian, that paved the way for further extremes of sexual ambivalence adopted by such Eighties performers as Boy George and Marilyn.   MARK WILLIAMS

Japan
Recommended Listening

Assemblage (Hansa HAN LP 1) (Includes: Adolescent Sex, Life In Tokyo, I Second That Emotion, Quiet Life, European Son, Suburban Berlin); *Tin Drum* (Virgin V2209) (Includes: Ghosts, Cantonese Boy, The Art Of Parties, Talking Drum, Still Life In Mobile Homes, Sons Of Pioneers).

Above left: Bassist Karn and vocalist Sylvian shine in the spotlight. Above: The band pose inscrutably in the Eighties, from left Richard Barbieri (foreground), Steve Jansen, Karn and Sylvian. Left: Drummer Jansen takes to the keyboard for a television appearance. Below: Early Japan. A shock-maned Sylvian (centre) with guitarist Rob Dean (right).

Video Stars

The persuasive power of pre-packaged pop

FROM THE MOMENT that Elvis Presley set the United States buzzing with his controversial TV appearances in the mid Fifties, it was to become ever more apparent that the spontaneity of rock and the conservative world of television made uncomfortable bedfellows. Although some of televised rock's most memorable moments were to occur live (Hendrix's unscheduled Cream tribute on a 1968 'Lulu Show', for example), the medium preferred to restrict the music, in the main, to programmes like 'American Bandstand' or the UK's 'Top Of The Pops', where backing tracks were pre-recorded, or disc shows like the perennial 'Juke Box Jury'; rarely were acts given an opportunity to present their music in a visually exciting way. The advent of the promotional video in the late Seventies provided the ideal solution – visual and musical entertainment in pre-packaged, three-minute segments.

Getting it taped

It was not unknown for pop stars to become film stars or vice versa, but the prohibitive expense of hiring film crews had previously restricted filming for promotional purposes to bands whose status guaranteed both a return on the investment and the TV exposure to warrant the time and trouble involved. Video, however, opened the field to all; it was both cheaper and quicker than film, required no processing and could even be monitored while shooting took place. If all failed to go according to plan, the tape could simply be wiped and used again. A quarter-century of research and development had brought the size and price of video cameras and recorders to reasonable levels; rock and television were set to reap the benefit.

Eighties superstars Eurythmics (opposite), Michael Jackson (above) and David Bowie (top).

Although all pop promotional clips came to be known as videos, film was still widely used. In comparison with videotape, film possessed more resolution and depth. Video stored sound and vision on magnetic tape in the form of electronic signals; when compared with film, its decoded pictures could appear 'flat', with subjects in the foreground having the appearance of being shot against a back projection. Film was cheaper to edit, but the process of cutting and sticking the celluloid was a time-consuming one. With video, editing was carried out not physically, but electronically by means of computer. Additional effects could be incorporated at this stage to intensify the visual impact of the end product.

The rapid growth of video was abetted by an influx of new personnel, many from the world of TV commercials. With the UK the undisputed world leader in the production of television advertisements, it came as little surprise to find young British directors like Steve Barron making an early impression on the pop video scene. Having worked his way from camera assistant on feature films and commercials to go freelance in 1976, Barron met the Jam while filming the Reading Festival two years later and the group hired him to direct videos for 'When You're Young' and 'Going Underground'. 'At the time [the Jam] weren't that big,' he commented later. 'They'd never had anything in the Top Ten – everything went to Number 25 or thereabouts.'

The Jam's video-assisted rise to greater fortune took Barron in its wake and his Limelight production company was to become one of the top video names of the Eighties. The company's roster of directors included two refugees from 'alternative' cinema in Julien Temple, maker of 1980's *The Great Rock'n'Roll Swindle*, and Don Letts, the one-time reggae DJ who chronicled the punk era on film.

Videos start life as storyboards – frame-by-frame guides to the visual action linked to the lyrics of the accompanying song. In the early days, most bands seemed overawed by the whole video process and so the storyboards tended to be devised by the director rather than the artists. This was the case with the Human League, whose

1981 UK chart-topper 'Don't You Want Me' caused Steve Barron some problems. 'I wrote a script where two of them were supposed to be driving cars, and out of four guys in the band none of them could drive... The same thing happened with Joe Jackson – we had him playing on a cliff top for "Real Men", and of course he had vertigo.'

The success (and consequent expense) of top directors ensured an influx of new talent to service bands with lesser budgets. Familiarity with the video-making process also encouraged a number of acts to follow in the footsteps of former art-school student Adam Ant and direct their own videos. Working in conjunction with former 'Supersonic' TV director Mike Mansfield, Adam successfully transferred his gaudy yet distinctive visual image to videotape, performing in and directing promos for such songs as 'Stand And Deliver' and 'Prince Charming'. Thomas Dolby and Ultravox's Midge Ure were among those to follow his lead.

Killer thriller

As video grew, new outlets opened up beyond the previously established TV pop shows. Most important of these was the American MTV cable channel, which began round-the-clock rock broadcasts, largely in video form, in August 1981. By the end of 1983, its audience had swelled to an estimated 16 million and it was being beamed to Canada by satellite. Some of the more lavish productions, such as Michael Jackson's 'Thriller' and the unexpurgated version of the Rolling Stones' 'Undercover Of The Night', even made it to the big screen as supporting features – a logical progression in some ways, since video directors had already cast overt glances at the cinema, with references to classic films a familiar standby. (Bowie's 'China Girl', for instance, echoed the 1953 movie *From Here To Eternity*.)

With its dancefloor orientation and traditional conservatism, soul music took time to accept the challenge of video. Motown artists like Stevie Wonder suffered in particular as the label debated its policy towards video. The wisdom of their decision was confirmed by the worldwide success in 1983 of Lionel Richie's 'All Night Long (All Night)', produced and directed by Bob Rafelson, who had directed the Sixties TV show 'The Monkees', along with millionaire ex-Monkee Mike Nesmith.

Former Motown stars such as Marvin Gaye, Diana Ross and, of course, Michael Jackson, had been among the first black stars to embrace video, and the results had been both striking and successful. MTV had found itself in the centre of controversy, however, when it was alleged that black acts were being excluded by the station's 'narrowcasting' policy of 24-hour rock; and soul groups like Earth Wind and Fire adopted a new 'rock' beat as pressure was applied to MTV to widen its musical policy.

Censorship ranked alongside discrimination as a subject for debate in the video

forum. The Rolling Stones' Mick Jagger openly invited controversy by having Keith Richards shoot him through the head in the video of 1983's 'Undercover Of The Night', although he subsequently allowed extensive editing to take place. Other reactions were somewhat less explicable; Eurythmics singer Annie Lennox was blacked out on MTV when she removed a long wig to expose her own close-cropped hair for fear that she might be promoting transvestism, while Paul Weller's affectionate fondling of fellow Style Councillor Mick Talbot was cut from their 1983 'Long Hot Summer' promo at the insistence of Polydor Records' managing director as contrary to Weller's 'masculine image'.

As sales of home video recorders grew apace, it was but a short step from preparing videos for TV to selling them direct to the viewer. The first of these were, perhaps inevitably, videos of concerts, but the choice later grew to include collections of promo videos (Madness even released a greatest hits and greatest videos package, *Complete Madness*, simultaneously) and even video singles. This form of commercial exploitation initially led to legal complications; musicians-turned-video directors Kevin Godley and Lol Creme sued Duran Duran when financial agreement could not be reached on the sale of a video collection of the steamy, soft-focus Duran Duran promo videos.

By 1983, BBC-TV's 'Top Of The Pops' could run a ten-minute sequence of the videos for the Top Ten singles, emphasising that the promo video had become an obligatory marketing device. If further proof were needed of the effect of videos on record sales, it was surely supplied by Paul McCartney's 'Say Say Say', a duet with Michael Jackson released in late 1983. A mediocre song by either artist's standards, it peaked at Number 10 in its second week in the UK charts, dropping to 13 and 14 in

Director Steve Barron (second from right) instructs Heaven 17's Glenn Gregory during shooting.

subsequent weeks. But its decline was to be arrested by the TV premiere of a lavish video production that – as with so many promo videos – bore little relation to the song's lyrical content. The clip was shown twice in the following week, and the record rose to Number 2.

Cable TV

The one problem that video failed to conquer was that of sound quality. However impressive the visuals, the music was invariably rendered in distorted mono through the tiny speaker of a domestic television set; indeed, the music of certain bands, Duran Duran among them, was held to have degenerated into mere film-soundtrack material as their videos hit new heights of sophistication.

The future of the rock video in the Eighties seemed inextricably linked with the prospects for cable television. With numerous channels bidding to emulate the Stateside success of MTV in the UK, it was hoped that the increased demand would grant fresh inspiration to video directors who had explored most of the obvious visual possibilities. The most promising variations on the pop promo theme might well lie in the fields of graphics and animation, where the work of Cucumber Video's Annabel Jankel and Rocky Morton for such artists as Tom Tom Club and Donald Fagen was outstanding.

What was certain, however, was that the genre that Adam Ant termed 'a three-minute Hollywood' had already consumed many ideas. And, from being hailed as a breakthrough that put visuals within the budget of many a rock act, the video's ascent to the status of an art-form had left all but the rich behind in its pursuit of perfection. MICHAEL HEATLEY

World Service

How the sounds of global rock changed from Sixties imitation to Eighties innovation

DURING THE SEVENTIES, as costs rose and profit margins were squeezed within the music business, international markets became essential for the survival of major record companies. Although the United States remained the world's biggest music market, with the UK the most important repertoire source, foreign markets were no longer seen as just icing on the cake. Countries like Japan, West Germany, France, Brazil, Mexico and Australia were spending increasing amounts of money on rock product and, consequently, most companies now signed acts only on a worldwide basis, while a growing number of artists from outside the UK and US became internationally successful.

The shock of the new
In the Sixties, throughout Europe and the English-speaking world, local bands had imitated the sound of the hugely successful British groups, often recording pale cover versions of British or American songs. But towards the end of the decade, the better Continental groups began to become more creatively adventurous, composing their own music. In the early Seventies a few, mainly Dutch, groups like the Cats, Focus, Shocking Blue and the George Baker

Above: Thijs Van Leer of Dutch band Focus.
Below: Australia's Men At Work.

Selection began to break internationally – Shocking Blue even had a US Number 1 in 1970 with 'Venus'. In 1974 Sweden's Abba, singing in English, began their phenomenal run of success, while the second half of the decade saw Germany become an important repertoire source with Munich the centre for Eurodisco producers like Frank Farian, Michael Kunze and Georgio Moroder. Though British or American in origin, major stars like Donna Summer and Boney M were launched from Germany. Bands like Can, Kraftwerk and the Scorpions gained international recognition, and Germany became renowned as a heavy-metal market.

The Eighties saw German new-wave bands help build an ever-increasing share of the German charts for German artists (although this trend was reversed in 1983 when the domestic share of the singles charts fell from 48 to 28 per cent). Meanwhile, a new phenomenon became apparent in the growing success of Italian records in Germany, fuelled by exposure from the many Italian radio and TV stations that could be picked up in parts of Germany. Italy itself, however, remained the weakest major market in Europe. Apart from the country's poor economic performance, the main problem seemed to be a surfeit of broadcast music.

While record sales in Europe climbed consistently throughout the Seventies, up to 80 per cent of album sales in parts of Asia were illegal pirate copies, making legitimate trade impossible. In India, on the other hand, EMI's Gramophone Company of India had a monopoly of the market until the mid Seventies, when Polydor stepped in to challenge their control. India has a population of around 700 million, yet record sales had always been low, peaking in the early Eighties at an annual eight million

albums a year. International repertoire traditionally accounted for about 12 per cent of the Indian market, with the Beatles and Cliff Richard the most consistently popular stars. It was not until the early Eighties, which saw the emergence of an Indianised disco sound (with Hazan's 'Disco Deewane' the most popular example), that India began building a lucrative pop scene of her own.

The rock scene in China, meanwhile, remained virtually non-existent. The China Record Company had released Maoist songs and revolutionary operas like *Taking Tiger Mountain By Storm* and *Producing Oil For The Motherland*, manufactured at the EMI Pathé factory in Shanghai, since 1949.

There was tremendous variety in Japan, however, with traditional music selling next to rock in a market worth over a billion dollars a year. In 1960 foreign records accounted for 60 per cent of all sales, by 1966 it was 50/50, and by the Eighties Japanese music had gained about 70 per cent of the market. Native acts like Alice and the Kai Band became popular at home while others, like Yellow Magic Orchestra, started to gain a foothold in the international market. Nonetheless, by the mid Eighties Japan had produced only one international hit in 30 years of trying: in 1963 Kyu Sakamoto took 'Sukiyaki' to Number 1 in America and into the charts around the world.

Danger! Men at work

South Africa and Nigeria were the biggest markets in Africa but poverty, piracy and political instability conspired to restrict the record industry throughout most of the continent. However, interest in African music grew over the years, with artists from Osibisa to Juluka and King Sunny Ade gaining an international following.

Jamaica has had a bigger impact on Western music than any other Third World country. Through calypso, ska and reggae, and singers like Desmond Dekker, Jimmy Cliff and Bob Marley, the music of Jamaica found its way, usually via the UK, to the rest of the world.

The biggest markets in Latin America were Brazil, Argentina and Mexico. Some major rock stars gained a foothold there, although few got as far as Queen, who had a very successful South American tour in the late Seventies playing to huge open-air audiences.

Australia was always considered an important market. In the Sixties, it produced best-selling acts in the Seekers, Frank Ifield, the Easybeats and others. The following decade saw AC/DC tread the path from local success in Australia to the US via the UK, breaking down many of the prejudices against Australian music along the way. The Little River Band, Australian Crawl and Men At Work followed, and the Eighties saw Australia finally recognised as an important source of new music in its own right.

Rock has moved from an American invention of the Fifties, through the British beat boom of the Sixties, to a degree of European and Australian success during the Seventies. Rock in the Eighties was still dominated by British and American music, but the rest of the world was gradually coming into its own.

DEMITRI ARGYROPULO

Below: Indian pop duo Hazan who emerged in the Eighties with an Eastern disco sound.

The bands that made it big in Japan

DURING THE EARLY EIGHTIES, it began to seem possible that Japan's domination of the world's car, motorcycle and consumer electrics industries might one day be repeated in the field of pop music. It was easy to scoff at the idea of diminutive Orientals with unpronouncable names regularly entering the British or American charts, but 15 years before, pundits had expressed similar disdain for the motorcycles being exported by Honda and Suzuki.

Blenders and Fenders

Notions of Japanese pop plunder looked even less laughable when one noted the similarities between the deliberate and systematic approach that lies behind the country's better-known export successes, and the development of its music industry. Immediately after the Second World War, Japan absorbed as much Western culture as it could; along with the gaudy sheet metal of Detroit and the home appliances considered obligatory by every American housewife, the huge influx of American servicemen introduced the music of Elvis Presley, Eddie Cochran and, to a lesser extent, Stax and Tamla Motown.

As with cars and electric blenders, the Japanese voraciously consumed rock's imagery to the point where their understanding of the genre became, if not completely natural, at least a convincing enough pastiche for an eager domestic market. And a healthy domestic market for foreign-influenced goods is the cornerstone of Japan's export strategy. In the

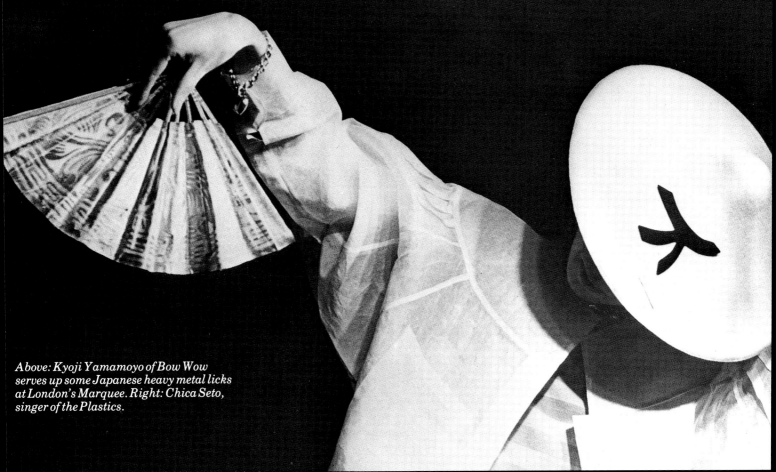

Above: Kyoji Yamamoyo of Bow Wow serves up some Japanese heavy metal licks at London's Marquee. Right: Chica Seto, singer of the Plastics.

LIFE IN TOKYO

stadium circuit (although the Beatles had played six nights at the Budokan in 1966). From their contact with these mega-bands, artists like Tetsu Yamauchi (ex-Samuri) and Hiroshi Min (ex-Silver Devil Babies) were recruited by English groups, Yamauchi becoming bassist with Free and later the Faces, and Min working first as High Tide's roadie and later guitarist in the revived Toefat. The hard rock/jazz-rock invasion quickly threw up mandatory plagiarists like Flower Travelin' Band and Condition Green.

Punks in plastic
Around 1973-74, blues copyist Haroumi Horono left his band Happy End to begin a solo career that would eventually lead to Yellow Magic Orchestra, while Kazohiko Katoh abandoned the pop muzak of the Folk Crusaders to form the Sadistic Mika Band. The Mikas' debut LP, *Black Ship*, was produced by Chris Thomas, chosen for his work with the band that most influenced them, Roxy Music. The cross-fertilisation continued when the Mika Band, fronted by Kazohiko's sister, Mika, toured Britain with their heroes and received rave reviews for their urgent,

Above left: Riuichi Sakamoto of Yellow Magic Orchestra. Below: The Sadistic Mika Band who won much praise for their Roxy Music-influenced rock.

early Sixties, Japanese teenagers were exposed to a similar volume of home-produced cover versions of American hits as were heard in Britain, and there were a legion of Elvis clones and Ventures-style instrumental outfits sporting tinny fake Fenders. But Japan's home-brewed pop music lacked sufficient originality to tempt any of the multi-nationals to try to export it to the rest of the world. It was not until American and British bands began regularly touring the country in the early Seventies that the West had any idea of the calibre of Japan's musicians.

John Mayall's Bluesbreakers, Grand Funk Railroad, Chicago and Led Zeppelin were some of the first to discover the rich pickings to be made on the Japanese

compulsive blend of Western and Oriental rock. But the imminence of international fame proved too much for them – they broke up after the tour, although Mika stayed behind and married Thomas.

The Sadistic Mika Band forged the way for other artists with global appetites, and the Plastics, Yellow Magic Orchestra and the Sunsetz were the next major competitors for foreign currency. Led by guitarist Hajime Tachibana, the Plastics grew out of the Tokyo art-club circuit in the late Seventies.

The Sunsetz, meanwhile, were formed by veteran guitarist/vocalist/keyboardist Kubota out of the remnants of his mid-Seventies Sunset Orchestra. Having won top trophies at Yamaha's 1976 World Music Festival, American singer Sandii joined the band the following year and married Kubota shortly afterwards. The Sunsetz' music was a homogenous mix of Spanish/American and Oriental influences; Sandii's sultry sex-appeal was undoubtedly a major factor in the group's growing reputation outside Japan, but the lilting, percussion-based tunes by Kubota, drummer Hideo Inoura and guitarist Keni Inoue had a strength that more than justified that reputation.

While progressive pop prospered in Japan, hard rock also had its devotees. Flower Travelin' Band clung tenaciously onto the loon pants of Deep Purple throughout the early and mid Seventies, making five best-selling albums. Their natural successors, Bow Wow, also made a lot of noise, two albums a year and completed a world tour at 1982's Reading Festival, while the Kodomo Band guested on Rainbow's 1982 Japanese tour.

Name check

The late Seventies also saw Japan throwing up a fair share of punk acts. The Mods, for example, were the Orient's answer to the Clash; initially called the Mozz and purveyors of post-Small Faces pastiche, the Mods recorded their first LP in London and, in order to dispel the image of their name, performed a few UK gigs under the name News Beat, which they then used as the title for their second album. Under their real name, they supported the Jam on their 1981 tour of Japan, and subsequently built up a substantial following with their zippy, three-minute punk anthems.

One should not under-estimate the Japanese teen-pop market either; bands like Zelda, the Virgin Vs (re-named Star Crazy for the world market) and Bongi-Bongi cut a suitably adolescent dash in the Eighties and backed it up with frothy pop that was certainly cleverer and arguably more substantial than much of the contemporary English pop product.

The Japanese rock world thrives quite openly on cross-pollination – a natural consequence, perhaps, of the 'plagiarism with honour' policies from which that country's original styles developed. Members of one band play on records made by another and often support each other on

live gigs; the extra-curricular dabblings of the three members of Yellow Magic Orchestra included collaborations with virtually anyone who was anyone in the history of Japanese rock.

Haroumi Hosono has already been mentioned as founder of Happy End (and before that, folk-rockers Apryl Fool), and Riuichi Sakamoto, though better-known in the West as David Bowie's co-star in *Merry Christmas Mr Lawrence*, has a long career behind him as a soundtrack composer and solo artist; his second album, *B2-Unit* (1980), was recorded with XTC's Andy Partridge. On his first LP, *Thousand Knives* (1978), Sakamoto worked with Sadistic Mika drummer Yukihiro Takahashi. After Takahashi, Sakamoto and Hosono got together as YMO in 1978, both Takahashi and Sakamoto continued to make solo albums using various YMO sidemen and, on occasion, some of the pro-Oriental international set drawn from

Above: Sandii and the Sunsetz pose decoratively. Below: Lizard – punks from the land of the rising sun.

Roxy Music and Japan (the band).

Although Takahashi was a fine singer, YMO became known primarily as an instrumental synthesiser band. Their second album, *Solid State Survivor* (1979), was a great critical success, sold over two million copies worldwide and won the group a sizeable following in America. The band toured there in 1979, along with guitarist Kazumi Watanabe and resident synth programmer Hideki Matsutake, and visited Britain in 1981. Western relations were further cemented in 1983 when they recorded their *People With Nice Smiles* LP with guitarist Bill Nelson. This album showed YMO developing a more lyrical approach to their music reflecting, perhaps, the progress of synthesiser pop elsewhere in the world.   MARK WILLIAMS

NEW EUROPEANS

The unsung heroes of Eurorock

ROCK'N'ROLL HAS BEEN one of the US's and the UK's most successful European exports. As a result, rock music in Europe can be divided into two parts – the first drawing on American and British models, the second based on what may be described as specifically 'European' sounds. Europe had played host to popular music from the US since the Twenties, when jazz first began to catch on there. However, jazz's influence was small compared to that of rock'n'roll, which supplied teenagers in a Europe still suffering from the after-effects of war with a complete, ready-made culture; as a result, English became the dominant lyrical language. It was to take a couple of decades and a great deal of thankless experimentation for European rock musicians to find their own voice and style.

Stormy Six
That voice first began to make itself heard in the late Sixties. In Germany, bands such as Tangerine Dream and Kraftwerk transformed themselves from rhythm'n'blues outfits into 'experimental' groups; diverse jazz, classical and pop influences conspired to produce bands like Can and Amon Duul. In France, Christian Vander's Magma launched the heavy, modern-classical style that subsequently informed much of French rock. Scandinavia, Belgium and the Netherlands came up with a gentle, often jazz-rock-influenced style, typified by the likes of Focus, Ekseption, Nektar, Wigwam, Tasavallan Presidentii and Samla Mammas Manna, perhaps its finest exponents.

Italy's main contribution to European rock was the complex work of Premiata Formera Marconi (PFM) and Banco, although the most interesting and notably 'Italian' band to appear was the radical folk-jazz-rock group Stormy Six. Neither Austria nor Switzerland contributed much to the musical Common Market until the eruption of punk, while the political climate of Spain did not allow a flourishing rock scene to develop until after the death of General Franco in 1975.

The major influences on these groups were not American but British – not the Velvet Underground or Jefferson Airplane but experimental, 'progressive' bands like Pink Floyd and Soft Machine. Indeed, 'Eurorock' was briefly quite popular around the world in the early Seventies, with several of the aforementioned groups touring the UK, signing to major labels and even making forays into the US market. However, the novelty soon faded; of all the European bands, only Tangerine Dream maintained their success and, in the Eighties, were still finding a ready audience for their sophisticated, if hardly

Left: Christian Vander of the innovative and influential French modern-classical band Magma.

taxing, electronic tone-poems. With the dissolution of Focus, both flautist Thijs van Leer and guitarist Jan Akkerman found new life as purveyors of cod-classical mood music for major US labels, while in 1977, Kraftwerk were belatedly hailed as heroes by the British new wave when they released *The Man Machine*.

However, the late Seventies record charts, radio and TV shows of Europe were dominated by the same names that were prevalent in Britain and America. The most successful European group was Sweden's Abba; the most successful rock label in Europe was Germany's Brain, a spin-off of the giant Metronome company.

Apart from seeing out the last years of Amon Duul II (an emasculated version of the late-Sixties 'progressive' group), Brain specialised in acts that aped well-known American or British acts, such as Guru Guru, Midnight Sun and Anyone's Daughter.

As in the UK, punk revitalised rock in Europe in the late Seventies and, for a while at least, reduced the disparity between what appeared in the charts and what was listened to in the clubs. In Germany, the controversial electronic funk duo Deutsche Amerikanisches Freundschaft (German-American Friendship, an intentionally sour irony) not only

Formed in 1968, Can were determined to do more than just copy the music of American and British bands such as the Velvet Underground and Pink Floyd. The band certainly had an intriguing musical background: bassist, producer and 'founder' Holger Czukay had been a pupil of Stockhausen; keyboard-player Irmin Schmidt had studied with composer Luciano Berio; drummer Jaki Liebezeit had played free jazz; and Michael Karoli had taught guitar in Switzerland.

Their first singer, black American Malcolm Mooney, left after the recording of their first LP, *Monster Movie* (1969); his replacement was the Japanese Kenji 'Damo' Suzuki, who had a manic vocal style.

He made his recording debut on *Tago Mago* (1971), the LP that marked the beginning of Can's most creative period. The band's diverse musical influences were increasingly apparent on *Ege Bamyasi* (1972) and the summery

Germany's Can whose eccentric style impressed many a 'serious' rock fan.

Future Days (1973), often considered their masterpiece. Suzuki quit after recording this LP to become a 'born-again' Christian. Can recorded *Soon Over Babaluma* (1974), their last album on United Artists, then signed to Virgin. Their next two LPs, *Landed* (1975) and *Flow Motion* (1976), remain Can's poppiest and most accessible records.

Czukay then relinquished his role as bassist to Rosko Gee, and Can's rhythm section was augmented by former Traffic percussionist Rebop Kwaku Baah; subsequent releases, however, saw a gradual dissipation of the group's identity. The band were unable to capitalise on the praise of later rock artists such as Brian Eno, David Byrne and Joy Division/New Order, all of whom cited the group at their early-Seventies peak as a formative influence. JOHN GILL

Gong

Gong were formed in France in 1969 by Australian emigré and former Soft Machine mentor Daevid Allen, an incorrigible beatnik/poet/revolutionary committed to psychedelia as a force for social change. Although Gong provided the music for Jerome Laperrousaz's *Continental Circus* (1970), their first genuine album, *Camembert Electrique*, did not appear until 1971. It featured a line-up of Allen (guitar), Welsh poetess Gilli Smyth (vocals), Christian Tritsch (bass), Pip Pyle (drums) and Didier Malherbe, an eclectic jazz musician (sax and flute).

Despite becoming among the most popular avant-garde bands working in France, Allen broke up the group in 1972 to concentrate on writing. A recording contract from Virgin Records persuaded him to re-form the band.

Gong became one of Europe's favourite avant-garde acts of the early Seventies.

Later that year a revised line-up, including synthesiser wizard Tim Blake and guitarist Steve Hillage, began work on *The Flying Teapot* (1973). However, the whimsical mysticism of this and LPs such as *Angel's Egg* (1973) and *You* (1974) did not appeal to more than a loyal cult following.

Allen left the band after the release of *You*, and Hillage soon followed to pursue a solo career. Drummer Pierre Moerlen (who had joined Gong for *Angel's Egg*) now took control of the group's music, which veered increasingly towards mainstream jazz-rock. The group continued to release albums in the Seventies and Eighties.

ALAN KINSMAN

achieved fame at home, but managed to reinvigorate German interest in home-grown talent, such as Can and Kraftwerk.

In France, bands like Telex and Telephone charted with their own 'new-wave' sounds, while in the Netherlands, Switzerland and Austria, cities such as Amsterdam, Zurich and Vienna became hives of furious musical activity. Bands like Zurich's Yello and Vienna's Monoton, as well as labels like Germany's Zick Zack and Belgium's Crammed and Crépuscule, even exceeded the achievements of their British and American counterparts.

In many ways, the ideas of punk and the new wave – in particular the placing of control in the hands of musicians, bands, fans and independent labels – gave European rock a real sense of its own identity for the first time. The success of Deutsche Amerikanisches Freundschaft and the consequent emergence of the so-called 'Neue Deutsche Welle' (German New Wave) undermined the established practice of never singing lyrics in German (a sin that 'unpopular' German bands had been committing for years). At last, a thorough knowledge of English was not essential for European rock success.

By the early Eighties, the achievements of Europe's new wave were undeniably impressive, resulting in an upsurge of interest in bold experimentation, with musicians borrowing ideas from percussive New York 'scratch' rapping, native folk traditions, contemporary jazz and classical music. The refreshing eclecticism and commitment of Eighties European rock may well serve as an inspiration to new bands in Britain and the US. JOHN GILL

Below: French new-wave outfit Telephone. Above right: Deutsche Amerikanisches Freundschaft.

Tangerine Dream

Like Kraftwerk, Tangerine Dream grew out of an Anglo-American influenced band, the Ones, formed in Berlin in 1965 by leader Edgar Froese. After numerous line-up changes, the group split in 1967, allowing Froese to form Tangerine Dream. At this time, Froese was influenced by contemporary classical composers Gyorgy Ligeti and Iannis Xenakis. With Klaus Schulze (keyboards) and Conrad Schnitzler (flute), both of whom became important figures on the German electronic music scene, Froese brought those influences to the fore on Tangerine Dream's first LP, *Electronic Meditation* (1970), followed by *Alpha Centauri* (1971), *Zeit* (1972) and *Atem* (1973), all for the German 'underground' label Ohr.

The stormy electronic improvisations of these albums gave way in 1973 to *Phaedra*, which made the British Top Ten. Subsequent albums followed its format, alternating formless electronic washes with fast, syncopated sequenced synthesiser. Albums such as *Tangram* (1980), *Exit* (1981) and *White Eagle* (1982) saw the group introducing funky dance structures.

In the Eighties, the band's basic line-up became Froese (synths, guitars), Christoph Franke (synths) and Johannes Schmoelling (synths). Still based in Berlin, the group became active in the peace movement, playing 100,000-strong free concerts for the cause. Tangerine Dream were, unquestionably, the progenitors of the uniquely German electronic rock boom of the Seventies.   JOHN GILL

Tangerine Dream: Michael Hoenig (left), Edgar Froese (above) and Christopher Franke.

Over the rainbow with Australia's brightest

AUSTRALIAN ROCK HAS been a significant contributor to the international music marketplace since the Fifties; even if the ties between Australia and the Bee Gees, Olivia Newton John, Rick Springfield and AC/DC were a little tenuous, the Great Southern Land could still lay claim to the Easybeats, the Seekers, the Mixtures, Sherbet, Tin Tin and quite a few other isolated global breakouts. But it was not until the late Seventies that Australian rock music really came into its own.

Equidistant from Britain and the United States, Australia absorbed the best of both pop cultures during the Sixties, gradually blending this input with an indigenous style that could best be described as 'pub boogie'. Aussie musicians were bred tough and tenacious; audiences who gathered during the Seventies in cavernous concrete

Wizards of Oz

beer barns in the suburbs to hear Rose Tattoo one night, Midnight Oil the next and Angel City the next would never have tolerated pimply synthesiser duos doodling about on stage.

By the late Seventies, Australian music had found a sense of self-confidence thanks to improved studio facilities, better-qualified producers and increased foreign releases of product. It set about achieving a position of equality in international music, not as 'flavour of the month' but as a reliable source of repertoire for the charts of the Northern Hemisphere. The timing was perfect; the 'new music' explosion had created a chasm between British and American music – the latter clinging to ponderous stadium rock and saccharine singer-songwriters, the former scrambling for a new trend every three months.

Into the void sailed Oz Rock, sufficiently based in tradition to please the Americans and adventurous enough to impress – eventually – the British. Without any overt national characteristics, the music embodied a freshness, vitality and optimism which reflected the down-under lifestyle.

Heroes of hoodoo

The penetration, in the US at least, was incredible. In 1981, *Billboard* observed that the biggest hard-rock group in the world was Australian (AC/DC), as was the biggest soft-rock group (Air Supply) and the most popular teen idol (Rick Springfield). Furthermore, the American Song Of The Year, 'Physical', was written, produced and sung by Australians (respectively, Steve Kipner, John Farrar and Olivia Newton John).

Eventually, critics began to refer to Australia as 'the Liverpool of the Eighties' – which was more than a little erroneous. Merseybeat had been basically a single style with minor variations whereas the music that Australia was giving the world was breathtakingly diverse, running the gamut from the mass-appeal love ballads of Air Supply to the alienated expression of the Birthday Party.

One vital aspect of the overall quality of Australian rock was the process by which it is nurtured. As opposed to the British situation, Australian bands enjoyed a demanding but rewarding multi-tiered performance structure that worked them hard and often. By the time they came to leave Australia their local 'baptism of fire' had equipped them to appear with any act on any stage in the world. Certainly AC/DC were not showered with media attention when they arrived in London in 1976; what support they gained was hard-won before audiences by the only way they knew how – sweat and steam.

Left: Graham Russell (left) and Russell Hitchcock of Air Supply toast their American success. By 1981, Air Supply had become one of the world's best-selling soft-rock groups. Above left: Australian new wave act the Models.

Little River Band

The international success of the Little River Band throughout the second half of the Seventies was a vital factor in the rise of antipodean rock music in general. Certainly there is barely an Australian musician enjoying the fruits of a global market who will not readily acknowledge the pioneering work of this polished, adult-oriented rock outfit. The band was formed in 1975 by veterans of such Australian bands as the Twilights, the Zoot, Axiom and Mississippi – all of which had undertaken disastrous trips to the Northern Hemisphere since the Sixties. Even manager Glenn Wheatley had tried to crack Britain on two occasions as bassist with the Master Apprentices.

Established with the specific aim of developing a mass-appeal sound based on mature musicianship and lush harmonies, the Little River Band effectively took 'coals to Newcastle' when they began touring the US in 1976: indeed, many of those who heard their records and even saw them live were unaware of their origins. But to many critics they were a new Eagles, free of hedonistic overtones. The *Denver Post* observed: 'How can the Aussies offer a

The Little River Band. In the late Seventies, the group conquered the US with their brand of country rock.

band with such great pop sense when all we can muster is wimps like Firefall?'

After breaking into the US Top Thirty in November 1976 with 'It's A Long Way There', the group commenced a regular chart profile that saw them honoured by *Billboard* magazine in 1982 as the only act in the world to score an American Top Ten hit every year for the previous five years. The biggest was 'Reminiscing', a gentle, almost traditional ballad, which reached Number 3 in 1978. The unbending musical attitude of founder-member Graham Goble resulted in a regular turnover of membership and, in 1982, lead singer Glenn Shorrock was replaced by British-born Australian pop superstar John Farnham. Although a fine singer, Farnham was unable to equal Shorrock's worldly, textured writing skill, which had been responsible for such classic tracks as 'Cool Change' and 'Home On A Monday'. Nevertheless, the group remained a top-ranking act in America.   GLENN A BAKER

By the Eighties, Australian bands were deemed so 'bankable' by foreign record companies that many A&R men were unwilling to wait for acts to be offered to them by Australian record companies. They slipped quietly into the country in increasing numbers to check out talent for themselves, resulting in bands being offered contracts not only by local concerns like Mushroom Records but also by CBS International.

The most exciting aspect of the Australian explosion was the vast reservoir of talent that emerged to take the place of those acts siphoned off by overseas markets. By the end of 1983, bands like Real Life, the Expression, Hoodoo Gurus, Kids in the Kitchen, Pseudo Echo, the Johnnys and Little Heroes were declaring plainly that the 'Australian Invasion', once begun, had no intention of running out of steam.   GLENN A BAKER

2371

Above: Cheetah deliver some raunchy, steamy rock. Right: Icehouse cool out for the camera.

Men at Work

Men At Work were the Australian rock success story of the early Eighties. In 1983, just three years after formation, the group was simultaneously holding down the Number 1 album and single position in both Britain and the United States, having previously topped the equivalent charts in Australia. Their 'Downunder' was adopted by the world in 1983 as a new national anthem for the continent; created with the right mixture of self-mocking lyrics and crisp, refreshing musical structure, the song expressed the bright, confident nature of Australians and their music in the Eighties.

Formed at the close of the Seventies, Men At Work secured a residency at the Cricketer's Arms Hotel in the Melbourne suburb of Richmond. The band – Colin Hay (vocals), Greg Ham (sax), John Rees (bass), Ron Strykert (guitar) and Jerry Speiser (drums) – were passed over by virtually every A&R manager in the country before Peter Karpin, a young CBS employee freshly returned from a New York posting, placed his job on the line to get them signed and into the studio with American producer Peter McIan.

The group's debut album, *Business As Usual*, shot to the top of the LP chart in Australia and afforded three hit singles. Accepted for American release

Men At Work, who formed in Melbourne at the end of the Seventies. Within three years, they were Number 1 worldwide.

by CBS more out of obligation than enthusiasm, *Business As Usual* broke the Monkees' record for the longest-running debut album in the Number 1 position, spending 15 weeks at the top. 'Who Can It Be Now?' gave Men At Work their first American Number 1 single and 'Downunder' gave them their first global chart-topper when a stubborn British public finally relented and took them to heart.

The outfit returned to the top in the US with a second album, *Cargo* (1983). Accused, initially, of sounding almost exactly like the Police – due to their use of reggae rhythms and the high-pitched singing style of Colin Hay – the band eventually defined their own unique musical position and established a stance noticeably less flippant than that shown by the hypnotic 'Downunder'.

GLENN A BAKER

THE JAMAICA OF THE mid Seventies was in a turmoil of political unrest. The 1976 election was fought in the shadow of a formal State of Emergency; one victim of the violence was Bob Marley, shot during a murderous attack on his home – an unsuccessful attempt to prevent his appearance at the 'Smile Jamaica' concert, seen by some as an endorsement of support for Prime Minister Michael Manley.

Reggae in the Seventies reflected this social unrest. Channel One studio led the way with endless versions of tunes plundered from the vaults of Studio One, while vocal trio Culture voiced a warning of an impending apocalypse in their 1977 recording *Two Sevens Clash*. Big Youth took up the theme with 'Four Sevens Clash', and the message reached London, where Joe Strummer and Mick Jones formed the Clash.

Amid the political warfare, the Rastafarian sect captured the cultural ground. With the journalists and the photographers came recording contracts. Prince Far I, Prince Hammer, Ranking Trevor and seemingly just about every other dread hanging out at Idler's Rest, just off Kingston's Parade, were quickly signed to

How crucial was Eighties reggae to world rock?

the Front Line, a subsidiary of the UK-based Virgin Records label.

Reggae had become international. Burning Spear, Culture and Peter Tosh all embarked on major European tours while DJs like Prince Far I, Hammer, Clint Eastwood and Trinity worked the UK rock circuit. Rema-based DJ Tapper Zukie's *Man A Warrior* album (1977) was hailed as a classic and he appeared on stage with American new-wave singer Patti Smith at London's Hammersmith Odeon.

Michael Campbell, better known as Mikey Dread, was the DJ who took Jamaica by storm at the end of 1978. He cut his teeth on radio, hustling his way from technician at the Jamaican Broadcasting Corporation to co-presenter of a late-night show on Fridays. Styling himself the Dread at the Controls, he devised a

Above: Vocal trio Black Uhuru who, following local fame in Jamaica, became international stars of the Eighties, thanks to their hard and modern sound.

show that captured the imagination of the nation. Laced together with jingles and sound effects, it featured strictly roots reggae.

'Barber Saloon' was the first of a string of his hit singles. Mikey initially recorded for producers Lee Perry and Sonia Pottinger, but wasted no time in launching his own Dread at the Controls and Forty Leg labels. As well as releasing his own DJ 45s, he recorded youth singers like Earl Sixteen, Rod Taylor and Edi Fitzroy and produced a succession of outstanding 'computer mix' dubs. Despite his status as JBC's top presenter, his contract was terminated and he left for England, where he worked as a television presenter and both performed and recorded with the Clash and UB40.

Throughout the Seventies, reggae continued to absorb new sounds and accents. The mellow-voiced Gregory Isaacs' 'Mr Know It All' ushered in a cool-stepping drum style, while dub master Augustus Pablo perfected the Far Eastern cadences of the melodica. Burning Spear became one of the most consistently powerful Rastafarian solo singers, while the unique harmonies of the Royal Rasses and Israel

Vibration added new dimensions to an already outstanding vocal tradition.

The music of Jamaica, steeped as it was in the cultural, political and religious traditions of its people, was quick to respond to the economic and political upheavals that beset the island in the Seventies. Big Youth's 'Green Bay Killing' sparked off a wave of musical protest over the so-called Green Bay massacre – a bloody confrontation between armed insurgents and the security forces in August 1978 – while Bob Marley was persuaded to return to Jamaica for the first time since the attempt on his life in 1976 to perform at a Peace Concert held at the National Stadium in April 1978.

Sadly, the concert had little – if any – effect on the volatile situation, and clashes between rival factions in the run-up to the 1980 election resulted in over 800 deaths. Describing the music he released during this period, Bunny Wailer explained that 'the reggae artist tries to deal with their experience and the experience of others; they try and soothe the stress and tension by letting others know that their feelings are shared'. His song titles – 'Innocent Blood', 'Tug A War Game', 'Cease Fire' and 'Power Struggle' – spoke for themselves.

Dynamic duos
But reggae could also make people forget their troubles and dance. Guaranteed to set the dancehall rocking were 'Rub A Dub Style' and 'Nice Up The Dance' from the DJ duo of General Smilie and Poppa Michigan. Based on the classic Studio One rhythms, their 'combination' style was taken up by Kojak and Liza, Archie and Lynn ('Rat In A De Centre') and in London by Clint Eastwood and General Saint.

Vocal trio Black Uhuru built a tremendous reputation with a series of Top Ten singles in Jamaica, and eventually became international superstars in the Eighties. The sound of their music was hard and modern and owed much to the production of one of the most illustrious teams in reggae – drummer Sly Dunbar

and bassist Robbie Shakespeare.

Starting out as the backbone of the Revolutionaries, a session band at the famed Channel One studio, Sly and Robbie ended up playing with virtually every influential session band in Jamaica, and as producers were responsible for work by the Tamlins, Junior Delgado, Jimmy Riley, Delroy Wilson, Ina Kamoza and the Wailing Souls. Sly and Robbie's distinctive sound was removed from the reggae mainstream, and as their reputation grew internationally so they became involved with artists as diverse as Grace Jones and Bob Dylan.

At the turn of the Eighties, a new generation of tough youth singers emerged. Two labels, Black Roots and Freedom Sounds, replaced the old producer/artist format with a more cooperative atmosphere in the studio, and between them these companies launched a wave of ghetto vocalists including Sugar Minott, Tony Tuff, Little John, Triston Palma, Barry Brown and Sammy Dread.

With little chance of these young singers getting consistent radio play, they relied on the 'sound system', mobile reggae discotheques, to popularise their singles, and a 'dancehall sound' evolved that was quite distinct from the international releases of Peter Tosh or Dennis Brown.

The principal mentor of this sound was a young producer, Henry 'Junjo' Lawes, whose reputation grew rapidly in the Eighties following a succession of hits which he produced for Barrington Levy. Junjo's sure touch in gauging audience demands resulted in an impressive and prolific output of records, while his own Volcano sound system, launched in 1983, rivalled such established systems as U Roy's Stereogav, Gemini or Jah Love in popularity. The sound system thus became an essential link between record producers and the grass-roots audiences in the clubs.

During the Eighties singers often had to take second place to the DJs and in order to maintain or boost their following, vocalists like Don Carlos and Sugar Minott

Above left: Third World. Above: The bizarre-looking Yellowman, an unlikely reggae star. Above right: Tapper Zukie. Above far right: Sly Dunbar (right) and Robbie Shakespeare, reggae's most illustrious production team. Right: Mikey Dread.

performed 'live and direct' on sound system alongside DJs such as Josey Wales or Charlie Chaplin. Two of the more bizarre dancehall heroes who rose to international prominence in this manner were Eek A Mouse and Yellowman.

Poetry in motion
Ripton Hilton, also known as Eek A Mouse, developed an offbeat 'Japanese' style of vocalese, probably from watching too many kung fu films, which he combined with an ultra-dread stage persona. His first single 'Wa Do Dem' highlighted a considerable wit, while 'Assassinator' revealed him to be one of Jamaica's most serious songwriters.

Yellowman (Winston Foster) was an albino raised in the Eventide Home, Kingston. His bizarre appearance, innovative lyricism and a devotion to what he called 'sing-jaying' or toasting along to well-known pop, country or soul hits made him perhaps the most unlikely rags-to-riches reggae star of them all. His output in the five years from 1979, in excess of 15 albums and innumerable singles, made him an international celebrity.

In contrast to the largely improvised lyricism of the DJs stood the phenomenon of dub poetry. Operating within the oral traditions of Africa and the Caribbean, the visionaries of dub poetry unleashed a radical and uncompromising torrent of imagery set to a reggae rhythm.

Perhaps Jamaica's most incisive and innovative poet was Michael Smith. His *Mi Cyaan Believe It* album, recorded with Dennis Bovell and Linton Kwesi Johnson, was released in Britain in 1982 on Island Records and Mikey, a powerful and evocative wordsmith, was a favoured performer on his visits to Britain. His murder in

August 1983, stoned to death by thugs thought to be associated with the Jamaica Labour Party, was a blow not just to reggae but to the whole of Third World literature. Oku Onuora rose to poetic notoriety while imprisoned for armed robbery. He later performed at the 1978 Peace Concert, and toured the UK with Mikey Smith. His 'Reflection In Red' stands as one of the great dub poetry singles.

Another dub poet to build a serious international reputation in the mid Eighties was Mutabaruka, a controversial militant Rastafarian easily recognisable by a distinctive forelock of white hair amid a mane of locks. Stalking the stage, shoeless and shirtless, Mutabaruka left no one unscathed by his swingeing poetic attacks.

The death of Bob Marley on 11 May 1981 was a serious blow to reggae music and its international advance. Despite major European tours by Peter Tosh, Dennis Brown, Black Uhuru, Jimmy Cliff and Gregory Isaacs, by the mid Eighties reggae music was finding it difficult to sustain its influence. America was gradually opening up to the music and in the hope of reaching a wider audience most artists introduced rock and funk influences, both on stage and on record. Even Bunny Wailer experimented with rapping and funk – but, apart from tunes like Third World's 1978 hit 'Now That We've Found Love', the majority of the fusion records were less than successful in the charts.

With the upsurge of interest in African music and the apparent popularity of reggae in parts of Africa, the Eighties offered the prospect of ever greater crossfertilisation of musical ideas, as more and more reggae artists turned their attention to touring Africa rather than the US.

But as the gap between the music of the ghetto dances and the sophisticated styles developed by its international envoys grew, reggae's future as a modern musical force looked uncertain. Like American blues or soul music, reggae derived strength from its very deep roots.   PAUL BRADSHAW

BACK IN THE

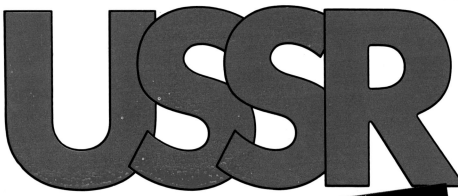

Red rock from the Eastern bloc

LONG BEFORE FRANK ZAPPA enquired raucously 'Who are the brain police?' or Johnny Rotten revelled in the joys of anarchy, rock music was indelibly associated with rebellion, bad manners and a mischievous tendency to ask questions calculated to embarrass adults. In most Western countries, the reaction of the establishment has generally been more entertaining than alarming (and in some cases more entertaining than the music); behind the Iron Curtain, however, Zappa's jibe against conformity, so easy to make from the comfort of southern California, would not have escaped the attention of real policemen. And the Sex Pistols would probably have been declared insane and promptly incarcerated.

Brainwashing blues
With the collapse of the hippie ideal, it was perhaps inevitable that rock should become political in the late Sixties. The acceptance of drugs, revolutionary sentiment that derived partly from Black Power and partly from fear of the Vietnam War, and outlandish modes of dress, all combined to make rock and its adherents a fearful spectacle in adult eyes. The anger and the rebellion were doubtless genuine, and caused even the Vice President of the United States, Spiro Agnew, to address himself to the problem. His speech, 'Talking Brainwashing Blues', lamented rock's interest in drugs, but was as nothing compared to one Gary Allen's essay, 'More Subversion Than Meets The Ear'.

Mr Allen, with the help of his friend Dr Joseph Crow of Seattle, concluded not only that CBS was a Communist front organisation but that for Lennon and McCartney 'to have written some of their songs is like someone who has not had physics or math inventing the A-bomb . . . it is possible that this music is put together by behavioral scientists in some "think tank".' And who owned the think tank? Mr Allen could tell you: '. . . the reason the Beatles and other folk-rock groups [sic] received such success . . . was because they were backed by the

Entertainment Section of the Communist Party'. Such occasional hysterical reactions in the West were as nothing to the way in which rock was treated in Eastern Europe, where musicians were ferociously persecuted.

Communist nations have always been wary of rock music, as have other totalitarian régimes, because of its intrinsic appeal to non-conformity. The Beatles were banned by the Greek military *junta* in 1967, along with such other evil influences as the mini-skirt and the composer Mikis Theodorakis – who was imprisoned and tortured. In 1969, the official Soviet organ *Sovetskaya Kultura* called the Beatles 'the property of . . . pop-art, the market, and business' and added pointedly: 'The Philistine must have his idols to worship.' In 1971, reporting on world record markets, EMI drily remarked of the USSR and its satellites that 'this huge potential market is unavailable to international record companies both for economic and political reasons' and could give no figures for them. Rock was, in effect, illegal behind the Iron Curtain; Western acts were heard there only by virtue of the black market.

The traditional insularity and xenophobia of the USSR, which have always informed Soviet murmurings about 'alien Western influences', account to some extent for the Communist aversion to rock. So does the deeply puritanical, indeed Victorian, attitude of Russians towards

the human body, on which rock music has always had a liberating effect. But the overriding reason is the authorities' need to control and censor what people may enjoy, both from ideological causes – rock being a form of capitalist corruption – and in order to sustain the Party's power over every aspect of people's lives.

In the late Seventies and early Eighties much rock music could actually be heard in the USSR, if only because the leadership, patiently awaiting the demise of Leonid Brezhnev, had other things on its mind. Within six months of his death in November 1982, the Party struck at artistic unorthodoxy, closing discotheques in Moscow and even banning dancing in some clubs, calling them 'sleazy dives'. Popular rock groups like Time Machine and Cruise and even out-and-out pop groups such as Vesyolye Rebyata (Happy Kids) were accused of offering songs of 'dubious ideological content' and told to toe the Party line or be banned.

Plastic People
In Czechoslovakia, where the local Party has been closely controlled by Moscow since 1968, matters are probably worse. For 14 years the underground band Plastic People of the Universe managed to survive despite continuous harrassment, until the spring of 1982. Then saxophonist Vratislav Brabanec was arrested: 'I was told to be careful of the edge of the table, since I could easily knock my teeth out on it.' Brabanec chose exile, shortly before fellow band member Ivan Jirous was jailed (for the fourth time) as a 'dangerous recidivist' for three-and-a-half years hard labour. All this followed a long campaign against Czech rock groups, including DG307, Midsummer Night's Dream and others, throughout the Seventies, when secret police would regularly disrupt concerts and beat up fans.

In Hungary, where a mixed economy of sorts operates and even the *International Herald Tribune* is on sale in Budapest, the repression is less obvious but consequently more chilling. Before being given a recording contract, top local band Beatrice were told in 1981 to provide songs, the 'texts of which won't hurt our social norms' and were reminded that 'The rules of the game are compulsory'. The appearance of a Soviet band, Autograph, in Live Aid in 1985 suggested a softening of attitudes but was derided by some as a gesture.

So, however Western bands may bemoan the rigours of capitalism and the nuclear threat, at least they are heard to do so. And so far no Western rocker has yet defected to the East.   PETER BROOKESMITH

Above left: Plastic People of the Universe's 1978 LP Egon Bondy's Happy Hearts Club Band. *Right, clockwise from left: Cruise on stage; Russian rock opera* Juno And Avas; *Bob Gzelenschikov of successful Russian rockers* Aquarium; *Hungary's Omega; East German punk exile Nina Hagen.*

AFRICAN CHILDREN

A new generation of dynamic sounds and styles

SAMPLER ALBUMS ARE the ideal *hors d'oeuvre* to introduce any kind of music to a new audience. In the early Eighties, British record buyers had a feast of such starters to give a peep into the immense variety of pop music being produced in Africa.

Between them, Rough Trade's *Soweto* (1982) and Earthworks' *Zulu Jive* (1983) spanned a decade's music born of the struggle in South African townships; the LPs featured the classic African jive, whose lurching rhythms and accordions can sound like misplaced cajun, traces of the bygone penny-whistle band era and the accordions and saxophone bands which replaced them, and acappella harmony groups an ocean away from the street corners of Harlem. While *Soweto* reached Number 66 in the UK album charts in 1982, a reworked version appeared much higher the following year on Malcolm McLaren's *Duck Rock* collection of holiday souvenirs.

Another Earthworks collection, *Go South – South Of The Sahara* (1985), was a thoroughly modern collection of sounds from Zaire, Zimbabwe, Lesotho, Nigeria and Kenya that had already successfully permeated the UK dancefloor scene. Zimbabwe's Thomas Mapfumo and the Blacks Unlimited's contributions were sunnier in mood than their previous *chimurenga* songs, which had provided a powerful inspiration for independence fighters back home. Rooted in the catchy music of the thumb piano, Mapfumo's music has been increasingly influenced by reggae.

The sound of *soukous*

The album leads with Souzy Kasseya's 'Mr Simon', a dizzy example of the Congolese music known in Europe as *soukous*. This style developed in central and Eastern Africa in the Sixties, performed by orchestras where ranks of electric guitars and horns vied with each other behind a charismatic and powerful male tenor or female lead singer. Souzy Kasseya represents the young generation of Zaireans, currently working out of Paris or Brussels, whose music is increasingly inclined towards synthesisers and slicker productions than their music back home.

Keynames in the development of this style are the Zairean legends, both now in their 60s, the singer/bandleader Seigneur Tabu Ley Rochereau, and the guitarist/ bandleader known simply as Franco. Soukous developed in the Congo in the Fifties, and was built around the contemporary passion for imported Cuban records, and particularly the rumba.

Franco

In 1982 Franco et le T.P.O.K. Jazz Band celebrated their 25th anniversary at the forefront of Zaïrois music. Since forming the first line-up of his 'Tout Puissant' (all-powerful) band in 1957, Franco (real name Luambo Makiadi) has helped to shape the music of a generation of East Africans. Working like James Brown as a somewhat browbeating bandleader, Franco acted as a nurseryman for a generation of young African musicians, tutoring them in his own, unique brand of *soukous* music.

Franco's own mentor was a guitarist called Kabassele who, in the early Fifties, first merged rumbas and sambas with the local dance music, laying the foundations of Franco's sound. One of Kabassele's bandboys was Tabu Ley Rochereau, who was to become Franco's partner at the head of the new Eastern African sound; while Franco's hand shaped the rippling, *tremolando* guitar style, Rochereau was responsible for the sweet vocal harmonies.

Central to Franco's style was his long love affair with Cuban music – the rumbas with their stop-start sense of drama and hip-swivelling cross-rhythms. Like the Cubans who were still mesmerising audiences half their age in New York's *salsa* clubs, Franco's prowess as an entertainer – a man who makes you dance – was undeniable.

SUE STEWARD

Above: Franco works up a soukous *storm with his T.P.O.K. Jazz Band.*

While the music of Southern Africa still showed signs of the jazz influence of the Fifties, particularly in the saxophone and solo improvisations of Central Africa – which showed the influence of Franco's guitar style and Rochereau's voice – was altogether gentler. Songs were repetitive, collective productions with choruses of undulating guitars and sweetly pitched voices, while the apparent fondness for hissing hi-hat and snares betrayed a remarkable similarity to the Zulu jive of South Africa.

Brothers of Africa

Newcomers to African pop music have often been surprised not only by its variety, but also by its modernity. Electric guitars were used in almost every form of African music to reach the UK, with the exception of the various Nigerian 'talking drum' percussion-and-vocal styles.

Although African pop music was designed – like all pop – for leisure, and heard in clubs, bars and concert halls, at the same time, the music was frequently linked with politicians, many countries boasting musicians whose sounds carried political messages. At his 1983 London show, Nigerian Fela Anikulapo Kuti revealed his charismatic powers as a politician; under a banner for his Movement of the People party, he sang and preached pan-Africanism, while his records have been vehicles for criticism of the corruption in post-colonial Nigeria. In 1984 he was jailed, ostensibly for currency offences.

Ghana's Mohammed Malcolm Ben also preached pan-Africanism in his records, and was simultaneously Ghana's top producer, famed for his work with the 20-year-old African Brothers Band. With his own African Feeling Association Band, his songs ranged from pleas for African unity – 'Africans are praying for the day African politicians will love one another . . .' – to outrage about Nelson Mandela's imprisonment. Like Fela, Malcolm Ben sang in English, taking his message beyond its Ghanaian source.

Language has always been a problem in a continent where a single country could house hundreds of different tongues. Prince Nico Mbarga's hit of the Seventies, 'Sweet Mother', was in English, but when he fled Nigeria during the Civil War and moved to the Cameroons he began to record in pidgin, which catered not only for all Nigerian tribes but people from neighbouring countries.

Musicians who wanted their work to reach beyond Africa often decided to sing in English but, as Sunny Ade's English verses revealed, this was not always a good idea. Transcribing a tonal language, involved in intimate rhythmic communion

Right: Nigeria's Lijadu Sisters. Far right: Yssou N'Dour, the national singing hero of Senegal. Below right: Mohammed Malcolm Ben, Ghana's top producer.

with the talking drums and percussions, invariably resulted in some loss of impact. Franco, who spoke only French and Lingala, the Zairois *lingua franca*, insisted that he would not compromise by singing in any other language.

Not all politicised musicians were struggling against their country. Marxist Guinea's government subsidised the instruments for the Bembeya Jazz National Band, whose 1969 album, *Regard Sur Le Passe* recorded Guinea's battle for independence. Les Amazones de Guinée chronicled the effects of the revolution on women from the informed position of being an 18-piece all-women band. Their *Au Coeur De Paris* (1983), complete with rapturous applause, was far from drab polemic – a euphoric blend of saxophone and guitar soloings, an unusual fluttering vocal and songs that were concerned as much with the struggles of love or the evils of drink as with women's role in post-revolutionary Guinea.

Religion, too, has invariably proved a major force within African pop. Nigeria, for instance, is divided roughly into three areas and two religions: Northern Hausa (Muslim), Western Yoruba (Christian) and Eastern Ibo (Christian and Muslim). Traditional religious practices were everywhere and the music, particularly the singing styles, reflected the differences. *Juju* music was basically Christian; both Sunny Ade and Ebenezer Obey mixed Yoruba parables and traditional metaphors with Biblical morality, and their Christian upbringing was evident in their sweet sense of choral harmony. Similarly, Franco, Rochereau and the bevy of younger *soukous* players from Central Africa with French-Catholic upbringing sounded closer to the gospel and soul styles of Afro-American music than to the harsh, nasal tones of the Muslim singers.

Vocal strains

Nowhere was the Muslim presence felt more in the vocal style than along the Eastern coast of Tanzania and Kenya, where a genre known as *tarabou* grew out of a blending of Arabic instruments, with hard, slightly dour vocal tones derived from the Koranic chanting style.

This same diversity was at work in the Mali band Les Ambassadeurs, whose 'Yellowman' vocalist Salif Keita had a charismatic strained voice, pitched against the heat-hazy langour of his band. And in neighbouring Senegal the national singing hero Yssou N'Dour similarly contrasted an urgent vocal torrent with the music of an impassive and relaxed backing band, whose fondness for wah-wah and muted trumpets made a delightful combination of opposites. After his first successful tour of

the US in early 1985, Youssou N'Dour looked set to be the next big African star to cross over into another continent.

In Nigeria, it appeared that *fuji* music was exclusively Muslim: Alhaji Sikiru Ayinde Barrister and Alhaji Chief Kollington Ayinla, both granted the 'Alhaji'

a number of African groups—the Bhundu Boys, Ladysmith Black Mambazo and others—secured contracts with major labels in the aftermath of Simon's success.

In addition, areas such as Senegal (Youssou d'Nour), Guinea (Mory Kante) and Zimbabwe (the previously mentioned

Bhundu Boys) added their voices to groups from Nigeria, South Africa and Zaire in making the West aware of the diversity and quality of African music. SUE STEWARD

Top: Ebenezer Obey's Adventure Of Mr Wise *LP. Above: Les Amazones de Guinée.*

title after visiting Mecca, performed in ensembles as large as the *juju* bands (around 20-piece) playing an array of percussion: squeezed talking drums and an assortment of shaken percussion and bells.

Elsewhere in Africa – and particularly amongst African musicians working in Europe and the US – there was an increasing tendency to experiment with blending synthesised sounds and electronic percussion on to traditional or local arrangements and rhythms. New styles of Afro-electro-disco arose in the mid Eighties, though this was no new thing: the international hit 'Soul Makossa' from the Camerounian saxophonist, Manu Dibango, was a successful Sixties blending of local Camerounian rhythms with Manu's passion for soul music.

Paul Simon's success with the backing of African musicians on his 1986 album *Graceland* aroused controversy and accusations of cultural piracy. But apart from bringing music from the continent to Western ears,

King Sunny Ade

In 1983, only a couple of years after he had declared a 'global strategy' for his Nigerian *juju* music, 'King' Sunny Ade introduced his 23-piece African Beats to a London audience, with a three-and-a-half hour show that guaranteed them a place on the English pop scene. Non-stop shimmering guitar choruses, pulsating talking drums and a fast banter of vocals converted the audience, and the momentum grew from that icy night. Sunny Ade performed twice more in England in 1983, and played the year out with a movie role in Robert Altman's *O.C. And Stiggs*.

The effects of Ade's travels beyond Africa were apparent throughout his music: his inveterate magpie attraction for new gadgets, studio technology and techniques introduced synthesisers and electronic percussion, experimentation which constantly stretched the definition of juju.

Together with the other king of *juju*, Ebenezer Obey, Ade re-shaped a dance

Above: King Sunny Ade in a juju *celebration with his African Beats.*

music which started life in low dives and was originally played on acoustic guitar and talking drums. Obey introduced more guitars and electric bass, but it was Ade's sharp ear that recognised the potential of the Hawaiian steel guitar, and this later became an obligatory instrument. In 1983, he began to combine synthesiser and talking drums with each other, also introducing elements of dub to the music.

Over the years, King Sunny Ade's music slowed down and became more relaxed. Meanwhile, the younger *juju* bands, led by the likes of Segun Adewale and Dele Abiodun, were producing a faster, brighter sound as their mentor Ade had shown them. By the Eighties, *juju* had become an infinitely elastic genre, the most dynamic music emerging from the African continent.

SUE STEWARD

Music For Chameleons

Eighties British pop was a bewildering kaleidoscope of sounds and fashions

Kajagoogoo a-go-go! Despite the somewhat flimsy nature of the group's music, the pretty-boy looks of bassist Nick Beggs (left) and singer Limahl (right) guaranteed success at a time when frivolous pop music had come back to the fore.

WHILE PUNK and the musical fashions that followed it had tended to emerge from an 'underground' scene of small clubs in London, Manchester or Liverpool, the wave of UK pop that swept the charts on both sides of the Atlantic in 1983 saw the mainstream of the record industry reassert itself. The showbiz-oriented, 'pop' end of the music business had done well enough through the late Seventies, but it had held little credibility with young, punk-influenced rock musicians. But now, the major record deal and the 'Top Of The Pops' appearance were once again seen as legitimate goals as bands like the Thompson Twins abandoned the benefit circuit for the Top Ten.

Who's that girl?
The UK charts featured an almost unprecedented variety of new music, from the passionate electronic soul of Eurythmics to the cool, reggae-influenced ballads of Culture Club, from the catchy glam stomp of Duran Duran to the wistful pop of Nick Heyward. The traditional male good looks of stars like Duran Duran's Simon Le Bon and Wham's George Michael reflected the fundamentally safe and conservative nature of their music. But two of the most striking new faces of the year overturned such stereotypes dramatically. Culture Club's Boy George combined dreadlocks, exotic robes, lipstick and rouge, while Annie Lennox of Eurythmics wore a man's suit and cropped orange hair.

While the mainstream pop world was dominated by the synthesiser, a backlash was underway as bands like Big Country, U2 and the Alarm brandished their guitars and found success on both sides of the Atlantic. Three of punk's crucial figures found themselves back in the limelight: John Lydon and his band Public Image Ltd had a Top Ten hit with 'This Is Not A Love Song', as did Siouxsie and the Banshees with 'Dear Prudence', while Tom Robinson returned after four years with 'War Baby'.

Sixties soul star Tina Turner also made a powerful comeback at the end of the year with a successful UK tour and a hit single, 'Let's Stay Together', while TV comedy star Tracey Ullman had a Top Ten hit with the Sixties-sounding 'Breakaway'.

Blue hit for a blue day
Another surprise hit was New Order's 'Blue Monday'. The best-selling independent record of the year, it reached Number 12 in the spring before re-entering the charts to make the Top Ten in October. Other independent acts to make a substantial impression were the mysterious Cocteau Twins, whose LP *Head Over Heels* went swiftly to the top of the independent LP charts, and Manchester's the Smiths, who had a Top Ten hit with 'This Charming Man' at the end of the year.

But despite the variety of music in the charts, record sales were actually falling quite drastically: in 1978, 88 million records were sold in the UK, but by 1983, the figure had dropped to 77 million. Chart return shops were inundated with posters, T-shirts and videos to be given away with singles to boost their chart position. But although the brief popularity of many bands may have been the result of such marketing ploys, this wave of UK pop had produced at least two substantial new talents in Culture Club and Eurythmics. REGINALD STINCUER

ROCK '83

A host of teen idols emerged in the UK in 1983. The most unusual of them was Culture Club's androgynous Boy George; rarely a day went by without his appearing in one of Britain's daily newspapers. Despite his outrageous looks, he actually came across as a sensible and talented performer, winning respect and praise. The other idols of the year – stealing young girls' hearts the world over – were Duran Duran, while soul revivalist Paul Young, disco duo Wham!, cute popsters Kajagoogoo and macho boys JoBoxers all provided pinups.

The US scene gave Britain chart hits by Billy Joel, Hall and Oates and Lionel Richie, while UK megastars the Police continued to enjoy chart success. Michael Jackson's *Thriller* became the best-selling LP ever, and his stylish dance music was accompanied by lavish videos and a slick new image.

Dominating the music scene worldwide was David Bowie, now sporting a classy line in suits and a new healthy image. 1983 saw him achieving success in the album and singles charts, making the headlines with his controversial 'China Girl' video, appearing in three films, undertaking a massive world tour and playing a benefit that raised £90,000 for community schemes in his birthplace of Brixton, London.

In the year the cruise missile arrived in Britain, peace festivals were abundant, with bands such as Madness, Fun Boy Three, U2, the Damned, Orange Juice, the Beat and ex-Jam Paul Weller's new band Style Council all playing for the cause.

After ten years working together, Toto—a West-Coast band of former session musicians—finally had a U.S. Number One hit with the song 'Africa'. Toto dominated the year's Grammy Awards by winning in six categories, including Record Of The Year with 'Rosanna' and Album Of The Year with *Toto IV*.

January

1 Daryl Hall and John Oates top the US singles chart with 'Maneater'.
12 Former Traffic percussionist Reebop Kwaku Baah dies in Stockholm of a brain haemorrhage.
15 Phil Collins' version of 'You Can't Hurry Love' tops the UK singles chart while in the US, Australian band Men At Work reach Number 1 with their single 'Downunder'.
19 London music venue Dingwalls opens a chain of clubs in Hull, Bristol, Liverpool, Sheffield and Newcastle.

25 Lamar Williams, bassist with the Allman Brothers Band and Sea Level, dies aged 36 in Los Angeles of cancer.
29 Veteran pop star Billy Fury dies at 41 of a heart attack.
Men At Work's 'Downunder' reaches Number 1 in the UK singles chart.

February

4 Karen Carpenter dies of a heart attack in Los Angeles aged 32.
11 A riot by punks at the Los Angeles Mendiolas Ballroom results in 41 arrests. The show had been heavily overbooked.
19 Kajagoogoo top the UK singles chart with their debut 'Too Shy'.

Above: Slick teen idol of the Sixties Billy Fury died in January. He had notched up 19 Top Twenty single hits in the UK.

March

2 Sony, Philips and Polygram launch a digital audio system with compact discs that reproduce sound by laser beam.
5 Michael Jackson's 'Billie Jean' tops the singles charts in the UK and US. His album *Thriller* is also at Number 1 on both sides of the Atlantic.
26 'Is There Something I Should Know' by Duran Duran enters the UK singles chart at Number 1. New Order have the best-selling indie single in 'Blue Monday'.

April

2 Pink Floyd's album *The Final Cut* reaches the top of the UK chart within a week of release.
9 David Bowie tops the UK singles chart with 'Let's Dance'.
16 Bass player Pete Farndon, who left the Pretenders in the summer of 1982, is found dead in the bath of his London home.
18 Cream producer and Mountain

bassist Felix Pappalardi is shot dead in his New York apartment; his wife is charged with murder.
27 Buckingham Palace intruder Michael Fagan fronts the band Bollock Brothers at London's outrageous nightspot the Batcave.
30 Spandau Ballet's 'True' tops the UK singles chart.
Muddy Waters dies in his sleep in Illinois at the age of 68.

May

7 Style Council, Paul Weller's new band, play a short set at a Campaign for Nuclear Disarmament gig at Brockwell Park in Brixton, London.
16 A former teacher storms into an elementary school and takes twelve children hostage. He uses WBLI Long Island DJ Rick Sommers as an on-the-air go between. They are on the air until midnight when the kidnapper finally surrenders to police.

June

4 The Police return to the Number 1 slot in the UK with their single 'Every Breath You Take'.
8 Dexys Midnight Runners are dropped as Bowie's support act in Paris after Kevin Rowland gets annoyed with impatient fans and insults Bowie.
17 Fun Boy Three, the Beat, Curtis Mayfield, Melanie and King Sunny Ade headline a three-day CND festival at Glastonbury.

July

9 The Undertones play their last ever British gig at London's Crystal Palace, supporting Peter Gabriel.
Fantastic, Wham!'s debut album, enters the UK chart at Number 1.
12 Traffic's former sax-player Chris Wood dies of liver failure at 39.
15 Fun Boy Three split after a tour of the US. Their last concerts featured a version of the Doors' 'The End'.
23 Newcomer Paul Young makes Number 1 in the UK with his single 'Wherever I Lay My Hat'.
30 The Beat split up. Dave Wakeling and Ranking Roger form a new band called General Public, signing to Virgin Records.

August

5 David Crosby, of the Byrds, and Crosby, Stills, Nash and Young, is sentenced to five years in prison for a 1982 drug and firearm offence.
6 On the 38th anniversary of the dropping of the atomic bomb on Hiroshima, Greater London Council stage a free Peace Festival in London's Victoria Park, Hackney. JoBoxers and Orange Juice headline.
10 Kajagoogoo sack their shiny-haired singer Limahl and bassist Nick Beggs takes over on lead vocals.
17 Michael Smith, Jamaica's foremost dub poet, is murdered. He was stoned to death by thugs suspected of being activists from the ruling Jamaica Labour Party.

20 Soft Cell's Marc Almond announces his intention to quit the recording side of the music scene a week after visiting rock critic Jim Reid at the *Record Mirror* offices, brandishing a whip.

21 Ramones guitarist Johnny Ramone is found unconscious in a New York street after a fight. He undergoes four hours of brain surgery.

27 The most famous nose on the pop scene, Barry Manilow, brings tears to the eyes of 40,000 (mainly female) fans at the historic setting of Blenheim Palace in Oxfordshire.

September

1 The Clash announce the sacking of Mick Jones after Joe Strummer and Paul Simonon claim Jones had 'drifted apart from the original idea of the Clash'. Jones says the allegation is unfounded.

15 Michael Williams, better known as dub master Prince Far I, is killed by gunmen who burst into his home in Kingston, Jamaica.

18 The re-formed Bay City Rollers headline the Futurama '83 festival held in Leeds.

20 A benefit for former Faces' bass player Ronnie Lane takes place at London's Royal Albert Hall. Among the performers are Eric Clapton, Jimmy Page and Jeff Beck.

27 Culture Club postpone part of their sell-out UK tour after drummer Jon Moss breaks his little finger. Their single 'Karma Chameleon' is top of the UK charts, as is their album *Colour By Numbers*.

October

1 The two-day Bowie World Convention opens at London's Cunard International Hotel. Afterwards, disappointed devotees slam the event, complaining about unfulfilled promises of rare Bowie film.

3 Paul McCartney and Michael Jackson's second duet 'Say, Say, Say', produced by George Martin, is released.

Goodbye Yazoo (top left); hello Paul Young (top right). Above: Lounging around in leather and lace at London's Batcave Club.

8 Paul Young's debut album *No Parlez* tops the UK charts.

20 Merle Travis dies of a heart attack in Nashville, aged 65. The country guitarist and songwriter has written such songs as 'Sixteen Tons' (later a hit for Tennessee Ernie Ford), 'Smoke, Smoke, Smoke That Cigarette' and 'Stick With Me' (also sung by the Everly Brothers).

23 Echo and the Bunnymen play at the Royal Shakespeare Theatre in Stratford-upon-Avon as the culmination of a two-week Youth Festival.

November

2 King Kurt are victims of a vicious gang attack after their gig at the Liverpool Venue and are forced to cancel concert dates. The band had built up a reputation for hurling sticky substances at their audiences during their wild sets.

The remaining members of The Doors hold a convention in London to promote a new album of previously unreleased live Doors tracks.

Public Image Limited open their first ever British tour at Brighton's Top Rank.

5 Topper Headon, former Clash drummer, is arrested for being 'staggering drunk while walking his mongrel dog' in Fulham Road, London. He is later fined £3.

7 Billy Joel's 'Uptown Girl' tops the UK singles chart.

17 Yet another lavish disco opens in London – the Hippodrome – on the old Talk of the Town site.

23 Ex-Badfinger bassist Tom Evans is found hanging at his home in New Haw, Surrey. He had recently been involved in a long legal battle over songwriting royalties for the Nilsson hit 'Without You' which he co-wrote with Peter Ham.

30 A 'secret' gig by industrial band Test Department is prevented by a police raid on the illegal venue in a warehouse near Waterloo Station. 150 police question members of the audience and the band are held overnight. The group are not charged but their equipment – including mallets, springs and mangled metal – is confiscated as potential offensive weapons.

December

1 The Poison Girls headline a benefit gig at North London Polytechnic to buy wirecutters for women at the Greenham Common peace camp.

Industrial music group SPK's concert at London's Venue is brought to a halt after chains are swung rather close above the audience's heads.

18 Elvis Costello, U2 and Ian Dury are among artists taking part in 'The Big One', a theatrical peace show at London's Apollo Theatre, Victoria.

23 Pete Townshend announces he is leaving the Who.

24 Acappella group Flying Pickets have a Number 1 hit single in the UK with their version of Yazoo's 'Only You'.

28 Beach Boy Dennis Wilson is found drowned in the sea near his Californian home.   ANNETTE KENNERLEY

Fantastic Days

Teen magic from Nick Heyward and Haircut 100

THE MUSIC BUSINESS traditionally extracts a high price for fame. Group members who have known each other since schooldays find their youthful enthusiasm and fellow feeling sorely tried and tested by the demands of success and the tour-album-tour merry-go-round of contractual obligation. Haircut 100 emerged from the pleasant London suburb of Beckenham, Kent, in the early Eighties to sweep all before them in scenes of teen adoration reminiscent of the Monkees. Like those Sixties kings of teen pop, Haircut 100 were to find that overnight fame brought its own problems. Unlike the American quartet, however, a genuine solo star would emerge from their ranks to repeat the group's success in his own right: Nick Heyward, their singer, songwriter and guitarist.

Haircut 100 was formed one Sunday afternoon in 1980. The whimsical trio of schoolfriends behind the nascent teen-dream were Heyward (born 20 May 1961), bass guitarist Les Nemes (born 5 December 1960) and second guitarist Graham Jones (born 8 July 1961). All three shared a love of such youthful pleasures as 'surfboards, yellow chocolate bananas and jumping over hedges', to quote three random responses from a teen-mag questionnaire of 1981.

Ski lift

'It was the perfect situation,' Heyward later recalled. 'Then suddenly the session players joined and it all got disjointed.' The musicians who rounded off the band's line-up were saxophonist Phil Smith (born 1 May 1959), drummer Blair Cunningham (born 11 October 1957) and percussionist Mark Fox (born 13 February 1958). The new recruits all boasted previous musical experience – in Cunningham's case, a string of session credits from his native United States – and *their* answers to the probing questions of *Blue Jeans* magazine revealed somewhat different concerns to those of the original trio, although the musical talents they brought to the band were undoubtedly invaluable.

Early 1981 had seen the band make its London debut in the unlikely surroundings of the Ski Club in fashionable Eaton Square and recording engineer Karl Adams subsequently offered studio time for a demo which aroused some record-company interest. A last-minute engagement at London's Rock Garden earned them a review in *New Musical Express*, and Arista Records were hooked, signing the band before they had clocked up half-a-dozen live appearances. The line-up had varied in both personnel and number in these early months, Cunningham edging out original drummer Patrick Hunt and Mark Fox flitting in and out of the ranks before finally committing himself. His comment – 'I wouldn't have given up an interesting teaching job just to play around in a little no future pop group'— betrayed a strength of character that was soon to lead him into confrontation with Heyward, the band's frontman.

Despite differences of outlook and opinion within the band, the first flush of success lent enchantment to the Haircuts' view of life. On the group's debut single,

'Favourite Shirts (Boy Meets Girl)', a four-to-the-floor beat and scratchy rhythm guitar was augmented by peppy brass to provide an infectious slab of pop that more than nodded to the dancefloor. Heyward's thin, mannered vocal was perhaps the weakest link at this stage, but his engaging grin and cheery, cherubic countenance played a major part in speeding the single to Number 4 in the UK chart.

The new year, 1982, dawned brightly enough with the January release of 'Love Plus One', which refined its predecessor's gauche charm while hinting that Heyward's lyrics allowed little scope for musical development. Apart from being a Number 3 single, the track made a swift reappearance on February's LP *Pelican West*. The fact that it was sequenced to follow 'Favourite Shirts', the album's opening track, was no coincidence, since these were the highlights of a somewhat one-paced set that nevertheless peaked at Number 2 in the album chart. The frothy 'Fantastic Day' completed the singles hat-trick, reaching Number 9, but for one band member at least the rot had set in.

Nobody's fool

Heyward had begun to resent the loss of the shared intimacy of the early days with Nemes and Jones. His songwriting skills, too, were being put under pressure – and suffering. Although their next single, 'Nobody's Fool', reached Number 9 in the UK in the autumn of 1982 the sparkle of old was lacking.

After their second US tour, Haircut 100 were steered into the studio to revive their flagging fortunes with an all-important second album. But the pressure proved too much for Nick Heyward; while the other members, once so musically ambitious, were content to clone past hits in safety-first fashion, he sensed that the formula had been played out. The album, scheduled for November 1982 release, was postponed twice – and never appeared. Announcing that percussionist Mark Fox – who had previously departed for a spell after losing a battle of egos with Heyward – would be their new vocalist, the band rejected Heyward's suggestion of a final tour and record release before the inevitable split. The boy wonder was out on his own.

The acrimony of the breakup plainly hit Heyward hard; he rashly appeared in *Melody Maker* as guest singles reviewer, and petulantly slammed nearly every release (an action that prompted Liverpool band Dead Or Alive to attack him with a fire-extinguisher); a period of depression followed. His former friends signed to Polydor Records for a reputed six-figure sum, retaining the group name, while Nick stayed with Arista, releasing 'Whistle Down The Wind' in March 1983. Heyward had come up with a reflective, mature composition that inspired him to turn in his best recorded vocal to date. Following this Number 13 solo success was 'Take That Situation', a song originally written for the Haircuts but invested with a

Favourite sweaters . . . Nick Heyward enjoys his brief heyday as frontman with Haircut 100 (left). Above: The boy goes it alone – a show of hands for the solo star on Tyne Tees TV's 'Razzmatazz'.

confident melody-line and a significantly fuller sound courtesy of co-producer Geoff Emerick that earned its Number 11 chart placing on musical merit.

Heyward's solo album *North Of A Miracle* (1983) featured the services of experienced session musicians whose careers, in some cases, had started before Heyward was born. The wisdom of this decision was fully demonstrated by such songs as 'When It Started To Begin', one of two tracks to feature the assured keyboard-playing of Elvis Costello sideman Steve Nieve, and the jazzy 'The Kick Of Love'. Although Nick's lyrics remained somewhat shallow and schoolboy-ish, his fast-improving vocal talents combined with finely-crafted arrangements to produce British pop in the best tradition; two further tracks, 'Blue Hat For A Blue Day' and 'On A Sunday', made moderate chart appearances as singles. Though his second album *Postcards From Home* didn't chart.

1988 saw him try again with the WEA label and *I Love You Avenue*.

While the gauche but charming youth with the semi-acoustic guitar gained both fans and pop credibility, his former companions were faring less well. After a series of unsuccessful singles, Polydor cancelled release of their album. Though Nick Heyward had still to justify *Music Week's* assertion in 1983 that 'like Cliff Richard, he will continue to be a major solo artist long after the screams have faded away', Haircut 100's six heady months of success seemed to have given the boy from Beckenham the taste for a continued spell in the pop spotlight.   MICHAEL HEATLEY

Haircut 100
Recommended Listening

Pelican West (Arista HCL 100) (Includes: Love Plus One, Marine Boy, Fantastic Day, Snow Girl, Calling Captain Autumn, Milk Film).

Nick Heyward
Recommended Listening

North Of A Miracle (Arista NORTH 1) (Includes: Blue Hat For A Blue Day, Whistle Down The Wind, Take That Situation, Atlantic Monday, Two Make It True, Club Boy At Sea).

SWEET DREAMS

Out of the Tourist trap with Eurythmics

RARELY DO POP STARS get a second bite at success, and few manage to top their previous achievements, especially when they have been in a band that became the target for some of the music papers' most vitriolic attacks. Annie Lennox and Dave Stewart are two people who achieved such a feat, rising from the ashes of the Tourists to form the immensely successful Eurythmics. The same pages that screamed at the Tourists' mediocrity and lack of originality at the end of the Seventies were pouring adulation on Eurythmics a few years later, with Annie Lennox's striking face running a close second to Boy George's on the news stands.

Red jazz academy
The secret of the duo's success seems to lie in the combination of their unquestionable talents and the survival of their unique partnership through the proverbial thick and thin of the music business. They cast aside compromise until they were eventually able to do just exactly what they wanted – writing all their own material, working within a flexible framework rather than a permanent band, and retaining control over the business and management side of their enterprise.

Annie Lennox was born in Aberdeen, Scotland, on Christmas Day 1954. Having learned to play piano and flute and having developed a passion for Tamla Motown, she left home in 1971 to study at the Royal Academy of Music in London. Disappointed somewhat by its limitations, she dropped out and joined a 10-piece jazzband called Redbrass, which included three female vocalists. The group toured social clubs and pubs.

Lennox was by now a strong and articulate singer. 'She sings and you get goosebumps,' her friend Paul Jacobs told Dave Stewart in 1976, when Stewart was looking for someone to write songs with. Whereas Lennox's background was working-class, Dave Stewart, born in Sunderland in 1952, came from a well-heeled family. At 15 his interest in music inspired him to stow away in the back of the Amazing Blondel's van after a gig. He subsequently played guitar in bands ranging from folk to blues, including Longdancer (on Elton John's Rocket label) and the Sadista Sisters.

Dave walked into Annie's life one night in 1976 at the health food restaurant Pippins in Hampstead, London, where she was working as a waitress. The spark from that introduction led to the couple living together for the next four years. Teaming up with fellow songwriter and rhythm guitarist Peet Coombes, bassist Eddie Chin and drummer Jim Toomey, they formed the power-pop band the Tourists and secured a deal with Logo Records in 1979. Annie sang and played keyboards.

In the following 18 months they notched up four UK Top Thirty singles, including a cover of Dusty Springfield's 'I Only Wanna Be With You' which reached Number 5 and went gold. Two albums, *The Tourists* and *Reality Effect* (both 1979), on Logo were followed by a third album, *Luminous Basement*, after the band joined RCA in the autumn of 1980. Manufactured for pop success and doomed by their own restrictions, the band split that winter in the middle of a Far East tour.

Dave and Annie's personal relationship suffered: Annie's confidence sank to an all-time low, and Dave spent several months of 1981 in hospital with a collapsed lung. However, their musical partnership survived, and the duo were now able to write and perform their own material.

At a New Year's Eve party at German producer Conny Plank's studio in Cologne, they had made some rough demos with DAF's drummer Robert Gorl, ex-Can members Jackie Liebezeit and Holger Czukay. (Plank was known for his work with Kraftwerk, DAF, Can and Ultravox.) The demos were taken up by RCA and provided the material for the first Eurythmics album, *In The Garden* (1981). Featuring Blondie drummer Clem Burke, the LP displayed a wide range of styles, from passionate pop to avant-garde electronics. The uptempo feel of the music was often undercut by Annie's moody, aching lyrics and powerful vocals, as in the track 'Never Gonna Cry Again': this effect was to be a characteristic element in her later work.

Framework of success
The LP was not a commercial success, however, and back in London the couple began writing new material, recording it on an eight-track in their rooms above a picture-framer's in Chalk Farm. They played most of the instruments themselves, beating picture frames against the wall to create the disco 'clacking' effect on 'Sweet Dreams' and a local café proprietor's breathings to add atmosphere to 'Love Is A Stranger'. Costing a mere £8000 to produce, the resulting album, *Sweet Dreams (Are Made Of This)*, released in 1982, launched the second stage of their career. The title track combined commercial appeal, an insistent dancefloor beat and strong vocals to make it one of the most successful singles of early 1983, rising to Number 2 in the UK chart in March.

Coupled with a sophisticated video, the single brought a new Annie Lennox to 'Top Of The Pops'. Escaping from the bland, 'girl singer' stereotype she had conformed to in the Tourists, Lennox now projected one of the most dynamic and confident images ever shown by a commercial female singer. Sporting a neatly-cut man's suit, tie and cropped orange hair, Annie played on her image, confusing audiences still further by donning a variety of guises for the video of the later single, 'Who's That Girl?'. Underneath the wigs, stubble, petticoats and outrageous glitter suits, her new-found confidence, embracing the sincere and frequently painful personal intimacy of her lyrics, won over audiences throughout the world.

Dave and Annie set up their own company, D&A, and started a small record label. They moved to a 24-track studio in a converted church in the North London suburb of Crouch End, which housed other

projects involving video and dance, and invited other musicians (including former Throbbing Gristle members Chris and Cosey and an androgynous street duo called Flex) to record there. Determined to maintain both control of and variety in their music, Dave and Annie added no permanent members to Eurythmics. On BBC2's 'Old Grey Whistle Test' in 1983, they appeared with a grand piano, an acoustic guitar and eight gospel singers, while their touring band included, at various times, former Blockhead keyboard-player Mickey Gallagher, saxophonist Molly Duncan (ex-Average White Band), drummer Pete Phipps from the Glitter Band and trumpeter Dick Cuthall, who had worked with various bands, including the Specials.

The professional touch

Their 1983 UK tour, undertaken to promote their third LP, *Touch*, was slickly professional entertainment. The colourful, expertly choreographed stage show featured a tongue-in-cheek chorus of three female backing singers, dressed identically in white suits and black wigs. The first single taken from the LP, 'Right By Your Side', seemed to point to a more optimistic sound: with its lilting calypso rhythm and lightweight lyrics. The next single, 'Here Comes The Rain Again' (which reached Number 8 in February 1984) was a subtle, haunting melody; her warm and sensual voice offset the light, airy string-playing of the Royal Philharmonic Orchestra and gave a melancholy, desolate edge to the love song.

In 1983 Eurythmics sold over six million records worldwide, with 'Sweet Dreams' topping the US singles chart; 1984 saw them embarking on a major tour of Europe, the US, Australia and Japan. In 1984 Eurythmics recorded the soundtrack for the film *1984*, and the following year released *Be Yourself Tonight* – an album that combined a harder rock edge with soul, spawning a UK Number 1 in 'There Must Be An Angel' with Stevie Wonder.

Further Top Five successes with *Revenge* and *Savage* in 1986 and 1987 respectively confirmed Eurythmics' position as one of Britain's top pop acts—a state of affairs repeated in the US with the success of the 1989 album *We Too Are One*, a chart-topper in the UK. ANNETTE KENNERLEY

Eurythmics
Recommended Listening
Sweet Dreams (RCA PL 70014) (Includes: Sweet Dreams (Are Made Of This), Jennifer, This Is The House, Love Is A Stranger, The Walk, I've Got An Angel); *Touch* (RCA PL 70109) (Includes: Who's That Girl?, Aqua, The First Cut, Here Comes The Rain Again, Cool Blue, Regrets).

Above left: The Tourists, from left Eddie Chin, Dave Stewart, Annie Lennox, Peet Coombes and Jim Toomey. Right: Annie and Dave – the nucleus of Eurythmics. Above: Annie's many disguises.

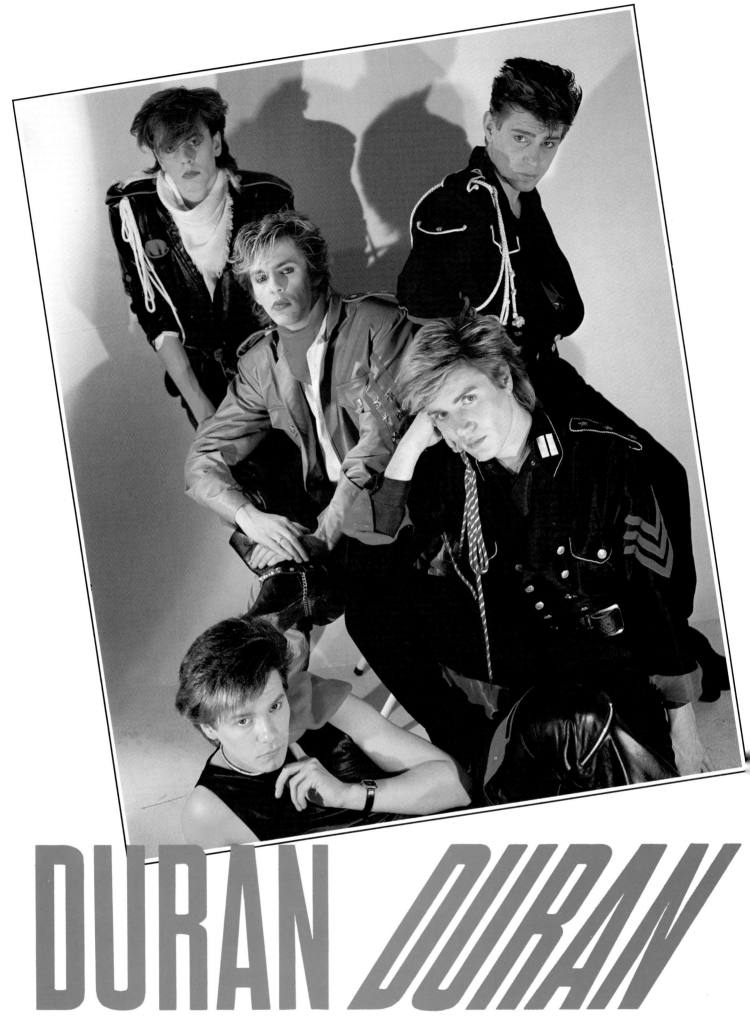

DURAN DURAN

Gloss and glamour from Birmingham's brightest

DURAN DURAN were a pop group *par excellence* – good looking, fashionable and great to dance to. They also made no bones about eschewing 'political messages and preaching' in favour of purely escapist music: 'We want to be the group to dance to when the Bomb drops' was one of singer Simon Le Bon's most quoted remarks. In the early Eighties, however, this attitude did not stop them wildly over-estimating their own artistic value and, in a series of carefully calculated moves, offering themselves as the new Beatles.

Dancing in the dark

It was in 1977, in their home town of Birmingham, that Nick Rhodes and John Taylor first hit on the idea of a group that crossed the Sex Pistols and Chic, combining the energy of punk with the danceability of disco. They took their name from the monster in the 1968 film *Barbarella* – Rhodes being something of a movie buff – and the first Duran Duran line-up consisted of Rhodes (synthesiser and rhythm unit), John Taylor (lead guitar) plus Steve Duffey (vocals, later to re-surface as Tin Tin) and Simon Colley (bass, clarinet). Duffey and Colley soon left in search of a more authentic rock'n'roll band and were replaced by Andy Wickett (vocals) from local band TV Eye; Wickett moved on shortly after the group acquired its first drummer, Roger Taylor, from another local band, Crucified Toad.

Guitarist Alan Curtis and singer Jeff Thomas meanwhile came and went, and it was around Rhodes and the Taylors that Duran Duran's fusion of disco and rock was knocked into shape. Rhodes later told the group's biographer Kasper de Graaf that they were influenced at the time by music like Rod Stewart's 'Da Ya Think I'm Sexy' and Bowie's *Young Americans* (1975), together with certain tracks by Sparks.

The group became part of the Birmingham new romantic scene based around a club called the Rum Runner that attempted to recreate the atmosphere of New York's Studio 54. The club held Roxy Music/David Bowie nights, dedicated to the artists who were Duran Duran's real heroes. Bryan Ferry's influence, for instance, could be heard as late as 'New Moon On Monday' on their third album, *Seven And The Ragged Tiger* (1983).

The band's next recruit was lead guitarist Andy Taylor, who joined through an ad in *Melody Maker*, despite making an unfavourable impression at his audition by turning up in jeans. A barmaid at the Rum Runner then mentioned to her boyfriend, Simon Le Bon, that the group was looking for a singer. Le Bon, who turned up for *his* audition in skin-tight, pink leopardskin trousers and sunglasses, went down inordinately well; the group liked his song lyrics, too. So by the summer of 1980, the final Duran Duran line-up had been

assembled: Simon Le Bon (vocals, born 27 October 1958), Nick Rhodes (keyboards, born Nick Bates on 8 June 1962), Andy Taylor (lead guitar, born 16 February 1961), John Taylor (bass guitar, born 20 June 1960) and Roger Taylor (drums, born 26 April 1960).

Gigs at the Edinburgh Festival, London's Marquee and the Lyceum were followed by a chance to support Hazel O'Connor on a national tour in late 1980. Michael Berrow, who with his brother Paul ran the Rum Runner and now managed the group, sold his house to finance the tour, during the course of which they were spotted by and signed to EMI. By March 1981, Duran Duran were heading their own national tour and their first single, 'Planet Earth', was on its way to Number 12 in the British charts (and Number 1 in Australia). Three months later, however, their second single, 'Careless Memories', proved a temporary setback when it stuck at Number 37.

1981 earned the group plenty of flak from British music papers like *New Musical Express* and *Melody Maker*, which accused them of being frivolous and trivial. However new magazines like the *Face* and *Smash Hits* enthusiastically welcomed the group. That same year their first album, *Duran Duran*, sold well, reaching Number 3; it contained their first two singles and the melancholic 'Is There Anyone Out There', the lyrics of which owed much to Bowie's 'Space Oddity'. Their third and fourth singles were also successful: 'Girls On Film' gave them their first Top Ten hit, reaching Number 5, and 'In My Own Way' made it to Number 14; Duran Duran seemed firmly established.

Opposite: Duran Duran, clockwise from bottom left Roger Taylor, John Taylor, Andy Taylor, Simon Le Bon and Nick Rhodes. Above: John and Roger.

Film fun

Meanwhile, the classy promotional videos for their singles had earned them much attention. The mildly pornographic clip for 'Girls On Film' (directed by Godley and Creme) suggested, however, that neither the group nor EMI then realised Duran Duran's potential teen appeal. It did, however, show that the group were thinking of themselves as artists: this impression was confirmed by the glossy and carefully constructed promos shot the following year in Sri Lanka and Antigua by Russell Mulcahey. 'We view videos as an art form,' said Rhodes, while Le Bon remarked that he saw himself as a 'very serious artist' who took video 'very seriously'.

These short films were approached with the same kind of energy reserved for the group's stylish appearance: fashion, from new romantic frilly shirts to Anthony Price suits, was an essential ingredient of the fantasy, escapist world Duran Duran provided for their fans. Rather than encouraging the viewer to see the world in new and fresh ways, however, all these promos – with their palm trees and sundrenched beaches – shared the imagery of Martini television commercials, an area long since abandoned by artists who laid claim to any integrity.

The same kind of criticism may be levelled against what Le Bon pretentiously chose to call their 'radial rather than linear lyrics'. Most of their compositions, while suiting the travel-brochure world

Below: Simple Simon sings for his supper.
Top right: The lads whoop it up on stage.
Centre right: Slinky Simon nestles down
amongst lily-white pillows.

Below right: On the rooftop of the BBC-TV
centre, Duran Duran exhibit the style that
propelled them to the top. Bottom right: A
racy scene from the 'Girls On Film' video.

the group conjured up with its promo films, were equally drenched in cliché. The images used – 'summer days', 'moonlight', 'shadows', and 'windy midnights' – might have answered the emotional needs of adolescent teenagers, but hardly constituted lyrical innovation. On the occasions when their meaning was clear, it was frequently trite.

In 1982, the group managed to ditch their new romantic label, thereby reaching a wider audience. As a result, that year brought a string of successes. Their second album, *Rio* (1982), which made Number 2 in the UK, was far more confident than the first album and produced four hit singles – 'In My Own Way' (Number 14), 'Hungry Like The Wolf' (Number 5), 'Save A Prayer' (Number 2) and 'Rio' itself (Number 9). After completing the Russell Mulcahey videos in the Caribbean, they started on an eight-month world tour, taking in Europe, Australia, Japan and the US (where, for the second half of their tour, they supported Blondie).

Fancy that?

All this hectic activity was beginning to pay off. Their live performances were exciting, entertaining and – increasingly – sold out. And in Britain the group swept the readers' poll of *Smash Hits* (the magazine most in touch with Britain's pop trends), winning the Best Album, Best Single and Best Male Singer categories; in typical *Smash Hits* style, Simon Le Bon was also voted Most Fanciable Human Being. The group also did exceedingly well in the Radio One Rock and Pop Awards.

Equally importantly, given Le Bon's obsession with world domination for the group by 1984, their videos were proving popular on America's rock-music cable TV channel, MTV. Their single 'Hungry Like The Wolf' reached Number 10 in the *Billboard* charts.

Duran Duran finally made the top of the British charts in March 1983 with their next single, 'Is There Something I Should Know'. The group themselves spent most of the year out of the country in tax exile – in France, the West Indies and Australia – writing, recording and mixing their third album, *Seven And The Ragged Tiger*. They composed the songs as a group in their usual way. Although each member was primarily concerned with the music for his own instrument – with Le Bon adding vocals – they all chipped in with ideas, often starting from an interesting beat laid down by Roger Taylor. In the middle of all this, they returned to Britain in July 1983, for two charity concerts.

At the first, in aid of the Prince of Wales Trust at London's Dominion Theatre, in the presence of Prince Charles and Princess Diana, the group suffered from all manner of technical difficulties: the bass-drum pedal broke twice, Andy Taylor broke a string and a flying box of chocolates knocked John Taylor's bass guitar out of tune. Compared to Dire Straits, who were topping the bill, the group sounded rather weak and unprofessional.

The second show, at Birmingham's Villa Park football ground, had slightly wider ramifications since it was organised by the group to raise £40,000 for Mencap, the organisation for the mentally handicapped. Poor planning meant that the promoter was caught on the hop when the local council restricted the audience capacity and insisted on postal booking. Promoter Derek Block later claimed they were unable to sell enough tickets to break even (18 to 20,000 people were apparently needed to cover expenses of £130,000) and the group ended up losing money.

Perhaps the most interesting thing about the concert itself, however, was the family audience of picnickers intent on a good day out. Here was the kind of pop group parents could breathe a sigh of relief over: no Johnny Rottens or John Lennons here, and no chance of any adolescent rebellion. It came as a shock to the group when their first single from the album, 'Union Of The Snake', reached only Number 4 in the British charts in 1983, although the album itself went straight in at Number 1.

In 1985 Duran Duran split temporarily to form the Power Station and Arcadia. The latter, with Simon Le Bon, released the single 'The Promise' in late 1985. Duran Duran's single 'A View To A Kill', however, proved the most successful of the band's output that year.

A permanent change came when Roger Taylor retired and Andy Taylor went solo amid acrimony. Bolstered by session players Steve Ferrone and Warren Cuccurello, Duran survived to cut *Notorious* (1986) and *Big Thing* (1988), but their chart-topping days were gone.

In the balance

Although it remained to be seen whether Duran Duran would have the talent to make the leap to becoming serious rock musicians, their achievements were already considerable.

However Duran Duran had shown a strong tendency to mistake 'style' for 'depth'. It is unlikely that a group that existed so much on the surface and put such emphasis on pop as mere entertainment could ever create an LP like the Beatles' *Rubber Soul* (1965). Musicians attempting to satisfy the wider emotional needs that classic rock music serves require a much wider vision. That, of course, is one of the aces that Duran Duran heroes such as Bowie and Ferry, despite their similar emphasis on style, have always had hidden up their own fashionable Anthony Price sleeves. COLIN SHEARMAN

Duran Duran
Recommended Listening

Duran Duran (EMI EMC 3372) (Includes: Girls On Film, Planet Earth, Anyone Out There, Night Boat, Friends Of Mine, Sound Of Thunder); *Rio* (EMI EMC 3411) (Includes: Hungry Like The Wolf, Rio, Last Chance On The Stairway, My Own Way, Hold Back The Rain, The Chauffeur).

HITSVILLE UK

The worldwide appeal of Eighties British soul

By 1984, ACCORDING to some trade journals, British acts accounted for nearly £600 million worth of business per year in the US; however, relatively little of this money was generated by Britain's black artists. This might well have been due to the influence of MTV, the cable television channel that supplied its subscribers with a diet of rock videos around the clock. Many observers claimed that MTV discriminated against black performers; although mainstream black videos such as Michael Jackson's 'Billie Jean' and 'Beat It', Eddie Grant's 'Electric Avenue' and Herbie Hancock's 'Rockit' received 'heavy rotation' (an

MTV expression that signifies three to four plays per day), they were the exception rather than the rule. MTV's somewhat inadequate answer to those who enquired about the lack of black music videos was that the station only played 'rock'n'roll'.

British soul music has always revealed an intriguing mixture of styles and influences, and it is no surprise that that two

Below: David Grant (left) and Sketch (right) made up the duo Linx and did much to put the new Brit-funk on the map.

of the bands to gain attention in the US in 1983, Freez and Level 42, were produced by Americans – Arthur Baker (Freez) and Verdine White and Larry Dunn (Level 42). This ploy was nothing new, for British soul bands had drawn upon America for inspiration since the Sixties.

During that decade, acts such as the Foundations, Geno Washington, Jimmy

James and Johnny Johnson found a profitable niche on the mid-Sixties UK live circuits, covering or imitating the latest sounds from Stax, Motown and Atlantic, whose big-name artists were only rarely available to tour Britain.

By the Seventies, British soul music had become more organised, and groups such as the Real Thing, Gonzalez, Kokomo and the Olympic Runners compared favourably with their American counterparts. Scottish soul group the Average White Band even hit the top of the US charts in 1974 with their instrumental 'Pick Up The Pieces'. As the decade drew to a close, many British groups had begun to 'do their own thing' at last, with little or no regard to what was happening in the US. Freez's first big hit, 'Keep In Touch' (released in 1980), owed very little to the latest American trends, while Linx, Central Line and Level 42 all found success by writing songs that appealed specifically to British kids.

Missing Linx

In contrast to the sophistication of American black music, British soul had a do-it-yourself air. Freez's hit had been financed by group member John Rocca, who even started his own label, Pink Rhythm; the song was subsequently issued by Pye on their Calibre label to reach Number 48 in the charts. The two members of Linx, David Grant and Sketch, also financed their first single, 'You're Lying', before hawking the finished masters around several record companies. The success of Freez and Linx revealed the commercial potential of Britain's black and black-influenced musicians to the major labels.

However, Linx's success was short-lived: after only two albums, *Intuition* (1981) and *Go Ahead* (1981), the duo split up. Sketch has since released nothing at all, but David Grant has established himself as one of British pop music's hottest properties. His success owes as much to his adroit changes of image as to his music – he switched from wearing spectacles to contact lenses and from suits to trendy sportswear, complete with matching sweatbands.

One of the more commercially successful bands of the early Eighties were Imagination, whose 'Body Talk' made Number 8 in 1981. Imagination have since gone from strength to strength: their flamboyant appearances on television have turned Messrs John, Ingram and Kennedy into teen-idols; and their concerts have attracted huge audiences.

While the majority of artists found American success hard to achieve, Junior found himself with the opposite problem – his success in America has far exceeded that attained in the UK. His 'Mama Used To Say' was released to little or no reaction

Right: Imagination adopted a slinky and glamorous image that made them into pin-ups and attracted large audiences to their concerts.

initially in the UK, but became a major hit in the US, in a remixed form. Its British re-release in 1982 redressed the balance, making Number 7; however he has experienced difficulty in maintaining his success in the UK.

One of Britain's most popular black groups is Shalamar, who comprise three Americans. However, group member Jeffrey Daniels has become an honorary Brit – his clothes are straight out of the King's Road, and his intention to live and work here in the UK bodes well for the growing black music scene.

Soul Spectrum

No review of the British black music world would be complete without mentioning some of the people who have worked behind the scenes, uncovering the hits and new talent. Of them all, none has worked as hard as Morgan Khan. As a club plugger at Pye he was instrumental in the birth of the Calibre record label, whose initial success came from licensing American product. Soon it began to unearth potential hits here in the UK, with Freez gaining a major hit in 1980. Morgan subsequently repeated his Midas touch with Excalibur Records and its offshoot R&B, where Imagination have become the label's major money-maker. By the mid Eighties, Morgan had moved to Streetwave Records, whose compilation albums of club hits have continually managed to feature on the charts.

Numerous club disc jockeys have helped record companies get a better idea of what the public want. Jeff Young works for Phonogram, Mick Clark at Virgin, Pete Tong at London, Theo Loyla was a longtime employee at Polydor, while Ensign Records' Chris Hill was instrumental in acquiring Light of the World for the label; although the group has since split, their off-shoots, such as Beggar & Co, continue to make good music.

In the same way that John Peel has done much to further rock music, there are numerous radio disc jockeys who have specialist programmes that highlight new black records, Greg Edwards and Robbie Vincent being probably the best known. Greg Edwards' 'Soul Spectrum' on Capital Radio was for a long time compulsive listening as Britain's music found its feet, while Robbie's Saturday show, on Radio London, made him something of a legend, as have his various club residencies.

Despite the upsurge of interest in black music in Britain in the Eighties, the UK's black artists have been largely upstaged by predominantly white, soul-influenced acts such as Culture Club, Eurythmics, Yazoo, Paul Young, Marilyn, the Style Council and the Thompson Twins. As the decade progresses it will be interesting to see if black soul artists can rival their white counterparts in accessibility as they have generally surpassed them in the past in passion and originality. GRAHAM BETTS

Top left: Isle Of Wight boys Level 42. Left: Junior Giscombe, whose 'Mama Used To Say' was a US hit. Below: Shalamar were a popular live band in the UK.

THE *NEW* PRODUCERS

At the controls of the UK's music machine

THE UPSURGE OF raw talent in British rock in the mid Seventies inevitably led to producers taking a back seat in the creative process. Punk rock was all about achieving a hard-hitting sound using simple instrumentation; there was thus little scope for the producer to exercise his talents. By the Eighties, however, when more expensive sounds had once again become fashionable, the prestige of the producer rose dramatically.

One of the decade's most notable success stories was that of Martin Rushent, who had built a solid reputation in the late Seventies working with the Stranglers and the Buzzcocks. In 1981 he recorded *Dare* with a revised form of the Human League – a group that had previously inhabited the avant-garde fringes of post-punk music. Their use of electronic instruments had been based on simplicity, melody and, often, rhythm, yet they had exuded an air of weirdness that had made them unlikely chart contenders.

Genetic engineering

The LP's songs by the League's principal new writers, Phil Oakey and Jo Callis, were catchy and danceable, while the band's visual appeal had been refurbished by the addition of two girl singers. However it was Rushent's adroit work at the mixing desk that proved the crucial factor in the group's success; his achievements would influence the tone and confirm the direction of much chart music to come.

Rushent took the group's mannered cosmeticism and inflated it, separating out each programmatic element, emphasising and texturing both its mesh of robotic pulses and Phil Oakey's cold, languid croon with a clarity that was a hi-fi fanatic's dream. This sound's prefabricated sheen only enhanced the suitability of the League's compositions for that most powerful of modern marketing devices, the video, while being ideal for the increasingly sophisticated technology of the discotheque. The album sold in truckloads, and former bizarre outsiders the Human League were suddenly as respectable as Abba or the Osmonds.

However, because its technical

Producer Andy Hill (left) moved into music from the slick world of advertising to add a surface sheen to the Eurovision pop fare of Bucks Fizz (above).

execution complemented and enhanced its artistic aspiration, *Dare* also showed how constructive the producer could be. Rushent later applied himself to Pete Shelley's solo work and, less successfully, to the more brittle sound of Altered Images. His Genetic Studios became synonymous with a particular and much-imitated contemporary engineering of sound – one that added a dimension of space and a vaguely futuristic detachment to the music.

Artifice is perhaps the key word when considering the types of sound taken to teenage (and not so teenage) hearts in the Eighties by a new flood of openly chart-conscious starlets who were glad to conform to the wishes of record-company promotional departments. In the developing computer

age, pop stars became creatures of spotless beauty, elevated, glamourised beings blithely assuming their positions in the alleged new age of leisure.

Genuine technological advances in the recording studio helped producers apply the icing to these fey pop pastries, thereby often disguising less original or charismatic artists as the 'real thing'. Bucks Fizz were rescued from their 1981 victory in the Eurovision Song Contest (traditionally an accident black-spot in terms of a future career in pop, Abba excepted) and transformed from a bleached blur of hair and teeth into main-street futurists for all the family. How? By the creation of sleeker haircuts, the application of perky pouts, and their complete subordination to a business team whose crucial studio specialist was Andy Hill, a man whose background lay in the advertising world.

Silicon treatment

Hill developed the perennial Eurovision thump into a big, glistening crash that dominated a string of hits, including 'The Land Of Make Believe' and 'My Camera Never Lies' (both UK Number 1s). So an otherwise tired musical approach was lent just enough up-to-date sheen to persuade impressionable adults and young teenagers to dip into their pockets. Rather less of a deception were the Belle Stars who, after failing to make meaningful progress in the wake of the vibrant 2-Tone phenomenon, finally opted to be wacky chorus girls, recycling old novelty hits or chanting empty aphorisms like 'Sign Of The Times'. Success finally came to them when, in Peter Collins, they found a producer to channel their ebullience into singalong hooks and build layers of glittering percussive cacophony around them.

Collins' nimble conversion jobs on Sixties bubblegum melodies further wooed the consumer when applied to the undeniably magnetic Tracey Ullman, who was seeking to expand on a flourishing career as a comedienne. Collins' other success threatened to be briefer. The mischievous junior reggae which took Musical Youth to Number 1 in 1982 with 'Pass The Dutchie' required only minimal exposure to standard reggae techniques. The song made the top because of its jaunty tune and the unpretentious charm of its performers. Similar success with the band proved hard to find, with reggae lending itself less easily to the established conventions of Eighties studio laundering.

The chart sound of the early Eighties then, was bright, smooth and synthetic. In the hands of Trevor Horn, ABC's producer, an extravagant dash of glossy melodrama was added to these qualities. Horn first made his name as half of the double act that was the Buggles – a studio-created

Top: Martin Rushent (seated) lent Altered Images (right) an electronic lustre.
Opposite: Trevor Horn (in specs) with fellow Buggle Geoff Downes and pop protégés Dollar (inset opposite).

group, whose 'Video Killed The Radio Star' soared to Number 1 amid a shower of silicon chips in 1979. After an unlikely liaison with fading progressive rock band Yes, Horn nurtured a handful of wholesome love-affair hits for male/female duo Dollar, and then produced Frankie Goes To Hollywood's 1984 Number 1 hit, 'Relax'.

ABC, with their singer/composer Martin Fry, had painstakingly conceived a kind of celluloid waltz full of romantic clichés. For the band's first LP, *Lexicon Of Love* (1982), Horn embellished their slightly wooden brand of pop-funk with dramatic, crashing drum treatments and flurries of epic strings. The album contained no less than four successful UK singles – 'Tears Are Not Enough' (Number 19), 'Poison Arrow' (Number 6), 'The Look Of Love' (Number 4) and 'All Of My Heart' (Number 5). Horn's gift for versatility was confirmed by his share in Malcolm McLaren's predictably patchy *Duck Rock* in 1983.

The opulence of ABC's presentation was but one example of how several producers of the Eighties owed a debt to the lavish sensuality of much early- to mid-Seventies soul. The team of Swain and Jolley illustrated their grasp of the extravagances that the pop-soul mode could bear in their work with Imagination. 'Body Talk', the group's first hit, comprised a flexing, homophonic rhythmic writhe and tremulous slithers of synthetic strings, amid which the lead singer warbled submissively. A series of reasonably engaging camp hits followed, and the production team moved successfully on to provide the perfect aural accoutrements for Spandau Ballet's consuming lust for grandeur.

Magi-mixers

During the early Eighties, Colin Thurston successfully persuaded the public that indelicate heart-throbs Duran Duran were disco as much as they were cumbersome glam-rock. Mick Glossop and Mike Howlett manoeuvred, sometimes erratically, in the wake of Rushent's innovations, while Mute Records' supremo Daniel Miller applied a refreshingly light touch to his delicate protégés Depeche Mode. Few followed his example, though Steve Levine, who manned the console for the engaging Culture Club, was (despite counter-productively swamping David Grant) a welcome contemporary pacesetter, adapting adroitly to the group's cosmopolitanism, accentuating their strengths without engulfing the group's melodic agility and ample personality with weighty trimmings.

Much of British mainstream pop in the Eighties proved to be remarkably backward-looking. As the record producer made a substantial comeback, all too often style outweighed content. The success of Stock Aitken and Waterman with artists as disparate as Kylie Minogue and Cliff Richard suggested that the balance was swinging back towards the studio at the expense of the true performer. DAVE HILL

MAD ABOUT THE BOY

Culture Club's instant karma

THE MOST REMARKABLE aspect of Culture Club's rapid rise to fame was the transformation of the group's lead singer, Boy George, from an emblem of London's bizarre transsexual demi-monde into an all-round family favourite. His appeal rapidly took him from the style-conscious pages of *I.D.* magazine to the cover of *Woman*.

Previously, male pop artists with a penchant for cosmetics and female clothing, such as Wayne County, Divine, the New York Dolls and David Bowie circa *The Man Who Sold The World* (1970), appealed to a marginal, mainly student audience. Their sexuality was regarded by others as deviant, an affront to middle-class family life. But in 1983, Boy George, self-confessed bisexual in lipstick and frocks, was basking in the sort of widespread affection reserved for the tame and un-threatening.

He was a sexual outlaw who could endear himself to a family audience by moral stands on cigarette smoking and drugs. He was a man-as-woman, paradoxically stressing his normality in photographs with Mum, Dad or his collection of dolls. He was a freak from the margins, singing hummable tunes for the masses. He was a boy in drag who was, in turn, imitated by the girls, a double-chinned 'boy wonder' who became a pin-up of the Eighties.

Sanctuary, sanctuary

Boy George was also a contradiction of his own origins in South-East London, where boxing was the way to prove your manhood and bricklaying the way to earn a decent living. He was born George Alan O'Dowd on 14 June 1961, the son of working-class Irish Catholics. His father, Jeremiah, was a strict ex-army man, a boxing instructor and a builder who administered instant and often violent punishment if disobeyed. His mother, Diana, who was softer and more liberal, raised a total of five boys and one girl in the O'Dowd household.

George was always the hardest child to handle. His truancy and insolence at school made him a subject for the Special Needs Department, who kept him in their quaintly-named Sanctuary Unit where he doodled as others studied. Then, in September 1976, after a confrontation with the headmaster, he was expelled.

At the age of 12 he had become enamoured of David Bowie and Marc Bolan, going to see Bowie in concert in 1973. Two years later he outraged his parents by arriving home with orange hair, white sandals, a shoulder bag and drainpipe trousers. At the same time he was frequenting the homosexual clubs of central London, where the dance music and display of style captivated him. It was here, through meeting such poseurs as Martin Degville and Philip Salon, that he

Opposite: The charismatic features of George O'Dowd. Above: Culture Club, from left Jon Moss, Mikey Craig, Boy George and Roy Hay.

began to develop his unique personal style.

Between 1976 and 1980, he worked as a salesman, window-dresser, model and makeup artist, but lived for the clubs where he became a minor celebrity, much photographed by chroniclers of the new romantic movement.

The beginning of Boy George's move into music came in 1980 when Sex Pistols' manager Malcolm McLaren asked him to join new protégés Bow Wow Wow as a second vocalist. Dubbed 'Lieutenant Lush', George made his concert debut alongside the teenage Annabella Lwin and, for the first time, began to recognise his own potential as a performer.

The association with McLaren and Bow Wow Wow proved to be short-lived, but the following year saw George branch out on his own. With bassist Mikey Craig (born 15 February 1960) and guitarist John Suede, George formed Sex Gang Children (the name was later used by an entirely

different outfit). Subsequently, drummer Jon Moss (born 11 September 1957) was added to the band.

At 24, Moss was the group's oldest and most musically experienced member. He had worked with London, the Clash, the Damned, the Edge and Adam and the Ants, developing a good business sense along with a determination to succeed commercially as well as critically. It was Moss who decided that the name Sex Gang Children would have to be changed and, after the band recorded two demo tracks for EMI, that guitarist Suede would have to go. He was replaced by Roy Hay (born 12 August 1961) and the group, now called Culture Club, made its performing debut in October 1981 at a small club in Essex.

Clowes horse

Moss's determination and George's artistic flair made Culture Club a promising entity; Moss believed the group should have 'religion, warmth and colour', while George collaborated with designer Sue Clowes to produce a unique visual image.

Early in 1982, Culture Club signed to Virgin Records; their first two singles, 'White Boy' and 'I'm Afraid Of Me', failed to make the charts. Their third attempt, the light, reggae-influenced 'Do You Really Want To Hurt Me?', released in September, reached Number 1 in 18 countries and sold over four million copies.

Culture Club's music was a clever blend of calypso, reggae, gospel, Detroit soul, dub, funk and Latin rhythms, all served up in a convincing pop format. 'Time (Clock Of The Heart)', which reached Number 3 in the UK at the end of 1982, was a melancholy ballad carried by the bitter-sweet tones of George's vocal, while 'Church Of The Poison Mind', their third UK hit at Number 2, was based unmistakably on the Motown sound of the Sixties and sold itself on a single hearing. Its follow-up, 'Karma Chameleon', revealed yet another side of Culture Club's musical makeup: described by George himself as a 'camp-fire song', the number was driven along by a jaunty C&W harmonica and had a catchy chorus.

Twankey panky

The single enjoyed a lengthy stay at the top of the UK charts and established the group as Britain's favourite pop act. Culture Club had taken the fashionable musics of the recent past and sold them back to the kids in a colourful, attractive package. Although two albums, *Kissing To Be Clever* (1982) and *Colour By Numbers* (1983), provided proof that there was ample substance beneath the packaging – in the form of strong, melodic songs, vibrant arrangements and musical performances, together with George's expressive voice – Culture Club's success was based, primarily, on the image and charisma of their singer.

The band ended 1983 with a triumphant UK tour, featuring vocalist Helen Terry, whose soaring voice had provided a stunning counterpoint to George's on 'Church Of The Poison Mind'. The following year saw the release of the LP *Waking Up With The House On Fire*, from which the single 'The War Song' reached Number 2 in the UK in October 1984, but the follow-up, 'The Medal Song', sank without trace. Boy George continued to make the headlines, but his career as a celebrity seemed to have overshadowed the achievements of the band as a whole, and by the mid Eighties their hold on the current pop scene had been lost.

It was no coincidence that Boy George's success came at a time when the traditional male role and stereotype were under constant challenge. His style caricatured this uncertainty and the uncritical acceptance of his bisexuality highlighted the moral confusion of the Eighties. 'I've made things acceptable that would have been considered outrageous 10 years ago,' he said. 'I take great pride in that.' STEVE TURNER

Left: George duets with Helen Terry whose soaring, soulful tones added another dimension to the band's sound in 1983. Below: George testifies.

Culture Club Recommended Listening

Kissing To Be Clever (Virgin V2232) (Includes: I'll Tumble 4 Ya, Do You Really Want To Hurt Me, Take Control, White Boys Can't Control It, Boy, Boy, (I'm The Boy), You Know I'm Not Crazy); *Colour By Numbers* (Virgin V2283) (Includes: Karma Chameleon, It's A Miracle, Church Of The Poison Mind, Victims, Black Money, Mister Man).

The Two Faces of Rock

How rock stars mixed pop with politics in the mid Eighties

THE CONTRADICTORY faces of the pop business were never more starkly juxtaposed than in 1985. On the one hand, a new breed of pop stars, such as Wham! and Duran Duran, spurned the idealism of their Sixties and Seventies predecessors in favour of an overt display of suntanned luxury. On the other, there was the unprecedented spectacle of virtually the whole of the new rock plutocracy going back to such idealism and burying their rivalry to work together on the Band Aid project. Ironically, it was not only the seasoned campaigners – Springsteen, Style Council *et al* – that made Band Aid. The participation of the Whams and Durans of this world ensured its huge success.

Close to the Wedge

Part of the reason that Band Aid exercised such a hold on the public's imagination – not to mention the public's wallets – was that its humanitarian appeal reached people of all political persuasions. But, by showing that pop stars could and ought to be concerned about the state of the world, it did open the doors for more overtly political projects. In the US, Springsteen's guitarist Miami Steve Van Zandt assembled a group of musicians as diverse as Bob Dylan, Miles Davis and Pat Benatar to make a record, 'Sun City', that publicised and raised money for the struggle against apartheid in South Africa. In the UK, artists such as Sade, Alison Moyet, the Style Council, Jimmy Somerville, Spandau Ballet, CP Lee and Billy Bragg teamed up to form Red Wedge, an organisation dedicated to ensuring a Labour victory at the next general election. Many of them had already given their support to political causes, particularly during the miners' strike, but Red Wedge represented a new level of coordination and publicity.

Above: 'Saint' Bob Geldof, the driving force behind Band Aid. Below: Cyndi Lauper, the archetypal glossy face of American pop.

Band Aid aside, the success story of the year was undoubtedly that of Madonna. A reasonably – but not spectacularly – talented individual, she had grafted her way to success, fuelled only by a hunger for fame and a powerful belief in herself. Her tacky, teasing image and her mildly salacious songs offended some: 'Young girls who listen to Madonna are learning how to be a porn queen in heat,' complained a Washington parents' organisation. But her appeal was not essentially sexual: she provided a role model for the aerobics generation, a fulfillment of the young American dream of money, self-expression and the respect of one's peers – something that the Everley Brothers had sung about 25 years before.

The fact that Madonna's success coincided with her move from club disco to an altogether rockier style of music is indicative of a wider reaction in taste both in the US and, to a lesser extent, in Britain. The smooth, synthesiser-based white soul sound of the early Eighties was out of favour. Guitars were back with a vengeance; the new heroes were Bryan Adams, Dire Straits and ZZ Top.

These manifestations of 1985 rock – idealism, a teenybop idol and the return of the guitar – could not disguise the fact, however, that essentially, very little new was taking place. The Eurythmics, Madness and the Style Council all produced magnificent albums – but for the most part, 1985 saw rock music in the doldrums, waiting, once again, for Something To Happen.   CHRIS SCHÜLER

2401

ALL IN A GOOD CAUSE

In 1985, Rock reached out to feed the world

Below: A galaxy of stars including Bob Geldof, Adam Ant, Roger Daltrey, Elton John and Sting lead the chorus at the Wembley finale of Live Aid.

THE BAND AID STORY began on the evening of 24 October 1984, with the transmission of Michael Buerk's television news report about the Ethiopian famine. In common with most people, Boomtown Rats singer Bob Geldof was shocked by the devastating scenes – but he was also moved to immediate action. His first idea was that the Boomtown Rats should make a record. But the group's career was hardly booming, and since raising money was the name of the game, he decided to try to produce a one-off record by the aristocracy of British pop music.

During a series of frantic phone calls, Geldof and Ultravox's Midge Ure (the first person Geldof contacted) quickly discovered that Britain's pop stars were willing. A song was put together by Geldof and Ure and a few weeks later a galaxy of pop stars, including Sting, U2, Paul Weller, Paul McCartney, Duran Duran, Boy George, Spandau Ballet, Phil Collins, Paul Young, Status Quo and George Michael, assembled to record the single 'Do They

Know It's Christmas?' under the collective name of Band Aid.

The record was an instant hit – it entered the UK singles chart at Number 1 and soon became the biggest-selling single ever in Britain. 'Do They Know It's Christmas?' went on to earn some £8 million for famine relief in Ethiopia and the Sudan. Unlike many charity acts by rock stars in the past – such as the Concert for Bangladesh (mounted by George Harrison and others) where the financing was so complicated that it took nearly two years to pay out the money to those it was intended for – Band Aid was efficiently organised. A born organiser, Geldof (who had started a CND youth branch in Dublin in his teens) got the artists to perform for free, persuaded Phonogram, his record company, to manufacture and distribute the single for free and the retailers to sell it for free. Only the British government refused to donate its 15 per cent (the amount due it for VAT) to the Band Aid Charity.

Virtually all the money raised by 'Do They Know It's Christmas?' was spent on relief work in Africa and none (bar the government's 15 per cent) was kept back. But the success of the Band Aid record was more than a matter of money or even of the number of lives Band Aid saved. 'Do They Know It's Christmas?' and the dozens of records it inspired, the most notable of which was US For Africa's 'Feed The World', helped raise the awareness of the Western World to the problems facing the poor of Africa *and* shamed governments into action.

Geldof in Africa

With hindsight, the bandwagon that Geldof had set in motion had an air of inevitability about it. Accordingly, it is worth noting that if 'Do They Know It's Christmas?' had not been such a *good* pop record, much of what followed might not have.

The simple emotional response to the Band Aid record quickly turned to anger when Geldof travelled to Africa to witness at first hand the misery of starvation. He spoke openly and directly about the gaping holes in governments' aid policies. More than any other organisation Band Aid helped to articulate the contradictions of the aid programmes of the West, contradictions that involved cutting aid programmes while spending more and more on storing and destroying surplus food (to protect the market price) that might have been shipped to Africa to alleviate the famine.

But, in addition to focusing the attention of the world on the African famine, Band Aid also achieved practical measures. It bought a vast amount of goods and set up 'Freight Free', a shipping operation through which Band Aid carried enormous quantities of aid to Ethiopia and the Sudan at no cost for the agencies fighting the famine. Similarly, in the summer of 1985, it established a trucking operation in the Sudan – at a time when there was little

transport available – and later helped set up another one in Ethiopia with USAID and the United Nations. To co-ordinate all these activities Band Aid relied on volunteers, all of whom were professional people. These included Kevin Jenden who became the organisation's project director, his wife, Penny Jenden, who bought all the supplies, and Ken Martin who organised 'Freight Free'. If Bob Geldof was the public face of Band Aid, the volunteers were the backstage stars of the show.

Global jukebox

From their trips to Africa, Band Aid soon realised that £8 million was but a drop in the ocean. Much more money was needed. And so the Live Aid project was born. The impetus behind Band Aid was so strong that the technical and logistic problems of mounting concerts simultaneously in Philadelphia and Wembley, with the greatest line-up ever in the history of rock, to be transmitted around the world by satellite simply evaporated. Thus it was that on Saturday 13 July 1985 the world saw an A-Z of rock'n'roll, from Adam Ant to Neil Young, the Beach Boys to the Who (who reformed specially for the event) and Bowie to Wham!, to list but six of the 50 acts that appeared. A further £50 million was raised for famine relief in Africa through telethons and television sales.

The spirit of the Live Aid effort carried on after the music itself had died away. It was David Bowie who commented in an interview during the Live Aid concert that he thought it should become an annual event. Organisers and performers alike were praised for their enthusiasm and commitment to the venture – none more so than the instigator himself, Geldof. The millions of viewers saw him exhausted and unshaven on their screens, making a heartfelt and desperate appeal for donations. He was acclaimed as the charity hero of the year and many people were outraged that Geldof's name did not appear on the New Year honours list. With Live Aid's contribution only amounting to the tip of an iceberg, Geldof started off 1986 with a vow to continue his campaigning, whatever the sacrifice to his own career. Geldof seemed to have touched the conscience of many rock artists to use their position for a good cause on a scale never seen before. Perhaps Live Aid heralded a new wave of socially-aware rock.

In the main, especially in the Sixties, rock music has been oppositional, has been against the status quo and the establishment. The wonder of Band Aid was that, at a time when the trend in post-punk Eighties rock was towards the more ephemeral charms of pop and entertainment, rock and the rock audience responded with great generosity to the plight of people thousands of miles away who had never before had anyone to speak for them. It may be ironic that so many lives were saved because of pieces of plastic with a hole in the middle and strips of video tape. But at least some *were* saved. PHIL HARDY

CHARITY ROCK

How music made millions to give away

Live Aid was the first and largest of a great number of charitable events as the Eighties progressed. Rock'n'roll, it seemed, had found a conscience—especially since the commercial spin-offs of the attendant media coverage could be more than beneficial—and it only remained to be seen how deep were the pockets of the rock audience.

The line between charity and propaganda was often a thin one: even Live Aid had a political edge not only in the implicit criticism of the Ethiopian government's handling of their own internal crisis—a view shared by 99 per cent of the world—but for example in the British Government's refusal to waive tax on the Band Aid record when all concerned had donated their services free.

Charity or controversy?

This reached a head in the Nelson Mandela 70th birthday party broadcast Live Aid-style from London's Wembley Stadium on 11 June 1988 to 40 different countries. Despite a BBC edict not to make political statements from the stage, many artists flagrantly ignored the ruling—and American television took the show only with a six-hour delay which enabled these statements to be edited out. Right-wing British MPs refused to let the matter rest on the grounds that the state-run BBC had a duty to be impartial, but the affair fizzled out.

As Live Aid had thrown up its hits, so Mandela Day revealed Tracy Chapman as its star. Playing solo with just an acoustic guitar, she played two spots, filling in when Stevie Wonder's computer-controlled synthesisers proved troublesome—and within three weeks found herself topping the UK charts. Her first eponymous album sold 12,000 copies on the Monday after the concert.

Amnesty International proved a big draw for rock stars with a conscience. In 1986, Sting re-formed the Police, albeit briefly, to play in an Amnesty benefit, while the following year U2—along with Lou Reed and others, played a series of US concerts. In 1988, perhaps the most attractive bill yet—Bruce Springsteen, Peter Gabriel, Sting, Yousso D'Nour and Tracy Chapman—toured the world playing to sellout audiences and pressing home the message. As Sting pointed out, Amnesty was easier for pop stars to identify with

Below: Amnesty International struck a chord with artists and audiences alike. A star-studded world tour in 1988 did much to advance their cause. Above right: Jackson Browne holds forth at the 1988 concert to celebrate Nelson Mandela's 70th birthday.

since it championed the rights of individuals.

Fighting for farmers
In the US, artists as diverse as John Cougar Mellencamp and Willie Nelson joined forces in Farm Aid, an organisation formed to save America's small farmers from bankruptcy. In a less public fashion, Kenny Rogers played benefits which involved his audience bringing gifts of food for the poor and destitute: a constructive protest against 'Reaganomics' that beat political sloganeering.

A parallel to Farm Aid could be found in Ireland's Self Aid. A 14-hour all day event on 17 May 1986, it brought together the survivors of Thin Lizzy and witnessed the last performance by the Boomtown Rats, as well as attracting such famous expatriates as Van Morrison. This event was unusual in spawning a couple of records: usually the labyrinth of record company connections and legal niceties were too complex to unravel to enable recorded highlights of such events to be preserved.

In Britain, the Campaign For Nuclear Disarmament's annual festival at Pilton Down, a staple of the Eighties and a foundation of that movement's financial situation, ceased in 1988—apparently for one year only—when the host farmer Michael Eavis found that the festival's popularity had outstripped the site's facilities.

Record receipts
Many attempts were made to produce one-off fundraising records. Ferry Aid in 1987 attempted to raise funds for the victims and families affected by the sinking of a British ferry at Zeebrugge, Belgium; the song was the Beatles' 'Let It Be'. Similarly, Mersey-beat survivor Gerry Marsden (of Pacemakers fame) took his band's 1963 hit 'You'll Never Walk Alone' back to the top of the UK chart in 1985 as part of the Crowd, a star-studded ensemble raising funds for victims of a fire at Bradford football ground.

Perhaps the most successful of all these fund raisers, however, was 'That's What Friends Are For', a Carole Bayer Sager-Burt Bacharach composition sung by Dionne Warwick, Stevie Wonder, Elton John and Gladys Knight, which topped the US chart in 1985. The cause was AIDS research.

Not all acts were keen on taking the spotlight for their charitable work. Huey Lewis pulled out of Live Aid but is known to have contributed more than generously to a number of causes including AIDS research, while Cliff Richard's UK chart-topper of Christmas 1988, 'Mistletoe and Wine', was just one of his records whose royalties have gone to Christian charities. One, the 1986 remake of his early hit 'Living Doll' with comedy quartet the Young Ones, was part of Comic Relief, a humour-based fundraising effort in the wake of Band Aid.

The danger was, of course, that record buyers might encounter charity overkill: this was almost evident in Smile Jamaica, a British fundraising exercise for the victims of 1988's Hurricane Gilbert which hit the Caribbean. Fearful of a poor turnout, the participation of Irish supergroup U2 was announced—allegedly before this had been finalised. Despite being off the road, the group agreed to appear at late notice—and the televised concert was spoiled by U2 fans impatient with the other acts who had originally agreed to participate.

Not that this mattered: at this, as with all other such events, it was the financial result that mattered and not the event itself. This is why we are unlikely to see another Woodstock motivated by caring concerns rather than musical or cultural merit. In the late Eighties, it seemed, rock was no longer the voice of rebellion but a channel for charity.

Going it

Bryan Ferry

Ever since his early days with Roxy Music, Bryan Ferry has cut a stylish figure across any stage and now, well into his 41st year, he remains the best-dressed man in rock. Even while fronting Roxy Music, Ferry has steadily maintained his own career (starting in 1973 with his first solo album *These Foolish Things*) and 1985 was a particularly good year for him, with his LP *Boys And Girls* going straight to Number 1.

Phil Collins

It's ten years since Phil Collins took over the vocals for Genesis, but only five since he's been involved in solo ventures. But he's certainly packed in a lot in that time, producing Adam Ant, Eric Clapton and Philip Bailey, singing and drumming on the Band Aid record, writing two film scores and finding the time to notch up huge international sales of his own three LPs. 1985 saw 'Easy Lover' (recorded with Philip Bailey) at Number 1 worldwide.

Sade

Sade has achieved phenomenal worldwide success in a relatively short time. In the space of two years she has gone from virtual obscurity to mega-stardom, from designing clothes and scraping a living to multi-million sales with her face on magazine covers everywhere. Her obvious good looks and exotic Nigerian background helped, but most importantly, she could sing. And that's what made *Diamond Life* such a successful album.

Alone

Old troopers and bright young things

Tina Turner

It's nearly thirty years since Annie Mae Bullock first sang with Ike Turner, and in 1985, as Tina Turner, she had her most successful period ever. After a ten year gap in the UK charts, she re-launched her solo career in 1983 with 'Let's Stay Together' and the LP *Private Dancer*, and with a rockier sound found a whole new (and much bigger) audience. In 1985 she stole the show with a lead role in the film *Mad Max (Beyond The Thunderdome)*.

The mid-Eighties was a good period for solo artists in general and witnessed a wide variety of them in the rock limelight. Old ones re-surfaced, and the message was that those with proven talent would survive comeback after comeback. Many big names split from their already established groups to launch their solo careers – often revealing hidden talents and exploring new musical directions. And there was, as always, a scattering of new faces on the scene – some would amount to no more than a passing fashion, while others would no doubt carry through their initial success on the quality of their output.

Old faithfuls such as Bryan Ferry and Phil Collins produced top-selling albums in 1985, Tina Turner made a massive impact with a string of hit singles (including her first Number 1 in the US, 'What's Love Got To Do With It?'), sell-out tours and a lead role in the movie *Mad Max (Beyond The Thunderdome)*.

Kate Bush and Midge Ure kept turning out the goods and having hits, Billy Bragg devoted his solo talents to causes and concerns, appearing at numerous benefits and rallies, and Adam Ant and Marc Almond strove to make it alone. Bonnie Tyler strengthened her hold on success, Aretha Franklin and Chaka Kahn were back in the charts, Style Council singer Dee C. Lee had a Number 2 hit in Britain and Prince percussionist and singer Sheila E. made an impressive solo debut.

New venturers into solo careers included Sting, proving his versatility and maturity with the jazz-laced *Dream Of The Blue Turtles* album, Alison 'Alf' Moyet establishing herself as a versatile singer whose vocals could extend to jazz, and Feargal Sharkey shaking off the angry-young-teenager image of the Undertones for the AOR UK Number 1, 'A Good Heart'. Outrageous New Yorker Cyndi Lauper brought a refreshing novelty to the solo scene, while elegance and sophistication were embodied in the highly successful Sade. Pouting peroxide blonde Billy Idol proved that old punks never die. Turned 30 and still sporting 1977's leather and chains, he has managed to carry the punk legend through into a successful, on-going commodity – perhaps demonstrating the selling power of nostalgia. Alongside the image-makers and the old stalwarts rest the clean-cut and popular solo artists such as Paul Young, Howard Jones and Nik Kershaw, all consistently, if not spectacularly, maintaining a high profile in the charts.

Whether or not the new faces will stay the pace remains to be seen, but there is no doubt that, whatever trends may come and go, there will always be a place in the rock field – and in the charts – for solo artists of all musical genres. The re-emergence and newly-won success of so many of the 'old guard' in the Eighties suggests that, for the forseeable future, rock audiences will remain faithful to music of the tried and tested variety.

ANNETTE KENNERLEY/DON PERRETTA

There can have been few more startling transformations than that of Feargal Sharkey. From the halcyon days of punk, singing with Northern Ireland favourites the Undertones, the gawky, spotty kid has become a suave, well-dressed, international celebrity. When the Undertones split in 1983, Sharkey's intense, quavering voice was quickly recruited by Vince Clarke to sing on the hit 'Never Never' with the Assembly, and soon after he signed to Madness' own Zarjazz label. A couple of minor hits followed, but then he hit the big time with the surprise Number 1 of 1985, 'A Good Heart'. His debut solo album, *Feargal Sharkey*, was produced by Dave Stewart of Eurythmics.

Feargal Sharkey

Paul Young

Billy Idol

Like so many British acts before him, Billy Idol (real name William Broad) had to go to America for his big break. But for him it's success a second time around, having already had a substantial bite of the cherry with punk band Generation X in the late Seventies. Generation X called it a day in 1980, and Idol went to New York to seek fame and fortune on his own. Retaining his punk image, his career suffered from a prejudice against his appearance until the arrival of MTV and the power of the video. His second album, *Rebel Yell*, released in 1983, went double platinum and yielded a string of US hit singles, and now he enjoys a status in the US second only to Duran Duran.

Billy Bragg is perhaps the man who most accurately fits the description 'solo artist' because, up to now, he has literally done everything with only a guitar and an amplifier to assist him. He's taken his radical, left-wing lone minstrel show up and down the UK and across Europe and America, and won over a big following. Bragg's punk band Riff Raff split in 1981 and he re-emerged in 1982 (after a 90-day stint in the army, which he bought himself out of – 'the best £175 I ever spent'). He took part in the first 1986 tour by Red Wedge, a left-wing cultural movement of which he is a founder member.

Paul Young spent years on the UK club and college circuit, most notably with the Soul/Motown revivalist band the Q-Tips, before his big breakthrough hit as a solo singer, a cover of Marvin Gaye's 'Wherevver I Lay My Hat'. Young had had a minor taste of chart success with one-hit-wonders Streetband and 'Toast', but it wasn't until his stint with Q-Tips that people came to notice his outstanding, resonant, white soul voice. CBS Records signed him on the strength of his voice, and after a difficult start, since his first solo hit, Young has rarely been out of the charts. Both his LPs, *No Parlez* and *The Secret Of Association* have sold well all over the world.

1985 was the year that Sting finally added a successful solo album to his already impressive list of achievements. Sting had always pursued ventures outside the Police, mainly in the field of acting, with parts in several major films, but it wasn't until the critically acclaimed *Dream Of The Blue Turtles* that he had put together any substantial solo recordings. In January 1985, Sting went to New York and recorded the album with local jazz musicians. They embarked on a world tour which ended in the UK early in 1986.

Sting

Billy Bragg

Alison Moyet

Alison Moyet ranks as one of the best vocal discoveries for years, her versatile, powerful voice providing one of the more memorable moments from Live Aid in a stunning duet with Paul Young. First emerging on the scene with the ultra-successful electro-pop duo Yazoo (remember 'Only You' and 'Don't Go'?), she found the format too limiting for her singing talents and decided to branch out on her own. Her first solo outing came in 1984 with the single 'Love Resurrection' which reached Number 10 in the UK, and paved the way for the international success of the LP *Alf*. In 1985 she scored another hit with 'That Ole Devil Called Love', a former Billie Holiday number, and won a new set of jazz fans.

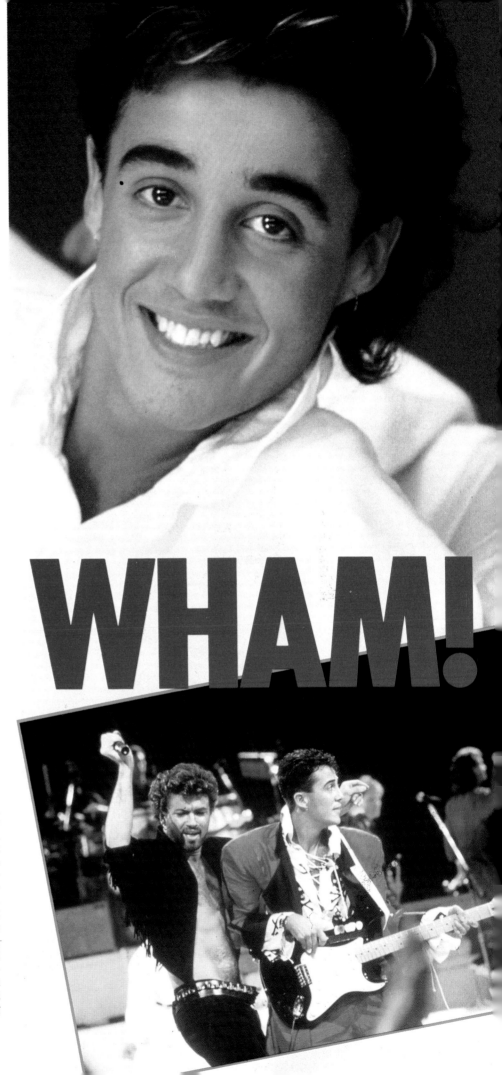

Two boys who took the world by storm

WHAM! NEVER LOOKED built for survival on the fickle pop scene of the early Eighties, as flamboyant new faces like Frankie Goes To Hollywood came and went and the once outrageous Boy George paled into insignificance after keeping Fleet Street in front page stories for many months. Perhaps the very secret of the duo's success lies in the fact that they were *not* particularly outrageous or shocking; they were promoted on the image of being two nice young men from a nice London suburb who were best of mates and showed a nice set of clean white teeth when they smiled. Every mother's dream . . .

The unique loyalty displayed by George Michael and Andrew Ridgeley seems to have been the key to their continued success after a somewhat chequered rise to world stardom. The two boys started their musical relationship at school in Bushey, on the outskirts of London. George (born 25 June 1963), of Cypriot origin, was the more self-conscious of the two; Andrew (born in Surrey on 26 January 1963) was the extrovert. They formed a band called the Executive in 1979, with Andrew on guitar and George singing.

By 1982 they had left school, changed their name to Wham! and produced a demo tape which they took to London's record companies. Several months later they signed a rather bad deal with a small independent label, Innervision. Their first single, 'Wham! Rap', released in June 1982, received only limited airplay but was overtaken by Wham's second single, 'Young Guns – Go For It', which made Number 3 in the UK singles chart in October and introduced Wham! to the fans on 'Top Of The Pops'. This brought them to the attention of manager Simon Napier-Bell who saw their potential as world superstars and took them under his wing.

Epic signings

Wham! became megastars worldwide – on a par with the success of the Beatles and the Rolling Stones in the Sixties. Their early days were marred by legal wrangles over money, however, as the band ended up broke, despite selling millions of records worldwide. The dispute was eventually settled and Wham! signed to Epic and began drawing in the cash. In September 1983, trouble hit again as an American band of the same name claimed their right to it – and damages. Again, Wham! survived the setback, though in December they failed to prevent their old company from releasing a medley single 'Club Fantastic Megamix' which reached Number 15 in the UK. In spite of these hitches, 1983 proved to be a successful one for the duo. They had a UK Number 2 single with 'Bad Boys' in May and their debut LP, *Fantastic*, reached Number 1 in the UK album chart and went gold. They embarked on their first tour that autumn with backing

singers Shirley Holliman and Pepsi Demacque (replacing Dee C. Lee who went on to sing with Style Council), but disaster struck when George lost his voice and 13 concerts had to be postponed.

The new year brought Wham! their first UK Number 1 with the single 'Wake Me Up Before You Go Go'. George – by now acknowledged as the songwriting talent behind Wham's success – made his first solo venture with the single 'Careless Whisper' in the summer of 1984. Its tone revealed a sensitive and more mellow side to George's songwriting.

Michael beats Frankie
Through the comparatively superficial gloss of Wham! shone a talent for writing quality songs with a popular appeal, a talent that might carry George Michael through a long and prosperous career. 'Careless Whisper' ousted 1984's flavour, Frankie Goes To Hollywood, from the Number 1 slot in the UK chart (with 'Two Tribes') in August. Andy and George seemed to approach fame and fortune in totally different ways. While Andy was in the news for his antics at a boozy student party in Bristol and for crashing his new Ferrari sports car, George was picking up the Ivor Novello Songwriter of the Year Award. Wham! – in particular George Michael – had entered the establishment; they appeared on Terry Wogan's chat show, and the Princess of Wales pronounced George 'gorgeous'. Their aptly named second album, *Make It Big*, went to the top of the UK chart on its release in November 1984 and went platinum.

At the end of a highly successful year, the Wham! single 'Last Christmas' – a sentimental confection aimed shrewdly at the Christmas stockings – took the Number 2 position to Band Aid's 'Do They Know It's Christmas?'. Andy announced that a donation from the royalties from 'Last Christmas' would go to the Ethiopia famine-relief cause. Wham! started 1985 with tours of Japan, Australia and China, and later that year, the US. George pursued his solo ventures, providing backing vocals for Elton John, including the hit singles 'Nikita' and 'Wrap Her Up'.

Late 1985 saw Wham! back at the top of the UK chart with the single 'I'm Your Man'. In February 1986, however, Wham! decided to follow separate careers. George was unable to reconcile his anti-apartheid beliefs with his management's investments in South Africa. In addition, both had grown weary of press reports citing George as the creative genius and Andy as a mere passenger. George Michael's *Faith* (1988) not only reached the top in Britain but also the US, suggesting a lasting solo career.   ANNETTE KENNERLEY

Above left: Andrew Ridgeley and George Michael with the smiles that sold millions. Bottom left and far left: The boys take the Wham! pop extravaganza on the road and show the Chinese another cultural revolution.

One cute navel and an awful lot of hits

THE LAST FEW YEARS have been bad ones for the girls, the argument goes, with female performers once more reduced to mindless onstage ornaments. The role of baddie in this depressing scenario always goes to the arch-collaborator who has, according to an unsigned letter in *Cosmopolitan*, 'put the women's movement back 30 years' with just one flash of her cute little navel. We're talking, of course, of Madonna Louise Ciccone, the pop phenomenon of 1985.

Born in 1959 into a middle-class Italian-American family in Rochester, Michigan, Madonna was the sixth child but the first of three daughters, and as such was blessed with her grandmother's name. Her childhood was disturbed by her mother's death and her father's subsequent remarriage to their housekeeper, but her ballet skills and academic grades were enough to ensure her a full scholarship to the University of Michigan after graduation, majoring in dance. She left after a year for New York,

Below: The changing face of Madonna Ciccone – fresh-faced in her high-school yearbook and (right) the sultry performer of the 'Like A Virgin' tour.

Madonna

eventually winning a scholarship with Pearl Lange and Alvin Ailey's modern dance group while working in a Dunkin' Donuts eaterie to support herself.

Trying to carve out a career, Madonna made a film, posed for photographs in the nude (the pictures were enthusiastically published by *Penthouse* and *Playboy* after her rise to fame) and formed rock bands (in one of which she was the drummer). That she had *something* was apparent: she was offered a solo spot in a French disco revue and Gotham Management – an agency run by Camille Barbone and Adam Alther – tried to groom her for stardom. She left Gotham after a year, dissatisfied with the clean-cut image they seemed to want for her.

In 1982 Madonna began recording a fusion of the music familiar to her from the New York clubs: new wave pop with a strong dance beat. Danceteria DJ and her then lover Mark Kamins touted the tape around the companies, hoping for a chance to move into production, and after a bizarre bedside meeting with label boss Seymour Stein in hospital, she signed to Sire/Warners.

Whips'n'furs

The first single was 'Everybody'. Written by Madonna, produced by Kamins and promoted in clubs, it sold over 250,000 copies in the US. 'Physical Attraction' followed with similar success, and the first album, *Madonna* – produced by Reggie Lucas – came out in June 1983 with 'Holiday' as the single, a song recorded in just one day with John 'Jellybean' Benitez.

'Holiday' was eventually a minor hit, but it was not until the fourth single, 'Burning Up', that Madonna made her debut on the rock video TV channel, MTV. It was 'Burning Up' which really broke Madonna. The promotional video featured the unholy one writhing on the ground, a rather nasty S&M image of a chain tightening round her neck, and the most outrageous lyrics from the girl so far: 'Do you wanna see me down on my knees/Or bending over backwards now would you be pleased?/Unlike the others I'd do anything/I'm not the same I have no shame.' Sweet submission: MTV loved it.

'Borderline' and 'Lucky Star' followed, the album *Madonna* passed the million mark with six singles drawn from its eight tracks, and its success continually delayed the release of the second LP, *Like A Virgin*. Madonna, meanwhile, passed the time with a role in Susan Seidleman's low-budget comedy *Desperately Seeking Susan*.

And then it happened. 'Like A Virgin' hit the top of both the Billboard single and album charts in early 1985, and broke her into the superstar bracket in Europe. She was on her way, and the retaliation for the Second British Invasion had begun.

Above right: Madonna with Rosanna Arquette in the film Desperately Seeking Susan. *Right: Madonna makes an increasingly rare public appearance.*

*Above: Madonna
takes Live Aid by storm and
(right) proves she can dance too.*

Hungry for quotes, the press pounced on Madonna's quip that she saw losing her virginity as 'a career move'. Few saw the humour in her words, and Fleet Street's usual combination of the salacious and the sanctimonious came to the fore, licking up titbits of gossip, leering over the pictures, but still adding that correct tone of moral disapproval.

The girl herself played the hypocrisies for all she was worth, thrusting her lingerie in the face of America's incensed Moral Majority and her tongue firmly into her cheek. In the film *Visionquest*, released in February 1985 (the story of a young wrestler obsessed with conquering the un-beaten state champion, Shoot, and in-fatuated by worldly wanderer Carla), Madonna makes a brief appearance, sup-posedly playing live in a sleazy downtown club. Her two songs 'The Gambler' and 'Crazy For You' both reached the US Top Ten, the latter also topping the UK charts in June 1985. The film was retitled *Crazy For You*, and launched on video for Christmas.

Pretty yet tough

Meanwhile, with 'Material Girl' nest-ling comfortably at Number 3 in the US, *Desperately Seeking Susan* made a timely New York opening in March, taking 16 million dollars before its UK opening six months later. It proved to be a gloriously funny film, with a bored housewife (played by Rosanna Arquette) learning to lose her inhibitions and Madonna playing her own myth – the wild, amoral city urchin – with a superb sense of comic timing. The critics loved it, and Madonna made a new set of fans and a step towards respectability.

By the end of the year, five singles had been released from *Like A Virgin* and it was still selling well. At one point, Madonna had six singles in the US Top Forty at the same time, and her only set-back was her failure to stop director Stephen Jon Lewicki cashing in with a re-release of her early film *A Certain Sacri-fice*. The shops were swamped with lace, lingerie and trash jewellery, lookalike contests abounded, and little Ms Ciccone was said to be worth eight million dollars. Her April tour broke box office records and grossed an estimated three million dollars a night.

Marriage to Hollywood brat Sean Penn was the next step. It was a private ceremony which just happened to be held

on a clifftop, giving the helicopter-borne cameras a prime view as the groom frolicked under the bride's white dress and the happy couple threw wedding cake. It was front-page 'news' everywhere, and a wise career move for both. Madonna was assured another plum film role in *Shanghai Surprise*, and Penn – whose *Falcon & The Snowman* was hardly a box-office stormer – would co-star with his wife.

Ciccone is an embodiment of the urban teen dream, a growing girl's fantasy made flesh. Pretty yet tough, sexy but never passive, a girl who transformed herself with make-up and junk jewellery rather than waiting for a fairy godmother. Madonna ignores the stares and dances her way through the clubs, the streets and the jeers with the confidence of a girl who knows her own mind.

For, no matter how submissive the lyrics, there's always a glint in those eyes to tell you its only a game. Sure, she's burning for your love, she'll do anything etc, but only because she *wants* to. Madonna, we know, always gets exactly what she wants, no more and definitely no less. She's terrifying to men (hence the sympathy so often ladled out to her ex-lovers by many male journalists) and irresistible to young women, especially. In the crudest form, what Madonna is telling her fans is that if you wiggle your fanny in the right direction ruthlessly and long enough, it'll get you to the top. It is this, presumably, that is supposed to have 'set the women's movement back 30 years'.

But what Madonna also conveys is a woman's right to pleasure and adventure – sex without romance or guilt, the freedom to ignore conventional roles and morality, and the courage to mock her critics. In her public persona at least, Madonna appears supremely self-confident, and as such is more convincing than say, the soul-less chant of 'Sisters Are Doing It For Themselves'. Annie Lennox followed this somewhat sloganeering duet with Aretha Franklin with the grovellingly abject 'It's Alright (Baby's Coming Back)'. Madonna, at least, is consistent.

The damage inflicted on female artists in general by The Year Of Madonna is less about the singer herself and more to do with what she is *assumed* to be. The surprisingly resilient myth of the girl who leapfrogged into the spotlight over the backs of her many male lovers ignores the years of struggling in New York. The many hours of writing, rehearsing, recording and filming are conveniently forgotten. Similar insinuations were made about Sade Adu, another hard-working singer whose star was assumed to have ascended effortlessly due to her classic looks and consummate sense of style.

Women in rock

Not all of the past two years have been artifice and glamour, however. The year 1985 also saw daffy Alf become solo star Alison Moyet, redefining how women were allowed to look onstage by performing throughout her pregnancy. As the baby was born, 'That Ole Devil Called Love' perched serenely at the top of the UK singles chart, promising Alf a long career as a showbizzy MOR jazz singer. Whitney Houston and Phyllis Nelson both celebrated the British public's new awareness of soul by producing a number one single apiece; Chaka Khan and Aretha Franklin both made chart appearances; and Tina Turner consolidated her comeback with 'Mad Max (Beyond The Thunderdome)'.

On another level of the business, female instrumentalists are no longer considered such a novelty, although many are still unsure whether they are there because of their talent or because they look good in the video. Trombonist Annie Whitehead has more than proved her worth as a session trombonist, and now leads her own band around the London clubs. Pianist Annie Hogan accompanies Marc Almond, as well as producing her own records; trumpeter Barbara Snow is often seen in the horn sections backing artists on 'Top Of The Pops'; Feargal Sharkey appeared in his 'Good Heart' video accompanied by two female drummers in his band, and so on.

Like Madonna, these women expected a career of their own and took what they wanted. Whether Madonna encourages or discourages such feminist attitudes remains to be seen.   SHERYL GARRATT

The follow-up to *Like A Virgin* took some while in coming. *True Blue* charted in the States on 19 July 1986, staying there for five weeks. It went one better than *Like A Virgin*—one US Top Ten single, that is. The creamy ballad 'Live To Tell' was a daring first choice that proved her seeming invincibility by hitting the top: it was followed by the uptempo 'Papa Don't Preach' (1), 'True Blue' (3), 'Open Your Heart' (1) and the mock-Spanish 'La Isla Bonita'. All also reached the UK Top Five.

One advantage of milking the album in this way was that it gave Madonna time to make another foray into the movie field and salvage the reputation she so nearly lost with *Shanghai Surprise*. Originally known as *Slammer*, *Who's That Girl* was appropriately retitled to direct attention towards the undoubted star of the show. Playing opposite Griffin Dunne as a modern-day gangster's moll with street-level wit, she took the honours as far as the critics were concerned.

Inevitably there was a soundtrack album—and though it contained only three tracks from her (all later issued as singles) it did well. For the record, the singles were the title track, 'Causing A Commotion' and 'The Look Of Love'. 1987 also saw Madonna tour the world, to tumultuous acclaim. She could rightly claim to be the female equivalent (or nearest to it) of Michael Jackson.

Disappointingly, her second album of 1987, December's *You Can Dance*, was merely a disco-mix of earlier hits—but the Christmas market lapped it up. Her marriage to Sean Penn, meanwhile, had its ups and downs: he served a brief jail sentence for violence, when it was rumoured the pair would split, but at the end of 1988 they seemed to be still together.

Encouraged by her screen revival, Madonna then took a chance that didn't come off—appearing in a Broadway production of the play *Speed The Plow* in which the critics showed no mercy. But such misjudgements were few as disco's first lady continued to tear up the Eighties.

Left: Madonna and husband Sean Penn. Their very public private life was rarely out of the headlines.

Bring On The Girls

How Madonna showed the way to stardom

Madonna's influence led to a shoal of good-looking young ladies intent on riding the same wave to fame and fortune. Debbie Gibson was one of the first with her hit-laden album *Out Of The Blue* containing her US Top Five single 'Shake Your Love'. Gibson was unusual in writing much of her own material.

Not surprisingly, 16 year-old Tiffany Darwisch dropped her surname in the search for stardom—and hit the top of the US (and UK) charts with that safest of bets, a Sixties cover (Tommy James and the Shondells' 'I Think We're Alone Now'). Her follow-ups included another cover, a sex-change version of the Beatles' 'I Saw Her Standing There'. Her particular Svengali was Smokey Robinson/Kim Carnes producer George Tobin.

Belinda Carlisle was unusual in being old enough to have a background—as a member of new wave group the Go Gos. Marriage to a Republican politico may not have done her rock credibility any favours, but the loss of puppy fat, the discovery of cheekbones and songwriting input from ex-Stevie Nicks producer Rick Nowels led to a year of hits in 1988 and a video directed by Diane Keaton.

Australian actress Kylie Minogue took the Tiffany route to success with Little Eva's 'The Locomotion', her first domestic hit and her second in the international sphere. But her handle on longevity was an association with producers/songwriters Stock, Aitken and Waterman. Starting with disco chanteuse Hazell Dean, whose 'Searchin'' they took to the UK charts in 1984, they built up a roster of interchangeable vocalists (including Minogue), often trying different singers over the same backing tracks. The result was a string of hits that dominated the UK chart in 1987-88 and influenced the whole of the rest of the music business.

Other singers turned to SAW: Samantha Fox, topless model turned singing star, looked to them to uplift her sagging chart fortunes—and this they did in 1987 with 'Nothing's Going To Stop Me Now'. Sabrina, an equally busty Italian, burst into the UK chart with the SAW-produced 'Boys'.

Just to prove the youngsters didn't have it their own way, 1988 saw the release of Sandie Shaw's first album for decades, *Hello Angel*—while Petula Clark, a 'bimbette' of the Sixties, returned to the UK charts with a remixed 'Downtown '88'. By contrast, Siouxsie (and her Banshees) was about the only survivor from the Seventies New Wave that had contained a fair share of women writing and singing their own songs. Madonna, paradoxically, had more in common with her than her younger, glitzier clones.

Left, from top: Madonna and followers, Australian actress Kylie Minogue and all-American Belinda Carlisle.

Left: Holly Johnson and Paul Rutherford front Frankie Goes To Hollywood. Below: Holly preaches to the masses. Bottom: 'Frankie Say' T-shirts, part of Paul Morley's marketing coup.

FRANKIE SAY

IN THE EARLY EIGHTIES, when for a number of years the idea of 'style at the expense of content' flourished, Frankie Goes To Hollywood caught the spirit of the times with uncanny precision. Possibly the ultimate pop style package, they left no detail to chance. The sound, image and word were carefully crafted, and their marketing and press coverage were immaculately arranged. The musical result was at times dazzling, inspired and outrageous, but time may prove them to have been the victims of the 'style' wave they so successfully rode.

Fronted by two outspoken homosexuals, dressed – in their early days – in sado-masochistic leathers and bondage wear, and armed with a debut single full of sexual innuendo, they caused an immediate controversy in the national press. Signed to the Island Records subsidiary Zang Tuum Tumb (ZTT), their lavish debut was packaged by former rock journalist Paul Morley and producer Trevor Horn, the former Buggle who put his stamp on 1980s production with ABC's *Lexicon of Love*. The three (heterosexual) band musicians, Brian Nash, Mark O'Toole and Peter Gill, insisted that they really did write and perform the music, but most credit was accorded to Horn, and during their first British tour estimates of how much music was on pre-recorded tape ranged from 50 to 90 per cent.

Frankie go to ZTT
Formed in their home town of Liverpool, Frankie made their first appearances supporting fellow Liverpudlians Hambi & The Dance at a series of local performances in 1982. Singer Holly (né Billy) Johnson had previously worked with cult new wave band Big In Japan. Fellow frontman Paul Rutherford had yet to join the group; the earliest line-ups were augmented by two female dancers/singers, The Leatherettes. In 1983 the group were asked to appear on the television rock show 'The Tube'. Trevor Horn caught the show, rang the group and offered them a deal with his new label, ZTT.

In October 1983 ZTT released their first single, 'Relax'. In the following weeks, it moved in fits and starts up into the Top Fifty. Radio airplay was considerable (thanks, no doubt, to high-powered radio and television promotion man Gary Farrow, an integral part of the operation), and by the second week of January 1984 the single was at Number 6. On 11 January Radio One disc jockey Mike Read, after studying the lyrics – notably, the couplet 'Relax, don't do it when you want to suck it,/Relax, don't do it, when you want to come' – took the record off the air before it finished. Two days later, 'Relax' was

The brief, bright meteor that shook the charts

banned from all Radio One shows.

Within two weeks, 'Relax' was at Number 1. In the manner of the Sex Pistols' 'God Save The Queen' before it, 'Relax' was banned from 'Top of the Pops'. It stayed at Number 1 for five weeks. The ban and the ensuing controversy made Frankie Goes To Hollywood into media stars. The outspoken homosexuality of Johnson and Rutherford, the lyrics and the outrageous public statements thrilled the national media. Morley, Fleet Street and the BBC had catapulted Frankie to the top.

'Relax' essayed a musical style that Frankie were to repeat on the subsequent singles 'Two Tribes' and 'Power Of Love'. At the time it was the most elegant, sophisticated pop most people had ever heard. In hindsight, while no less sophisticated, its devices become all too obvious: a mix of heavy funk beat and European electronic experimentation, wrapped together by Horn's undeniable ability to use the studio as a musical instrument. Yet the style took those singles to Number 1, and even managed to win respectable sales for the various re-release 'mixes' of the singles.

In October 1984 ZTT released *Welcome to the Pleasure Dome*. Somewhat longer than a normal single album, it was stretched out on to four sides, and came in a gatefold sleeve. The inner sleeves were covered with quotes from the band and from literature. In one typically mischievous piece of spin-off marketing, there was also a press-out order form for, among other Frankie ephemera, Jean Genet boxer shorts, the Kurt Weill sweatshirt, the Andre Gide socks and the Edith Sitwell shoulder bag.

The album took the listener on a guided tour of Horn's studio. As well as 'Relax' and 'War', it featured covers of 'Ferry Cross The Mersey' and Springsteen's 'Born To Run', all wrapped in long, exotic intros and segues featuring jungle noises, opera singers, you name it. It went straight to Number 1 in the UK album charts.

This was for many the snapping point. It was a brilliant piece of packaging, but the content was decidedly thin – a few powerful tunes padded out with what increasingly sounded like art-rock sound effects. In November ZTT released 'The Power Of Love', their most downbeat, traditional pop song, which also reached Number 1. On the band's first British tour, an 18-day round Britain trip, they played lengthy sets to rapturous audiences, and even had the doubters crediting Horn's 'puppets' with live abilities.

The power of marketing
At the end of 1985, rumours were flying around that, having staged the most outlandish smash-and-grab raid on pop in history, ZTT were moving on to concentrate on a newer signing, the German electropop group Propaganda. Frankie have been suspiciously quiet for some time, but were known to have been writing new material, due for release in 1986.

It is unlikely that Frankie could repeat that initial, delirious burst of success and stardom, and indeed it could be said that the idea of a 'comeback' is contrary to the very notion of Frankie Goes To Hollywood.

Armed with lessons learnt from an earlier put-on artist, Malcolm McLaren, Frankie, Morley and Horn took on the music industry from the *inside*. Even they were surprised by their success. Where McLaren had charged the doors of the music industry with a battering ram, Frankie were already inside with their feet up before even their first single reached the shops. And despite all the controversy and shock tactics, this was in fact little more than the classic factors of pure, disposable pop dressed up for a stylish cocktail party. It had that essential beat, it was about dressing up, and rebellion, and even if 'Relax' verged on the risqué, in 'The Power Of Love' they had a pining love song worthy, indeed reminiscent, of the Sixties boom.

What *was* different, however, was that they were doing it in the early Eighties, when many artists had responded to the warning of punk by ignoring it and adopting a pose of cynicism and decadence. Morley had adopted a term, 'post-modernism', from architecture theory, which holds that you can mix and match any manner of styles, the more outrageous the better, and ponents. The band split after 1986's poorly received and musically disappointing *Liverpool*. Though Paul Rutherford attempted a solo career, the three musicians vanished. Holly Johnson was the only band member to find subsequent fame, hitting Number 1 with his first solo album *Blast* after winning a lengthy court case over publishing rights.   JOHN GILL

ROCK '84

The flavour of the year in the UK was undoubtedly the flamboyant and expertly marketed Frankie Goes To Hollywood, who dominated the singles charts in 1984 with their saucy offerings 'Relax' and 'Two Tribes', proving that rock music still had the power to shock.

Michael Jackson, meanwhile, was still riding high on both sides of the Atlantic, Tina Turner made Number 1 for the first time in the US and rock stars took a stance against drugs and raised money for famine-relief.

Rock said a sad farewell to two soul giants – Jackie Wilson and Marvin Gaye – the latter tragically shot by his own father.

January
1 British R&B pioneer of the Sixties, Alexis Korner, dies at the age of 55, of lung cancer.
14 Paul McCartney's anti-war song 'Pipes Of Peace' is at Number 1 in the UK.
17 Linda McCartney is charged with importing cannabis at London's Heathrow Airport and later fined £75.
21 Soul artist Jackie Wilson, who had been in a coma since suffering a stroke on stage in 1975, dies, aged 49.
26 Michael Jackson's hair catches fire while filming a commercial.
28 'Relax', by Frankie Goes To Hollywood, tops the UK singles chart after being banned from Radio One.

February
16 Ethel Merman, the Broadway musical queen, dies at the age of 75.
Elton John marries studio engineer Renata Blauel in Sydney, Australia.

March
3 The Smiths debut album of the same name goes into the UK chart at Number 2.
15 Michael Jackson's *Thriller* LP's sales reach over 30 million.
31 Lionel Richie is top of the UK singles and album charts with 'Hello' and *Can't Slow Down*.

April
1 Soul superstar Marvin Gaye is shot dead by his father during an argument.
26 Jazz band leader Count Basie, aged 79, dies of cancer.

May
5 Duran Duran's single 'The Reflex' makes Number 1 in the UK.
19 A compilation album of Bob Marley's hits, *Legend*, enters the UK chart at Number 1.

June
2 'Wake Me Up Before You Go Go' is top UK singles chart, giving Wham! their first chart-topper.
16 Frankie Goes To Hollywood have their second UK Number 1 single with 'Two Tribes', which tops the chart for a record nine weeks.

July
7 Bruce Springsteen's LP *Born In The USA* is top of the US album chart.
21 Status Quo play their farewell gig at Milton Keynes Bowl.

August
Captain Sensible leaves The Damned. Virgin boss Richard Branson announces that London's Venue is to close.

September
1 Tina Turner, at 48, has her biggest hit yet with 'What's Love Got To Do With It?' which makes Number 1 in the US.
Helen Terry leaves Culture Club.

October
A nationwide anti-heroin campaign is aided by rock stars including Pete Townshend, Tom Robinson and Madness.

November
8 Fela Kuti, the African musician convicted of currency smuggling charges in Nigeria, is sentenced to five years in prison.
25 Band Aid's single 'Do They Know It's Christmas?' is released. It features, among others, Paul Weller and Midge Ure. All proceeds go to famine-relief in Ethiopia.

December
2 Islington's famous pub venue the Hope and Anchor closes down.
ZZ Top bass player Dusty Hill accidentally shoots himself with a gun he keeps in his boot. He makes a successful recovery after surgery.

ROCK '85

The big event of 1985 was the hugely successful Live Aid concert in July, staged in both the UK and the US, with a cast of hundreds and broadcast to an audience of millions. It was the culmination of Bob Geldof's Band Aid project and added a new dimension to political rock. The concert saw old faithfuls like David Bowie and Bob Dylan rubbing shoulders with newcomers Madonna and George Michael.

Paul Weller continued his commitment to causes with his involvement in campaigns in support of school leavers and the labour party, Stevie Wonder was arrested at an anti-apartheid demo, and Jerry Dammers teamed up with Robert Wyatt to raise money for African freedom fighters.

On the chart scene, the elegant Sade completed 23 weeks in the UK album chart Top Ten with her debut LP *Diamond Life*, and Madonna stormed in with a string of hits.

January
7 Sade's debut album, *Diamond Life*, becomes the best-selling UK LP of 1984, after 23 weeks in the UK Top Ten. Prince's album *Purple Rain* has been top of the US LP chart for almost six months.
11 Iron Maiden, Queen, AC/DC and Whitesnake appear at the Brazilian Rock Festival in Rio.
29 The US version of Band Aid release 'We Are The World', featuring over 40 artists.

February
2 Foreigner top the US and UK singles chart with 'I Want To Know What Love Is'. Stevie Wonder is arrested at an anti-apartheid demo in Washington.

March
28 Michael Jackson visits Madame Tussaud's – the famous waxworks – to witness the unveiling of his wax effigy.
29 Thompson Twin Tom Bailey collapses from exhaustion and has to take a break from work.
Sting plays his debut solo concert in New York.

April
6 Phil Collins dominates the charts: his LP *No Jacket Required* is top in the UK and US, his single 'One More Night' is Number 1 in the US, and the duet with Philip Bailey 'Easy Lover' is top of the UK chart.
7 Wham! play a concert in Peking.

May
US heart throb Bruce Springsteen marries Julianne Phillips in Oregon.

June
15 Bryan Ferry's first album for three years – *Boys And Girls* – goes straight into the UK LP chart at Number 1.
21 Sixties rock show 'Ready Steady Go!' is repeated on Channel Four.
27 Jimmy Somerville (ex-Bronski Beat) unveils his new band The Communards at London's Heaven club in a benefit for Gay's The Word bookshop.
30 John Lennon's psychedelic Rolls Royce fetches over two million dollars in a New York auction.

July
13 Live Aid – the massive marathon rock event – takes place in the UK and the US.
19 The three-day WOMAD Festival on Mersea Island, Essex, begins. It features artists from all over the world.
27 'There Must Be An Angel', by Eurythmics, reaches Number 1 in the UK.

August
Duran Duran singer Simon Le Bon is rescued after his yacht 'Drum' capsizes in the storm-tossed seas off Cornwall.

September
14 David Bowie and Mick Jagger make Number 1 in the UK with their version of the single 'Dancing In The Street'.
20 The Communards, Billy Bragg and Everything But The Girl play at the Nicaragua Libre! concert at Brixton Academy.
28 Madonna's album *Like A Virgin* tops the UK LP chart.

October
24 Siouxsie Sioux dislocates her knee on stage at Hammersmith Odeon. She continues the tour with her leg in plaster. Robert Wyatt, ex-Specials Jerry Dammers and the SWAPO singers release the single 'The Wind Of Change' to raise money for African freedom fighters.

November
2 Iron Maiden top the UK album chart with *Live After Death*.
12 The revamped Virgin Megastore on London's Oxford Street opens. It now boasts its own radio station, cafe and waxworks of stars including Meatloaf and Prince.
16 Feargal Sharkey has a UK Number 1 with the single 'A Good Heart'.
Paul Weller and other musicians join the Red Wedge – dedicated to return a labour government at the next election.

December
25 Former Thin Lizzy frontman Phil Lynott is rushed to hospital after a drink and drugs binge at his Richmond home. He dies 11 days later of heart failure and pneumonia.
27 Simon Le Bon marries model Yasmin Parvenah at an Oxford registry office.
31 US Fifties rock star Rick Nelson and his band are killed in a plane crash on route to appear at a concert in Dallas.

Above left: Marvin Gaye, shot by his father in April 1984. Far left: The Smiths charmed their way into the charts with their debut album. Left: Old timers David Bowie and Mick Jagger camp it up together. Above: Another of rock's casualties, Phil Lynott, who overdosed late in 1985.

The Charts

Waiting for something to happen...

THE EARLY EIGHTIES was an exciting period for rock music, with a wealth of new groups, sounds and images exploding on to the scene. The mid Eighties saw many of those groups consolidating their new-found success, but as the original impetus of London's club scene faded, there was a sense of emptiness, of waiting for something to happen.

The rock audience waited to see if the clubs could give them another star to follow Boy George. Marilyn thought he was that person and had a solitary hit with 'Cry And Be Free' before disappearing as quickly as he had arrived.

Meanwhile the world's attention, for so long fixed on the UK, had begun to drift away, looking towards America – the destination for many of Britain's top groups. Most of Britain's élite toured the States, with just as many American acts successfully visiting the UK.

At the front of the pack was Prince, Detroit's diminutive wonder. Thanks to an enormously lucrative movie, *Purple Rain*, and an accompanying soundtrack, Prince finally cast off the shackles of a cult following. In his wake, but still playing that curious blend of rock and disco (so acceptable on America's music video station MTV), were Kool And The Gang. Their singles 'Straight Ahead', 'Joanna', 'Fresh', 'Misled' and 'Cherish' certainly kept their accountants happy during 1984 and 1985. The biggest act to come out of the US in this period was Madonna. She had a couple of moderate successes in 1984 with the singles 'Holiday' and 'Lucky Star' before taking the charts by storm the following year with six massive hit singles (on both sides of the Atlantic) that included 'Like A Virgin' and 'Material Girl'.

The boys make it big ...

For Britain the flame of Frankie Goes To Hollywood had burned both brightly and briefly in 1984 with their long-running hit singles 'Relax' and 'Two Tribes'. But in 1985 the group released only one single – the title track from their LP *Welcome To The Pleasuredome*, highlighting the demise of the 'pop single' in the Eighties, when album tracks were increasingly released to sell the album, in a blatant and simple piece of marketing.

In the end it was left for Bushey's Wham! to carry the torch for Britain. Worldwide George Michael and Andrew Ridgeley were Britain's most successful act since the days of the Beatles and the Rolling Stones. Wham!'s LP *Make It Big* did just that: virtually every track became a hit. Meanwhile, Culture Club slowly disappeared from view. 'War Song' proved a popular single for them, but the follow-up, 'The Medal Song', barely made the Top Forty and a planned third single from the LP *Waking Up With The House On Fire* was scrapped. Rivals Duran Duran fared better, thanks largely to shrewd management which, amongst other things, forced the group to re-mix the single 'The Reflex' (it eventually made Number 1) as well as maintaining control over publicity and performance. In 1985 the group split temporarily to form the Power Station and Arcadia. Both were successful projects, but the Duran Duran song of 1985 'A View To A Kill' outsold both ventures.

One of the surprise success stories of 1985 must surely be that of Tears For Fears. The end of 1983 saw them floundering with the dismal offering 'The Way You Are', but their excellent second LP, *Songs From The Big Chair*, broke them into the big time. 'Shout', 'Everybody Wants To Rule The World' and 'Head Over Heels' were huge worldwide hit singles. By the end of the year Tears For Fears were one of the world's top bands – proving that good music with no frills could still take a group to the top.

... And so do the ladies

If Tears For Fears had no recognisable image, then Sade Adu had a surfeit. She oozed class and produced an album that somehow bottled it. Her debut LP *Diamond Life* shimmered with sophistication; it was the best-selling album of 1984 and was followed up with the million-selling

1985

album *Promise* at the end of 1985. No less talented than Sade, if not as successful, was Alison Moyet who had a trio of great pop songs: 'Love Resurrection', 'All Cried Out' and 'Invisible'. Sade and Alison Moyet led the way for British women with Eurythmics' Annie Lennox continuing to impress and Bonnie Tyler enjoying success with the single 'Holding Out For A Hero' in September 1985. American women more than held their own – the Pointer Sisters, Sister Sledge and Chaka Kahn all enjoyed hit singles. Tina Turner outdid them all, though, turning in an energetic performance with the huge hits 'What's Love Got To Do With It?' and 'Mad Max (Beyond The Thunderdome)'. Two other prominent female solo stars were Princess and Dee C. Lee (vocalist with the Style Council), who had hits with 'Say I'm Your No. 1' and 'See The Day', respectively.

In fact, 1985 saw many of music's 'old guard' re-surface – Foreigner, for instance, had the year's first Number 1 single with 'I Want To Know What Love Is', and later that year evergreens David Bowie and Mick Jagger made Number 1 with the classic 'Dancing In The Street'. Bryan Ferry

Below left: Lionel Richie, on stage at Live Aid. Below centre: Bronski Beat before Jimmy Somerville's departure to form the Communards. Right: The male Madonna? – glamour, glitter and lots of frills from Prince in Purple Rain.

reappeared, as did Slade, and Queen and Dire Straits increased their following.

There was a host of singles during this period that came from movies. Glenn Fry and Harold Faltermeyer had hits from *Beverly Hills Cop*, Kenny Loggins had 'Footloose', Ray Parker did 'Ghostbusters', Stevie Wonder's Number 1 'I Just Called To Say I Love You' came from the movie *The Woman In Red* and Simple Minds' hit 'Don't You (Forget About Me)' came from *The Breakfast Club*.

The return of rock

Rock music in all forms made a real comeback in the mid Eighties, whether it was on the tail end of punk (Simple Minds and U2) or genuine throwbacks to the Sixties and Seventies like Marillion and Dire Straits. It seemed that some kind of reaction against pure pop had set in and that people were looking for a harder edge to their music. The music of Simple Minds and U2, if at times rather pompous, always retained that 'smell of the street' that had been so important for Bruce Springsteen. The success of his world tour in 1984-5 highlighted this. Combining a dynamic performance with rock'n'roll, Springsteen had audiences clamouring for more. In the wake of such bands trailed the Alarm, the Waterboys and The Cult, all looking to build on the foundations laid by them.

Alternatively, for those who wanted to dance away from pop music rather than hit guitar chords, there was the music that spilt over from the clubs and discos into the charts, 'Trapped' by Colonel Abrams being the biggest dance hit of 1985. The watered-down soul of groups like Loose Ends and Five Star proved a welcome diversion from the usual pop attractions.

Overall, perhaps the most significant feature of the mid Eighties was the erosion of pop's boundaries. For the first time all the above categories became acceptable pop music. One could listen to Jesus And Mary Chain's barrage of noise (hiding surprisingly sweet melodies) and yet still like the more traditional form of Dire Strait's 'Money For Nothing' or 'Brothers In Arms'. People were going into shops and coming out clutching Marillion records in one hand and Spandau Ballet ones in the other, the tribalism of previous years having all but disappeared.

It was hard to say whether this was particularly good or bad; the general public's perception of what was good popular music had certainly broadened and diversified but at times there seemed to be a general merging of sound, with the oldest and newest talents sounding alike.

PAUL BURSCHE

Above left: Tears For Fears shout it out. Centre: Dee C. Lee – from Wham! to the Style Council and finally into the chart as a solo artist. Left: A-Ha, pop's most unlikely superstars from Norway, who finally broke into the UK charts in late 1985 with 'Take On Me' and look set to achieve world domination in 1986.

The best-selling records of the late Eighties showed few new names—and one or two surprising old ones. The Grateful Dead's return to the top of the US chart in 1987—and a hit single with 'Touch Of Grey'—was perhaps the most surprising, but the charts of that year had a familiar look: Pink Floyd, Bruce Springsteen, George Harrison and Foreigner followed the Dead at the top, with only John Cougar Mellencamp—at a 'youthful' 36—flying the flag for new acts.

In Britain, young teenage girls held sway. In the wake of Madonna came the flood: Kylie Minogue, Tiffany, Belinda Carlisle, Hazell Dean, Debbie Gibson all popped up with strings of hit singles. Most of these stars were in fact American—so it was fitting that British George Michael should set a record by scoring six Top Five singles in the US from his *Faith* album.

This was one of the few records Michael Jackson didn't hold—at least, not at the time of writing. He and his *Bad* album continued to define black music at its most popular. While his former patron Diana Ross re-signed to Motown in an attempt to rescue her flagging fortunes, Whitney Houston took up her mantle and monopolised the US Number 1 slot for two years with singles from two finely crafted albums. Elsewhere, Prince gave Jacko notice of his challenge for his crown, while UK trio the Christians found great success with some home-grown soul.

INTO A D·I·G·I·T·A·L FUTURE

While familiar names littered the charts, alternatives to vinyl were changing the face of musical entertainment

Below: The multi-platinum success of Foreigner emphasised the United States' continuing late-Eighties' fascination with adult-oriented rock, bought on compact disc and watched in studio.

Where to now?

If the charts of the late Eighties showed an alarming conservatism, there was enormous uncertainty and confusion as to the format in which the music fans of the Nineties would purchase their favourite sounds.

1988 was the first year in which British record companies made more money from the compact disc sales than vinyl—and the trend looked set to continue worldwide. Cassette tapes still took the lion's share of the UK market—thanks largely to the Walkman phenomenon—but even this looked likely to change given the rapidly falling price of 'Discmen' and the new, smaller 3-inch CD format which had become the industry standard for singles. Portable players were already being manufactured specifically to play the smaller disc, with consequent size and weight savings to the hardware. And compact disc video (or CDV) was being marketed as successor to the ill-fated laserdisc system to provide visuals alongside digital sounds.

The vinyl single itself was once more said to be in terminal decline—a spate of affairs pundits had been predicting since the advent of progressive album-orientated rock in the late Sixties and early Seventies. Yet this time the death knell could be sounded with some justification: in reaching the UK Number 1 position with the re-released 'He Ain't Heavy' in 1988, the Hollies failed to sell enough records to place the single in the Top Twenty of the year in which it was originally released, 1970.

One factor that had harmed the single, in the UK at least, was the wide availability of single material on compilation albums, which repeatedly hogged the top album spot—especially at Christmas. As a response to this, the British Phonographic Industry banned 'various artist' compilations from the charts from the beginning of 1989, though reaction to this move was mixed. Record companies would benefit in

Above: US chart-topper Debbie Gibson showed more talent than most of her teenage 'bimbette' rivals by writing her own material. Unlike Madonna, however, her fashion sense found few takers.

Below: Michael Jackson indulges his fantasies in the Captain Eo *film. Jackson's appeal transcended musical boundaries, as sales of albums like* Thriller *and* Bad *proved.*

the long term, it was felt, but they also had a stake in the financial success of these albums which could be threatened by the ban.

Compact discs were also clearly affecting buying patterns. Groups like Dire Straits, with fans clearly in the 20-35 age range said to be the format's chief adherents, saw their albums—*Brothers In Arms* was a prime example—registering a large percentage of total sales in the new, more lucrative format. The Beatles' re-releases on CD saw millions of fan re-purchasing albums they already possessed on vinyl, pushing the records back into the charts. In 1988, EMI released all 22 Fab Four singles as 3-inch discs as well as marketing the set of albums, cassettes and CDs with a wooden embossed case. As ever, marketing was the name of the game.

Digital piracy?

The status of DAT (Digital Audio Tape) remained unclear. At the end of 1988 there had still been no industry agreement as to a spoiling device to prevent digital copies being taken of compact discs—a practice that could result in master-quality pirate copies and a consequent effect on sales. It was widely assumed that Sony's takeover of CBS had been a tactical move to promote DAT by forcing competing record companies to release their software in the format, but there were no early signs of this happening.

The satellite and cable TV revolution promised for Europe in the Nineties looked set to have an effect on pop viewing and buying habits. In the US, MTV had abandoned anything but rock, but were forced to change their tune—coincidentally or otherwise, just before Michael Jackson unleashed *Bad*—and re-admit dance music. In an ideal world, cable and satellite should provide unlimited choice for fans of all genres . . . but this remained very much in the lap of the programmers.

NEW COUNTRY

Taking tradition into the '90s

Hank Williams Jr follows in his late father's footsteps, bringing country music to a new audience.

With the pop crossover success of country music in the Seventies, it was difficult to see how it could improve on its position. Its audience profile was ageing rapidly—and, as established stars like Dolly Parton moved towards Hollywood and the middle of the road, country in the Eighties appeared sorely in need of rejuvenation.

This came in the shape of New Country, a movement some saw as a marketing exercise but which had a fair degree of artistic validity. Sometimes known as New Traditionalists, these were artists in their twenties and thirties who typically utilised time-honoured country instrumentation—steel guitar, fiddle and mandolin—to reach a new audience raised on rock'n'roll.

Country had enjoyed a brief renaissance of popularity with the rock audience around the time of the film *Urban Cowboy* in 1980, one of John Travolta's decreasingly successful *Saturday Night Fever* follow-ups. But country itself couldn't at that point supply the music and the artists to capitalise on that brief exposure.

Tony Brown, A&R head of MCA Records in Nashville, summarised the roots of the movement thus: "What happened in the Sixties and Seventies was country music was getting watered down, losing its focus. From the Seventies, anyone who was in country didn't want to be associated with country so they tried to dress up as pop singers, tried to make their music close to pop so they wouldn't be associated with hillbillies. So now you find these new artists who love the art form and are determined to bring it back: they like the music, the way it's recorded, the way people are dressed."

Skaggs appeal

Instrumental virtuosity—an attribute prized by country and rock audiences—saw Ricky Skaggs rise to fame. For several years, he was a stalwart of Emmylou Harris's Hot Band—and this was particularly appropriate since Harris was a former girlfriend of Gram Parsons, a country music rebel in his day.

Coming from a bluegrass background, Skaggs's use of largely acoustic instruments was a reaction against the excesses of the 'Nashville Sound' with its all-pervading strings. And though the Eighties ended with Skaggs approaching Nashville establishment status, no-one would deny his trailblazing work earlier in the decade.

Austin, Texas's Steve Earle's rootsy brand of music exemplified by his debut *Guitar Town* (1986) might have been called country rock had the softer, mid-Seventies music of Eagles, Poco and their like not become synonymous with the term. Earle owed more to Hank Williams and the country of the Fifties that, along with black music, had been one of the twin inspirations of Elvis Presley.

Family favourites

Country had always been about families. And New Country recognised this by including in its first wave a plethora of family-based acts. One in particular the Judds were worthy of mention—not only for their music but for the fact that the act spanned a generation. Mother (Naomi) and daughter (Wynonna) harmonised beautifully to simple, acoustic backing—and

Above: Old country meets new as Randy Travis accepts an award from old-timer Charley Pride. Juice Newton looks on.

found great success.

In the wake of the Judds, New Country threw up the McCarters, Sweethearts of the Rodeo and others, while the children of famous country stars like Rosanne Cash and Hank Williams Jr brought familiar names to the New Country roster.

Perhaps the biggest New Country star was Randy Travis, whose first album *Storms Of Life* (1986) sold two million. His second album *Always And Forever* topped the country chart in

Left: Dwight Yoakam found success with a rough-hewn country sound he brought to Nashville from California.

1987, while *Old 8x10* provided the Top Twenty crossover in 1988. Fresh faced good looks, a great voice and a willingness to use outside writers marked Travis, a former dishwasher from North Carolina, down as a long-lasting talent.

New Country stars didn't *have* to hail from near Nashville—or even from Tennessee at all. Female Canadian vocalist k. d. lang (the absence of capitals is intentional) was exceptionally popular, while David O'Donnell hailed from Ireland. Dwight Yoakam brought his Buck Owens/Merle Haggard influences all the way from California, while Lyle Lovett, like Earle and Nanci Griffith, was a Texan—a fact that could be divined, claimed an anonymous Nashville music publisher, because "there's too many words in his songs".

Like Griffith and many others, Lovett survived his formative years on independent labels before being signed up in the record companies' search for New Country talent. To put this in context, it should be noted that Seventies superstar Barbara Mandrell ended 1988 without a current record contract.

A new breed

John Cowan of New Grass Revival, Nashville's 'house band' who session for Skaggs, Williams Jr, Travis and others when not recording as themselves, explained the appeal of New Country by describing himself and his band as "Beatles kids. As we've grown older we've gravitated towards this kind of music." He continued: "The guy in the K-Mart doesn't have girls, motorcycles and drugs, he's got his bills to pay but he can't pay 'em. So maybe people can relate to these country songs."

By the late Eighties, country was feeding back to rock and pop as a prime influence. U2 played a country set as their own support act in their 1987 US tour, following up by recording at Memphis's Sun Studios. Neil Young's *Old Ways* (1985)—ironically labelled 'uncommercial' by his label, Geffen—saw him duetting with Waylon Jennings, Willie Nelson and other country greats.

But it was Bruce Springsteen's adoption of the country idiom for 1987's *Tunnel Of Love* that set the seal on a couple of years that without exaggeration ensured a new generation of white Americans would inherit the music of their fathers.

As for Nashville itself, it really hadn't changed that much—or if it had, there was still evidence of the old order. Hank Williams Jr's souvenir supermarket vies for trade with Conway Twitty's 'Twitty City' and Dolly Parton's 'Dollywood' twin theme parks. And alongside George Jones' Car Collectors Hall of Fame stands hoardings advertising George Strait menswear. Austin might have put in a bid to become the New Country capital—but Nashville was still Music City.

Left: The winsome Nanci Griffith filled Emmylou Harris's shoes as female star of the New Country Show.

Michael Jackson

Solo success for black music's baddest star

Michael Jackson's solo career (see pages 1582-1585) had always threatened to outshine his brothers—and in 1983 the success of *Thriller*, its associated singles and videos did just that. Then, despite a mammoth five-year gap that would have seen most teen idols lose their constituency completely, he proved he remained the world's Number One solo performer with the triumphant *Bad* (1988).

1979's *Off The Wall*, with its six-million sales, had proved conclusively he had the attributes required for a solo career away from Motown, where his career and that of his brothers had been nurtured. The estimated 40 million sales success of *Thriller* took him into another league altogether.

We are family

Michael's professional divorce from his brothers followed the concerts to promote 1984's *Victory*, a tour much criticised for the over-zealous and expensive merchandising operation that accompanied it, quite apart from any shortcomings of show and music. Shortly afterwards, Jermaine left his brothers and Motown—he'd stayed on having married into the Gordy family—for a solo career with Arista. Michael, however, seemed in no hurry to follow *Thriller*. He did, however, make a film for Walt Disney entitled *Captain Eo*, which leaned heavily on ET-style special effects.

A huge contract to promote Pepsi nearly ended in tragedy when his hair was set alight during the filming of a TV commercial. But Jackson proved his motivation was more than just money when he co-wrote (with Lionel Richie) the USA For Africa anthem 'We Are The World'.

The Jackson myth was fuelled by rumour: facelifts, skin lightening, life in an oxygen tent, his constant companionship with monkey Bubbles, romance with Elizabeth Taylor, Brooke Shields, Diana Ross—all these fanciful (or some not so fanciful) tales kept him in the news. He even tried—and failed—to buy the skeleton of John Merrick, the Elephant Man, from a London hospital. But sooner or later he was to let the music answer for him.

The wait is over

When *Bad* was finally released in September 1987 it predictably entered charts worldwide at the very top. Pre-orders broke CBS's record figure at an amazing 2.25 million—and though the songs couldn't live up to *Thriller's* uniform excellence they did pretty well regardless: five consecutive US Top Five singles compared with *Thriller's* four-in-a-row feat—and five Number Ones by April 1988's 'Dirty Diana'. What was more, he certainly managed to worry Bruce Springsteen, whose *Tunnel Of Love* was delayed a month so CBS's record pressing plants could take a breather.

Jackson started his world tour in September 1987 in Tokyo, where touts offered tickets at 17 times face value. The story was the same elsewhere: in the UK his outdoor concert at Aintree Racecourse was the biggest ever by a single artist. Ticket applications for his first two Wembley concerts exceeded 1.5 million—20 times capacity—and he played eventually to 750,000 people.

But certain records remained immune from

Opposite: Michael Jackson hails the huge fan following which flocked to see his 1988 world tour. Top: Reminiscing about Motown days with the company's founder, Berry Gordy. Above: Shy and reclusive, Jackson sought the company of fellow celebrities like Elizabeth Taylor.

Bad's best efforts: *Thriller* had won eight Grammy awards: its successor failed to win one. But manager Frank Dileo summarised the official feeling to *Rolling Stone* "What happens if *Bad* doesn't match *Thriller* but ends up selling 23 million and becomes the second largest album of all time—are people gonna say we're losers?"

The last tour?

By the end of 1988, worldwide sales of *Bad* were estimated as approaching 20 million—but it wasn't the only best-seller he released that year, *Moonwalk*, his autobiography, shot to the top of the lists, despite revealing little of Jackson's own personality.

This suggested that Michael's future was probably not as a book author—a fact confirmed by his manager. He suggested the world had witnessed Jackson's last tour: "then we'll probably go into making movies." In his own time, of course.

243

U2

The continuing story of Eire's most famous sons

By 1984, U2 had established themselves as Eire's biggest rock act (see pages 2270-2271 for an account of their early career).

If *War,* U2's first UK chart-topping album had pushed their US-inspired brand of power-chord rock to its limit: *Under A Blood Red Sky* (1983) took it to the stage. The biggest effect of the album was to cut the profits of the bootleggers who'd been following the band around and releasing almost every show since each was different in some way. One such moment, captured on original copies of *Blood Red Sky,* was an improvisation of two show tunes, 'Send In The Clowns' and 'America', in the middle of 'The Electric Co'.

The performance at Red Rocks, Colorado, was completed in spite of torrential rain that had continued for two days solid—and the album was sold at a cheaper price than usual as a bonus to fans who responded by making it a UK Number 2. Bono described it as "The full stop at the end of a sentence . . . we are beginning a new paragraph."

Eno in charge

Former Roxy Music keyboardist Brian Eno was employed with Canadian Daniel Lanois to produce 1984's *The Unforgettable Fire.* Adopting a completely new approach with Eno, who'd achieved fame as an unorthodox producer with Talking Heads, the band freed themselves of the self-imposed straitjacket of playing 'live' in the studio. The sound was now built up gradually and deliberately, using random guitar tunings to achieve interesting effect.

Despite the Celtic setting of Eire's Slane Castle, it was again America and matters American that occupied the lyrics of songs such as 'Indian Summer Sky', 'Elvis Presley And America' and 'MLK'—like the first single, 'Pride', dedicated to Martin Luther King.

The religious aspect to the band that first surfaced on *October* was now even more obvious. Bono was quick to qualify all this in case they were misunderstood—or, worse, claimed by either side in the Irish troubles. "Because we come from Ireland," he explained, "we are

Below: U2 pick up a Grammy. From left, the Edge, Adam Clayton, Larry Mullen, Bono. Above right: Bono and Springsteen share a joke on the Amnesty International tour, 1988. Below right: The singer in full flight on stage. The Rattle And Hum *film was acclaimed as a concert classic.*

aware that religion can be divisive, bigoted and elitist. We are all alienated from most forms of organised religion."

'Pride (In The Name Of Love)' reached Number 3 in the UK, the title track reaching Number 6—and the album went straight in at the top. In America, the source of so many of Bono's lyrical ideas, they hit the Top 20 and made the cover of *Rolling Stone*—a first for an Irish group.

Words from the wise

After their appearance at Live Aid, the band retired with Eno to record *The Joshua Tree*, finally released in 1987. This was the first album since their debut that Bono had come into the studio knowing exactly what he was going to sing—and it showed. 'Bullet The Blue Sky' contrasted New York's hustle and bustle with US oppression in El Salvador and Nicaragua. 'Mothers Of The Disappeared' concerned political oppression. And 'One Tree Hill'—dedicated, as was the album as a whole, to roadie Greg Carroll who died in a motorbike accident—cited the late Chilean folksinger and political activist Victor Jara.

'I Still Haven't Found What I'm Looking For' was the first of three successful singles from the album, which topped the UK charts. The band then took the whole of 1987 to tour the United States—a period documented by 1988's double LP and film *Rattle And Hum*. Both film and record were full of contradictions about the nature of the rock'n'roll life, the state of America (Bono's obsession these past few albums) and the endless search for spiritual satisfaction.

Bono found a kindred spirit in his search in Bob Dylan, with whom he collaborated on some material. The LP also included U2's version of Dylan's 'All Along The Watchtower'. His presence, together with a cameo appearance by BB King, confirmed—if proof indeed were needed—that U2 had entered the supergroup league. There seemed no limit to their achievements and influence on late Eighties rock.

DIRE STRAITS

The relentless rise of the first CD supergroup

Dire Straits' early career is covered on pages 2218-2200. Their elevation to Eighties supergroup status could be traced to two major factors: the rise of the compact disc and the high profile of Mark Knopfler as a solo artist, producer and session guitar-for-hire.

In 1982, he had announced his intention to specialise in film scores with the haunting soundtrack to *Local Hero*. Two years later he found time to release two more celluloid collaborations: a three-track 12-inch EP of music for *Comfort And Joy* and a full album's worth of Irish-flavoured soft rock for *Cal,* on which he was assisted by Paul Brady on whistle.

Producing was another of Knopfler's fortes: June 1984 saw him at the desk for Aztec Camera's *The Knife* following his work on Dylan's *Infidels* the previous year.

Below: Straits survivors John Illsley (left) and Mark Knopfler (centre) trade licks with the besuited Little Steven. Above right: Knopfler wrings every last ounce of emotion out of his Fender Stratocaster. Below right: Having fun with another well-known guitar exponent, Eric Clapton.

Arms and the men
Brothers In Arms was released in May 1985 and saw a new Dire Straits built around the nucleus of Knopfler and John Illsley. New guitarist Jack Sonni was recruited from a New York guitar shop, while Guy Fletcher and, later, Chris White were added on second keyboards and sax respectively. Terry Williams and Alan Clark retained their positions.

The album was the largest-ever 'ship' (advance orders) in compact disc history—and appropriately the 'Live In '85' tour was sponsored by CD specialists Philips. A tour sampler CD of highlights from the album rocketed in value and is now perhaps the world's most collectable compact disc. The album hit the top spot in Canada, the US, UK, France, Germany

and 20 other countries within weeks of release.

July 1985 was a significant month for Dire Straits: they appeared for 13 consecutive record-breaking nights at London's Wembley Arena, on the 4th before the Prince and Princess of Wales: Knopfler was thenceforth a leading figure in rock events organised by the Prince's charitable Trust. On the 13th they played a major part in Live Aid—and the single 'Money For Nothing' gave them a US Number 1 in its wake.

With Sting guesting on backing vocals, that track was later to supply the title of their 1988 hits compilation. It inspired an especially inventive video with animated figures complementing concert film of the band. The title track, when released as a single, also featured animation in its video, placing Dire Straits as unlikely forerunners in the genre. Cynics would suggest this was in an attempt to compensate for the band's lack of visual identity.

By mid 1986, *Brothers* was a six times platinum seller in the UK (1,800,000 copies sold) and five times in the US. Significantly, too, it was the world's best-selling compact disc. Not surprisingly, the band elected to release single after single from the album as they enjoyed a deserved break—and this, apart from anything else, allowed Straits soundalike Chris Rea the chance to prosper with his album *Dancing With Strangers*.

More scores to settle

Knopfler himself refused to rest, however: summer 1986 saw him contribute music to Scorsese's *Color Of Money* and produce a couple of tracks for Tina Turner's *Break Every Rule*. His first collaboration with Turner, on the album *Private Dancer* (1984), had been his title track, also a best-selling single.

In 1987 he collaborated with country legend Chet Atkins for an Amnesty International Ball and a TV documentary. Later that year he returned to the soundtrack arena with an album's worth of music for *The Princess Bride*. Fearful, perhaps, of Dire Straits comparisons, he chose to employ Willy De Ville as vocalist on the non-instrumental title track.

In June 1988, shortly after John Illsley released his second solo LP *Glass*, Dire Straits reformed to appear at the 70th birthday celebrations of Nelson Mandela. But shortly afterwards Knopfler and keyboardist Alan Clark, still a mainstay of the band, chose to submerge themselves in Eric Clapton's ensemble for a US tour.

Such anonymity couldn't last, however, and October saw the release of the compilation *Money For Nothing*. Typically, however, Knopfler preferred to be interviewed about his latest production job—an album, *Land Of Dreams*, for Randy Newman. Future plans at this juncture were another soundtrack LP—for the long awaited *Last Exit To Brooklyn*—and a new Dire Straits album for 1989 release.

Few would have predicted Dire Straits' metamorphosis from Seventies pub-rockers to Eighties supergroup. But Mark Knopfler and sidekick John Illsley, together with sundry hired hands, have managed the feat without breaking sweat or losing the appeal of their music. In this image-conscious video era, theirs is a refreshing success story.

PRINCE

Purple reign of the soul sex symbol

'The new Hendrix': 'the next Michael Jackson': 'the black Bowie'. Just three of the more printable epithets applied to Prince as the young Minneapolis-born guitarist (born 7 June 1960) bumped and grinded his way to fame and fortune. And even after he hit the top of the charts, critics were still left looking for words. One thing seemed certain, however: that Prince Rogers Nelson (his real name) would be a major force in Nineties music.

From the beginning, his career seemed full of contradictions: his first album—*For You*, released in 1978—bore a dedication to God, while song titles like 'Soft And Wet' betrayed a less than religious lyrical content. Conflict between the sacred and the secular had been a constant thread in black music from the outset: it was a problem which Prince never quite resolved.

Impure thoughts
Prince (1979) contained the US Number 11 single 'I Wanna Be Your Lover', a track which brought the flamboyant artist to the attention of a wider audience. But the aptly titled *Dirty Mind*, released in 1980, shocked many would-be fans with songs of incest and oral sex. Such outrageousness was better accepted by a rock audience, brought up on Alice Cooper and Frank Zappa, than the innately conservative black music establishment. Thenceforth, Prince was to be filed under rock.

1981's *Controversy* predictably created just that, Prince chanting the Lord's Prayer during the title track which stood alongside such sexually explicit cuts as 'Do Me Baby'. But it was the following year's double *1999* that brought the commercial breakthrough he'd waited for. Five million copies later, Prince was finally a star.

MTV took to him immediately: the video for his US Number 6 single 'Little Red Corvette' was one of the first by a black performer to be played regularly on the network. His visual similarity to Jimi Hendrix plus the predominant electric guitar in his R&B-orientated material made him a natural soul-pop crossover.

Purple Rain (1984) was not only an album but a full-length film, naturally starring Prince himself. Low-budget and patchily produced, the film merged live footage—a wise move, since Prince's stage shows were never less than spectacular—with a vague showbiz plot. Reviews likened the five foot two Prince to Marlon Brando, while the semi-nude appearance of sultry singer Apollonia, once one of Prince's backing vocalists in Vanity 6, merely added to the sleaze appeal. Within weeks, *Purple Rain* headed the box-office charts.

Revolutions of the mind
His Minneapolis empire was growing apace: aside from Vanity 6, now stars in their own right, his group the Revolution spawned a spinoff in Wendy and Lisa, while several

associated artists appeared on Prince's Paisley Park label. Percussionist Sheila E launched a successful solo career from Prince's shadow, while in the strangest move of all Sheena Easton, once marketed as Britain's answer to Anne Murray, was transformed into a slinky vamp singing risque lyrics (for example, her Prince-penned hit single 'Sugar Walls').

Prince was also writing for other artists besides Easton: the Bangles and Chaka Khan were just two acts to benefit from his compositions, while Minneapolis band the Time achieved two gold records, sales of which undoubtedly benefited from the association.

Though *Purple Rain* and its hit singles—'When Doves Cry' and 'Let's Go Crazy' were US chart-toppers, the title track a Number 2—brought Prince to a wider audience, long-time followers saw his music as a dilution of his earlier work. This was inevitable given the restrictions imposed by radio, but the rewards were clearly worthwhile.

In early 1985 Prince announced his retirement from live performance—but like Bowie and countless others, this resolution was not to last.

Prince of psychedelia
1985's *Around The World In A Day* dabbled

Opposite: Prince in typically flamboyant action. His provocative lyrics and exciting music may well make him the black music star of the Nineties. Above: Prince's film career seemed likely to continue in parallel with his musical efforts.

with psychedelia rather unsuccessfully, yet still spawned two US hits in 'Raspberry Beret' (2) and 'Pop Life' (7). It was his own first album on his own label, and was followed by the more consistent *Parade* in 1986. Subtitled 'Music From Under The Cherry Moon', another Prince film project, it contained a US chart-topping single in the superb 'Kiss'.

1987 saw *Sign O The Times*, a double set inevitably compared with *1999*—but Prince's next project, known as *The Black Album*, was not to see commercial release, allegedly due to its controversial lyrical content. Instead came *Lovesexy*, an album on which Prince exacted revenge for real or imagined censorship by posing nude with a giant flower stalk protruding between his legs! The compact disc, too, was one in the eye for authority: it was impossible for individual tracks to be programmed and had to be listened to in its entirety.

Always outrageous and rarely predictable, Prince continued his entertaining if unorthodox path through popular music. In the late Eighties, he was the only black music act to rival Michael Jackson in terms of sales or influence. Like Sly Stone before him, he combined elements of many different musics to create something unique—and while this continued he seemed likely to retain his importance.

ROCK '86

The charts were dominated by solo artists as groups seemingly go out of fashion. No discernible musical movement emerges, though Scandinavia produces a pop group to rival Abba in Norway's A-Ha. However, the three-man teen idols top the US and, later, UK charts with their first two releases.

January
11 The Pet Shop Boys register their first UK Number 1, 'West End Girls'. It goes on to top the US chart later in the year.
25 One-time Bob Dylan manager Albert Grossman, owner of the Bearsville label, dies on a transatlantic flight.

February
10 The British Phonographic Industry vote Phil Collins Best Male Artist.
15 Sade tops the US album charts with her second album *The Promise*.

March
8 Diana Ross tops the UK singles chart with 'Chain Reaction'. Her last UK Number 1 was in 1971 with 'I'm Still Waiting'.
29 Cliff Richard's 'Living Doll' scores its second UK Number 1 hit—the first was in 1959, this version a re-recording for charity.

April
Duran Duran announce the retirement of drummer Roger Taylor who, tired of the rock life, decides to manage a farm. Dave Clark, Sixties pop star turned impresario, opens *Time* in London's West End: Cliff Richard and David Cassidy both pass through the lead role in its two-year run.

May
17 Eire's Self Aid event in aid of the unemployed takes place in Dublin.
31 Former Genesis singer Peter Gabriel registers his second ever UK Number 1 album with *So*.

June
28 Wham! hit the top in the UK for the fourth time with their final, posthumous single, 'The Edge Of Heaven'.

July
5 In the absence of brother Michael, Janet Jackson grabs top spot in the US LP charts with *Control*.
24 Bob Geldof's pioneering work with Band Aid is recognised by an honorary knighthood from the Queen.

August
16 Madonna registers her second Number 1 album in the US with *True Blue*.
A US court clears former Black Sabbath vocalist Ozzy Osbourne and his song

Above: February chart-topper Sade. Below left: Neil Tennant (left) and Chris Lowe, the Pet Shop Boys, made it big in January.

'Suicide Solution' from responsibility for the suicide of American youth John McCollum.

September
22 Top UK independent band the Smiths sign to EMI despite being under contract to Rough Trade. The band split before EMI can release anything. Madness, one of Britain's best-loved pop groups to emerge from the Seventies ska revival, announce their dissolution. They return in 1988 with a smaller line-up as *The* Madness.

October
4 Paul Simon's *Graceland* LP, partly recorded in South Africa, is the UK's Number 1 album.

November
29 The five-album live set from Bruce Springsteen, *Live 1975-85,* tops the US chart.
Prince's backing band, the Revolution, split up.

December
27 Aided by an animated video, the late Jackie Wilson's 'Reet Petite' tops the UK singles chart—a record 19 years after first release.

ROCK '87

Record companies receive a much-needed boost as the compact disc catches on: it's the most significant new musical format since the cassette. Heavy rock is back in vogue with Bon Jovi among the front runners, while on the pop front George Michael, once of Wham!, emerges as the year's most notable new solo star.

January
Elton John enters hospital for an exploratory operation on his throat. Happily, he makes a full recovery.

February
14 Bon Jovi's *Slippery When Wet* becomes the first album of the year to be certified five million sales, just five months after release.
21 Philips and Sony announce they are collaborating on the 3-inch compact disc format later to become the industry standard for CD singles. They intend this to eventually replace the 7-inch vinyl 45.
26 The first four Beatles albums are released on compact disc.
28 The CDV (compact disc video) format makes its public debut.

March
The Grammy Awards bring wins for Anita Baker, Steve Winwood, Paul Simon, Bobby McFerrin, Robert Cray, Bruce Hornsby and others.

April
5 Paul Simon's London dates are picketed by Artists Against Apartheid, led by Jerry Dammers of the Specials.

May
9 The UK album chart is dominated for a month by two new, unknown acts—Curiosity Killed the Cat and Swing Out Sister.
George Michael's 'I Want Your Sex' is limited to night-time play by the BBC in Britain and banned entirely by some US radio stations, but still manages to make the Top Five in both countries.

June
4,000 East Germans riot near the Berlin Wall while a concert by Bowie, Eurythmics and Genesis takes place 400 yards to the West.

27 Whitney Houston becomes the first female artist in the history of the US chart to debut at Number 1 with her album *Whitney*.

July
The British Government announces a copyright bill containing a levy on blank cassette tapes. They drop this four months later in the face of criticism.

August
1 The Grateful Dead top the US LP charts with their comeback album, *In The Dark*.
2 Producer Alex Sadkin, who worked with Bob Marley, Duran Duran and Grace Jones, dies from injuries sustained in a Nassau car crash.
MTV invades Europe! The all-day music video station starts broadcasting in 14 countries.

September
1 Michael Jackson's long-awaited *Bad* album is released, with CBS Records'

Above: June was an historic month for America and Whitney Houston. Below left: Elton John, hospitalised in January, with his wife Renata.

best ever pre-order figure—2.25 million.
11 Peter Tosh, founder member of the Wailers, is murdered by gunmen in his Jamaica home.
12 Dead Kennedys' singer Jello Biafra walks free from an obscenity hearing on an allegedly obscene poster included in the band's album *Frankenchrist.*
21 Jaco Pastorius, virtuoso bass player formerly of Weather Report, dies after a fight in a Florida club, age 35.

October
MTV returns to playing dance (ie black) music after a year of 'rock only' programming.
16 Dave Robinson resigns as managing director of Stiff Records, the label he started with Jake Riviera in 1976.
17 Bruce Springsteen's *Tunnel Of Love* tops both US and UK album charts.

November
13 U2 play an open-air concert in San Francisco. The 'Save The Yuppie Show' was distinguished by vocalist Bono spray-painting a local monument with the slogan 'Rock'n'roll stops traffic'—an action for which he later apologised.
18 Japanese electronics giant Sony buys CBS Records.
21 George Harrison tops US LP charts with his album *Cloud Nine.*

December
5 The hits compilation *Now That's What I Call Music 10* tops the UK LP chart—the fifth year in succession a compilation has monopolised the top spot at Christmas.
10 Abba's Bjorn Ulvaeus and Agnetha Faltskog start a court case in Sweden in which they face tax evasion charges.
12 Zydeco legend Clifton Chenier dies, age 62, in Louisiana.

ROCK '88

This was undoubtedly a year for reformations: Led Zeppelin; The Who; Crosby, Stills, Nash and Young were just three big names to follow the lead of recently revived rock giants like Status Quo and Pink Floyd. The career of new supergroup the Traveling Wilburys—messrs Harrison, Dylan, Petty, Lynne and Orbison—was tragically shortened by the death of 'The Big O' in December.

January
11 Whitney Houston's 'So Emotional' hits the top of the US chart, giving her a record 6 successive Number 1s—a distinction shared with the Beatles and Bee Gees.
16 Tina Turner's appearance before a 180,000 audience in Rio de Janeiro sets a world rock concert record.

February
1 US AOR group the Cars announce their split.
8 The Who reform to play at the British Phonographic Industry awards.

March
10 Andy Gibb, younger brother of Bee Gees Maurice, Barry and Robin, suffers a fatal heart attack, aged 30.
26 *Viva Hate,* Smiths lead singer Morrissey's first solo LP, enters the UK chart at Number 1.

April
5 James Brown is arrested for the alleged attempted murder of his wife. The charges are later dropped.
9 R&B pioneer Brook Benton dies in New York, age 56.
20 *Moonwalk,* Michael Jackson's autobiography, goes on sale.

May
13 Bon Jovi manager Doc McGhee is convicted of drug smuggling. His five-year sentence is commuted to community service in a drug rehabilitation centre he offers to found.
14 Atlantic Records' 40th Anniversary celebrations at New York's Madison Square Garden sees the reformation of Led Zeppelin and Crosby, Stills and Nash, Zeppelin bring in Jason Bonham to replace his late father John.
17 Wet Wet Wet top the UK chart with a cover of the Beatles' 'With A Little Help From My Friends'. The other side of the charity single features Billy Bragg's version of 'She's Leaving Home', also from the *Sgt. Pepper* album.

Below: Hope I die before I get old? The Who bury the hatchet for a February reformation.

June
11 Black African leader Nelson Mandela's 70th birthday is celebrated by a day of music and dance at London's Wembley Stadium—like Live Aid, it is televised to a massive worldwide audience.
The Moody Blues' *Sur La Mer* enters the US Top Five despite failing to make the Top Twenty at home.
28 American singer Tracy Chapman tops the UK charts with her first, eponymous album due largely to appearing on the Mandela bill.

July
18 One-time Velvet Underground singer Nico dies from a brain haemorrhage in Ibiza after falling off her bicycle.

August
20 Fleetwood Mac's *Tango In The Night* clocks up its 70th week in the UK charts. Its sales of 1,500,000 confer five times platinum status.

September
17 The Smiths' final live album *Rank,* released by their former label Rough Trade, becomes the fifth of their eight LPs to stall at Number 2 in the British charts.

October
16 U2 enter the UK album charts at Number 1 with *Rattle And Hum.* Sales of 320,000 copies in a week add to advance sales to assure double platinum status.
23 Dire Straits' hits compilation *Money For Nothing* displaces U2 at the top of the UK LP chart by selling 'just' 100,000 copies in a week.

November
5 The Beach Boys top the US chart for the first time in 23 years with 'Kokomo'.
13 A Coca Cola commercial, 'The First Time', by US female vocalist Robin Beck, tops the UK chart. Ironically, Bon Jovi top the US listings with 'Bad Medicine'.
30 The British Phonographic Industry announces that various artist compilations are to be banned from the UK chart since they restrict opportunities for up and coming groups.

December
6 Roy Orbison, veteran Sun rocker famed for his trademark dark glasses and quavering falsetto, dies in Tennessee. He is 52.
12 In an out-of-court settlement, the British *Sun* newspaper pays Elton John £1 million for libel.

ROCK '89

A full decade after the disco craze, dance music made a big chart comeback — chiefly in the hands of Mike Stock, Matt Aitken and Peter Waterman. Their productions dominated the British Top 30, duelling for pole position with manufactured Italian acts like Black Box and the 49ers — whose vocals were often sampled from other peoples' records. Meanwhile, the 'acid house' dance cult carried out at illicit warehouse parties continued to attract adverse publicity as the Eighties' punk equivalent, due to its perceived drug links.

Elsewhere, three notable independent records companies fell to the majors, while reformation fever continued to hit anyone and everyone over 40.

January
Former Yes members Jon Anderson, Steve Howe, Rick Wakeman and Bill Bruford are injuncted by one-time band-mate Chris Squire who owns the Yes name. They had intended to advertise their concerts as 'An Evening of Yes Music Plus'.
28 A remake of his 1967 hit 'Something's Gotten Hold Of My Heart' brings Sixties crooner Gene Pitney back to the UK chart partnering Marc Almond. It is the first single to go gold at the new lower sales figure of 400,000 copies. REM put out a single, 'Stand', from their *Green* album - appropriately in a recycled paper sleeve.

February
4 'When I'm With You', a six year old track by the now-defunct Canadian group Sheriff, becomes the oldest single to reach Number 1 in the United States after being picked up by regional radio. Marillion announce that Steve Hogarth, formerly of the Europeans, is their new singer, replacing Fish.

March
18 Donna Summer scores her first Top Ten hit for over a decade with 'This Time I Know It's For Real', produced by Stock Aitken and Waterman.
18 In the wake of his death, Roy Orbison's *Mystery Girl* album and his superstar collaboration with George Harrison and others, *Traveling Wilburys Volume 1*, stands at Numbers 2 and 1 in Canada, 6 and 4 in the US. Both are in the UK Top 30.
Sixties popsters the Monkees start a British 27-date tour, minus original member Mike Nesmith on guitar. Drummer Micky Dolenz: "We were a television show about a rock'n'roll group . . . it's like comparing *Star Trek* to NASA". EMI acquire 50 per cent of independent label Chrysalis, with an option on the remaining 50 per cent.
Simple Minds 'Belfast Child' becomes the

UK's top-selling CD single with 40,000-plus, over twice the previous record.

April
David Bowie launches a heavy metal project called Tin Machine. Pet Shop Boys win "substantial damages" against *The Sun* newspaper and singer/columnist Jonathan King for allegations of plagiarism. King claimed their 'It's A Sin' was copied from Cat Stevens' 'Wild World'.

June
3 Cliff Richard's 100th single, 'The Best Of Me', enters the charts. It reaches Number 2 two weeks later.
10 Australian soap actor-turned-singer Jason Donovan's *Sealed With A Kiss* gives producers Stock Aitken and Waterman their third consecutive Number 1 for the PWL label, the first time a label's achieved this since Decca in 1965 and only the fifth time ever.
The Who celebrate 25 years of rock'n'roll.
15 Echo and the Bunnymen drummer Pete de Freitas, 27, dies in a motorcycle accident in Staffordshire.
20 'Ferry Cross The Mersey', recorded by Liverpool artists Gerry Marsden, Paul McCartney, Holly Johnson and the Christians, enters the charts at Number 1. It raised funds for those bereaved by the soccer disaster at Hillsborough.

July
Long-running US punks the Ramones lose bassist Dee Dee, who leaves to become a rap artist. Their new bassman rejoices in the name of CJ.
A tribute album to Neil Young, *The Bridge*, is released. With covers from several leading alternative artists, the royalties go to sufferers of cerebral palsy. Sex Pistols manager Malcolm McLaren returns to the pop scene with *Waltz Darling*, a fusion of pop and the classics featuring the disparate talents of rocker Jeff Beck and funkmaster Bootsy Collins.

August
5 'Swing The Mood' by DJ duo Jive Bunny and the Mastermixers is Britain's Number 1 single. Sampling Fifties hits from Bill Haley, Chubby Checker, the Everly Brothers, Elvis Presley, Danny and the Juniors and others, it is declared a 'single artist' record by the chart authorities, thus enabling its inclusion.
12 Richard Marx hits the top in the US for the third time in just over a year with 'Right Here Waiting' . . . while Liza Minnelli scores her debut hit in the UK — her first British single came out in 1972 — with the Pet Shop Boys collaboration 'Losing My Mind'.

12-13 US metal superstars Bon Jovi headline the two-day Moscow Music Peace Festival to two sell-out 140,000 crowds in the Lenin Stadium.
Adam Clayton of U2 is charged with possession of cannabis with intent to supply. He is fined 25,000 Irish punts. Chris Blackwell sells Island Records to PolyGram, reportedly for over £200 million.

September
9 'Ride On Time' gives Italian producers/musicians Black Box a British Number 1. But with vocals sampled from Loleatta Holloway's 1980 'Love Sensation', a legal altercation follows.
2 Paula Abdul's 'Cold Hearted' becomes the first B-side of a Number 1 ('Straight Up') to make the US Number 1 in its own right.
16 Madonna's American Top Ten entry, her 17th, with 'Cherish' makes her pop's most successful female soloist, taking over the mantle from Connie Francis.
26 Paul McCartney starts his first tour since 1976 in Oslo, Norway.

October
28 Brazilian dance craze single 'Lambada' by black multinational Paris-based group Kaoma still on top of French charts after 11 weeks and 1,700,000 copies. It is top in 9 other European countries.
The third independent label of the year falls as Herb Alpert and Jerry Moss sell A&M to PolyGram.
Ozzy Osbourne appears before magistrates in Buckinghamshire on a charge of attempting to murder his wife. She drops charges at the last minute, but is required to undergo treatment for alcoholism.

November
4 Roxette's second US chart-topper is a record for a Swedish group. 'Listen To Your Heart' follows April's 'The Look' and puts them above fellow countrymen Abba and Blue Swede.
The British police crackdown on 'acid house' reaches new heights when a 25 year old council youth leader is jailed for ten years for organising three acid house parties where police claimed to have found LSD, cocaine and other drugs.

December
16 Billy Joel tops US singles and album charts simultaneously with 'We Didn't Start the Fire' and *Storm Front*, repeating a feat he managed in 1980.
23 'Do They Know It's Christmas?' by Band Aid II tops the UK chart five years after Bob Geldof's original effort. Geldof does not appear on the remake.

INDEX

Numbers in *italics* refer to illustrations.

U.S. HIT SINGLES

1989

JANUARY

7 EVERY ROSE HAS ITS THORN *Poison*
14 MY PREROGATIVE *Bobby Brown*
21 TWO HEARTS *Phil Collins*
28 TWO HEARTS *Phil Collins*

FEBRUARY

4 WHEN I'M WITH YOU *Sheriff*
11 STRAIGHT UP *Paula Abdul*
18 STRAIGHT UP *Paula Abdul*
25 STRAIGHT UP *Paula Abdul*

MARCH

4 LOST IN YOUR EYES *Debbie Gibson*
11 LOST IN YOUR EYES *Debbie Gibson*
18 LOST IN YOUR EYES *Debbie Gibson*
25 THE LIVING YEARS *Mike and the Mechanics*

APRIL

1 ETERNAL FLAME *The Bangles*
8 THE LOOK *Roxette*
15 SHE DRIVES ME CRAZY *Fine Young Cannibals*
22 LIKE A PRAYER *Madonna*
29 LIKE A PRAYER *Madonna*

MAY

6 LIKE A PRAYER *Madonna*
13 I'LL BE THERE FOR YOU *Bon Jovi*
20 FOREVER YOUR GIRL *Paula Abdul*
27 FOREVER YOUR GIRL *Paula Abdul*

JUNE

3 ROCK ON *Michael Damian*
10 WIND BENEATH MY WINGS *Bette Midler*
17 I'LL BE LOVING YOU (FOREVER)
   New Kids On The Block
24 SATISFIED *Richard Marx*

JULY

1 BABY DON'T FORGET MY NUMBER *Milli Vanilli*
8 GOOD THING *Fine Young Cannibals*
15 IF YOU DON'T KNOW ME BY NOW *Simply Red*
22 TOY SOLDIERS *Martika*
29 TOY SOLDIERS *Martika*

AUGUST

5 BATDANCE *Prince*
12 RIGHT HERE WAITING *Richard Marx*
19 RIGHT HERE WAITING *Richard Marx*
26 RIGHT HERE WAITING *Richard Marx*

SEPTEMBER

2 COLD HEARTED *Paula Abdul*
9 HANGIN' TOUGH *New Kids On The Block*
16 HANGIN' TOUGH *New Kids On The Block*
23 GIRL YOU KNOW IT'S TRUE *Milli Vanilli*
30 GIRL YOU KNOW IT'S TRUE *Milli Vanilli*

OCTOBER

7 FOREVER YOUR GIRL *Paula Abdul*
14 DR FEELGOOD *Motley Crue*
21 MISS YOU MUCH *Janet Jackson*
28 MISS YOU MUCH *Janet Jackson*

NOVEMBER

4 LISTEN TO YOUR HEART *Roxette*
11 WHEN I SEE YOU SMILE *Bad English*
18 WHEN I SEE YOU SMILE *Bad English*
25 BLAME IT ON THE RAIN *Milli Vanilli*

DECEMBER

2 BLAME IT ON THE RAIN *Milli Vanilli*
9 BLAME IT ON THE RAIN *Milli Vanilli*
16 WE DIDN'T START THE FIRE *Billy Joel*
23 ANOTHER DAY IN PARADISE *Phil Collins*

1988

JANUARY

2 ALWAYS ON MY MIND   *Pet Shop Boys*
9 ALWAYS ON MY MIND   *Pet Shop Boys*
16 HEAVEN IS A PLACE ON EARTH   *Belinda Carlisle*
23 HEAVEN IS A PLACE ON EARTH   *Belinda Carlisle*
30 I THINK WE'RE ALONE NOW   *Tiffany*

FEBRUARY

6 I THINK WE'RE ALONE NOW   *Tiffany*
13 I THINK WE'RE ALONE NOW   *Tiffany*
20 I SHOULD BE SO LUCKY   *Kylie Minogue*
27 I SHOULD BE SO LUCKY   *Kylie Minogue*

MARCH

5 I SHOULD BE SO LUCKY   *Kylie Minogue*
12 I SHOULD BE SO LUCKY   *Kylie Minogue*
19 I SHOULD BE SO LUCKY   *Kylie Minogue*
26 DON'T TURN AROUND   *Aswad*

APRIL

2 DON'T TURN AROUND   *Aswad*
9 HEART   *Pet Shop Boys*
16 HEART   *Pet Shop Boys*
23 HEART   *Pet Shop Boys*
30 THEME FROM S'XPRESS   *S'Express*

MAY

7 THEME FROM S'XPRESS   *S'Express*
14 PERFECT   *Fairground Attraction*
21 WITH A LITTLE . . .   *Wet Wet Wet*
   SHE'S LEAVING HOME   *Billy Bragg*
28 WITH A LITTLE . . .   *Wet Wet Wet*
   SHE'S LEAVING HOME   *Billy Bragg*

JUNE

4 WITH A LITTLE . . .   *Wet Wet Wet*
   SHE'S LEAVING HOME   *Billy Bragg*
11 WITH A LITTLE . . .   *Wet Wet Wet*
   SHE'S LEAVING HOME   *Billy Bragg*
18 DOCTORIN' THE TARDIS   *The Timelords*
25 I OWE YOU NOTHING   *Bros*

JULY

2 I OWE YOU NOTHING   *Bros*
9 NOTHING'S GONNA CHANGE MY LOVE FOR YOU
   Glen Medeiros
16 NOTHING'S GONNA CHANGE MY LOVE FOR YOU
   Glen Medeiros
23 NOTHING'S GONNA CHANGE MY LOVE FOR YOU
   Glen Medeiros
30 NOTHING'S GONNA CHANGE MY LOVE FOR YOU
   Glen Medeiros

AUGUST

6 THE ONLY WAY IS UP   *Yazz and the Plastic Population*
13 THE ONLY WAY IS UP   *Yazz and the Plastic Population*
20 THE ONLY WAY IS UP   *Yazz and the Plastic Population*
27 THE ONLY WAY IS UP   *Yazz and the Plastic Population*

SEPTEMBER

3 THE ONLY WAY IS UP   *Yazz and the Plastic Population*
10 A GROOVY KIND OF LOVE   *Phil Collins*
17 A GROOVY KIND OF LOVE   *Phil Collins*
24 HE AIN'T HEAVY, HE'S MY BROTHER   *The Hollies*

OCTOBER

1 DESIRE   *U2*
8 DESIRE   *U2*
15 ONE MOMENT IN TIME   *Whitney Houston*
22 ONE MOMENT IN TIME   *Whitney Houston*
29 ORINOCO FLOW   *Enya*

NOVEMBER

5 ORINOCO FLOW   *Enya*
12 ORINOCO FLOW   *Enya*
19 FIRST TIME   *Robin Beck*
26 FIRST TIME   *Robin Beck*

DECEMBER

3 FIRST TIME   *Robin Beck*
10 MISTLETOE AND WINE   *Cliff Richard*
17 MISTLETOE AND WINE   *Cliff Richard*
24 MISTLETOE AND WINE   *Cliff Richard*
31 MISTLETOE AND WINE   *Cliff Richard*

x

1989

JANUARY

7 ESPECIALLY FOR YOU
  Kylie Minogue and Jason Donovan
14 ESPECIALLY FOR YOU
  Kylie Minogue and Jason Donovan
21 ESPECIALLY FOR YOU
  Kylie Minogue and Jason Donovan
28 SOMETHING'S GOTTEN HOLD OF MY HEART
  Marc Almond featuring Gene Pitney

FEBRUARY

4 SOMETHING'S GOTTEN HOLD OF MY HEART
  Marc Almond featuring Gene Pitney
11 SOMETHING'S GOTTEN HOLD OF MY HEART
  Marc Almond featuring Gene Pitney
18 SOMETHING'S GOTTEN HOLD OF MY HEART
  Marc Almond featuring Gene Pitney
25 BELFAST CHILD   *Simple Minds*

MARCH

4 BELFAST CHILD   *Simple Minds*
11 TOO MANY BROKEN HEARTS   *Jason Donovan*
18 TOO MANY BROKEN HEARTS   *Jason Donovan*
25 LIKE A PRAYER   *Madonna*

APRIL

1 LIKE A PRAYER   *Madonna*
8 LIKE A PRAYER   *Madonna*
15 ETERNAL FLAME   *The Bangles*
22 ETERNAL FLAME   *The Bangles*
29 ETERNAL FLAME   *The Bangles*

MAY

6 ETERNAL FLAME   *The Bangles*
13 HAND ON YOUR HEART   *Kylie Minogue*
20 FERRY CROSS THE MERSEY   *Various*
27 FERRY CROSS THE MERSEY   *Various*

JUNE

3 FERRY CROSS THE MERSEY   *Various*
10 SEALED WITH A KISS   *Jason Donovan*
17 SEALED WITH A KISS   *Jason Donovan*
24 BACK TO LIFE   *Soul II Soul featuring Caron Wheeler*

JULY

1 BACK TO LIFE   *Soul II Soul featuring Caron Wheeler*
8 BACK TO LIFE   *Soul II Soul featuring Caron Wheeler*
15 BACK TO LIFE   *Soul II Soul featuring Caron Wheeler*
22 YOU'LL NEVER STOP ME LOVING YOU   *Sonia*
29 YOU'LL NEVER STOP ME LOVING YOU   *Sonia*

AUGUST

5 SWING THE MOOD   *Jive Bunny and the Mastermixers*
12 SWING THE MOOD   *Jive Bunny and the Mastermixers*
19 SWING THE MOOD   *Jive Bunny and the Mastermixers*
26 SWING THE MOOD   *Jive Bunny and the Mastermixers*

SEPTEMBER

2 SWING THE MOOD   *Jive Bunny and the Mastermixers*
9 RIDE ON TIME   *Black Box*
16 RIDE ON TIME   *Black Box*
23 RIDE ON TIME   *Black Box*
30 RIDE ON TIME   *Black Box*

OCTOBER

7 RIDE ON TIME   *Black Box*
14 RIDE ON TIME   *Black Box*
21 THAT'S WHAT I LIKE   *Jive Bunny and the Mastermixers*
28 THAT'S WHAT I LIKE   *Jive Bunny and the Mastermixers*

NOVEMBER

4 THAT'S WHAT I LIKE   *Jive Bunny and the Mastermixers*
11 ALL AROUND THE WORLD   *Lisa Stansfield*
18 ALL AROUND THE WORLD   *Lisa Stansfield*
25 YOU'VE GOT IT   *New Kids On The Block*

DECEMBER

2 YOU'VE GOT IT   *New Kids On The Block*
9 YOU'VE GOT IT   *New Kids On The Block*
16 LET'S PARTY   *Jive Bunny and the Mastermixers*
23 DO THEY KNOW IT'S CHRISTMAS?   *Band Aid II*